Contents at a Glance

About the Author xiii

About the Technical Reviewer. xv

Acknowledgments xvii

Introduction. xix

CHAPTER 1 Introducing Enterprise Java Application Architecture
and Design 1

CHAPTER 2 Simplifying Enterprise Java Applications with the
Spring Framework. 21

CHAPTER 3 Exploring Presentation Tier Design Patterns 41

CHAPTER 4 Exploring Business Tier Design Patterns. 135

CHAPTER 5 Exploring Integration Tier Design Patterns. 179

CHAPTER 6 Exploring Crosscutting Design Patterns 223

CHAPTER 7 Case Study: Building an Order Management System 269

INDEX 311

Contents

About the Author xiii

About the Technical Reviewer. xv

Acknowledgments xvii

Introduction. xix

■CHAPTER 1   **Introducing Enterprise Java Application**
              Architecture and Design. 1

              Evolution of Distributed Computing 2
                    Single-Tier Architecture 2
                    Two-Tier Architecture. 3
                    Three-Tier Architecture. 4
                    N-Tier Architecture 4
                    Java EE Architecture 5
              Java EE Application Design 11
                    Simplifying Application Design with Patterns 11
              The Java EE Design Pattern Catalog 12
              Java EE Architecture and Design with UML 14
                    Class Diagram 15
                    Sequence Diagram 18
              Summary. 19

■CHAPTER 2   **Simplifying Enterprise Java Applications**
              with the Spring Framework 21

              What Is Spring? 21
              Why Is Spring So Important?. 22
              Spring Framework's Building Blocks. 24
                    Spring Core. 25
                    Spring AOP 34

Spring DAO 34

Spring ORM. 35

JEE 35

Web MVC. 35

Building a Layered Application with Spring 35

Presentation Tier 36

Business Tier 37

Integration Tier 38

Spring Enterprise Java Design Pattern Directive 38

Name 38

Problem 39

Forces 39

Solution 39

Consequences 39

Summary. 39

■CHAPTER 3   **Exploring Presentation Tier Design Patterns**. 41

Front Controller 42

Problem 42

Forces 45

Solution 46

Consequences 49

Application Controller 50

Problem 50

Forces 51

Solution 52

Consequences 68

Page Controller 68

Problem 68

Forces 69

Solution 69

Consequences 89

Context Object 90

　　Problem 90

　　Forces 91

　　Solution 91

　　Consequences 98

Intercepting Filter 98

　　Problem 98

　　Forces 99

　　Solution 99

　　Consequences 106

View Helper 107

　　Problem 107

　　Forces 107

　　Solution 107

　　Consequences 116

Composite View 117

　　Problem 117

　　Forces 118

　　Solution 118

　　Consequences 123

Dispatcher View 123

　　Problem 123

　　Forces 124

　　Solution 124

　　Consequences 130

Service to Worker 130

　　Problem 130

　　Forces 131

　　Solution 131

　　Consequences 132

Summary 133

∎CHAPTER 4   **Exploring Business Tier Design Patterns** 135

Service Locator 136

Problem 136

Forces 139

Solution 139

Consequences 150

Business Delegate 151

Problem 151

Forces 151

Solution 151

Consequences 154

Session Facade 155

Problem 155

Forces 156

Solution 156

Consequences 162

Application Service 162

Problem 162

Forces 163

Solution 163

Consequences 167

Business Interface 168

Problem 168

Forces 169

Solution 169

Consequences 176

Summary 176

∎CHAPTER 5   **Exploring Integration Tier Design Patterns** 179

Data Access Object 180

Problem 180

Forces 183

Solution 183

Consequences 194

Procedure Access Object 195

    Problem 195

    Forces 195

    Solution 195

    Consequences 199

Service Activator 199

    Problem 199

    Forces 200

    Solution 200

    Consequences 208

Web Service Broker 209

    Problem 209

    Forces 209

    Solution 210

    Consequences 221

Summary 221

CHAPTER 6 **Exploring Crosscutting Design Patterns** 223

Authentication and Authorization Enforcer 224

    Problem 224

    Forces 225

    Solution 226

    Consequences 247

Audit Interceptor 248

    Problem 248

    Forces 249

    Solution 249

    Consequences 256

Domain Service Owner Transaction 256

    Problem 256

    Forces 257

    Solution 257

    Consequences 267

Summary 267

▉CHAPTER 7   **Case Study: Building an Order Management System** 269

Requirements 270
    Story Card: Sign In Users 270
    Story Card: Look Up Services 270
    Story Card: Save Order 271
Iteration Planning 271
Architecture 272
    Presentation Tier 273
    Business Tier 274
    Integration Tier 275
Design 276
Security 277
    Problem 277
    Forces 277
    Solution 277
Java Server Pages 277
    Problem 277
    Forces 278
    Solution 278
Page Controller 278
    Problem 278
    Forces 278
    Solution 279
Development 280
    Setting Up the Workspace 280
    Setting Up the Projects 282
    Adding Dependencies 285
    Constructing the Project 287
    Deploying the Project 297
Summary 309

▉INDEX 311

About the Author

DHRUBOJYOTI KAYAL is an agile developer architect with almost a decade of experience working with Java EE. During this time, he has actively contributed to the architecture, design, and development of products and applications using enterprise Java technologies. His areas of interest include the Spring Framework, JBoss SEAM, OSGi, refactoring and prefactoring, rich Internet applications, Scrum, and XP. He currently works with Capgemini Consulting, where he helps project teams with the architecture, design, and development of Java EE projects for leading vendors in the telecom, media, and entertainment sectors. Prior to Capgemini, Dhrubojyoti worked for TATA Consultancy Services, Oracle, and Cognizant Technology Solutions.

About the Technical Reviewer

 **PROSENJIT BHATTACHARYYA** has been working with software ever since he was introduced to computers during his early school days. Starting with BASIC and Logo, he soon graduated to C, C++, and Java. Currently he concentrates on designing enterprise solutions based on the Java EE platform. An ardent supporter of open source, Prosenjit contributes to the community through his open source projects—JavaTrace and Dissect Framework—hosted on SourceForge. His enthusiasm about open source has earned him the sobriquet of "open source evangelist" amongst his acquaintances. Working for companies such as BEA Systems, Oracle Corporation, and IBM has enriched his experience and honed him into a thoroughbred software professional. Prosenjit's hobbies include playing the guitar and working on the pit crew of an amateur racing team. He hopes to have his own racing team in the near future. Prosenjit can be contacted at `prosenjit.bhattacharyya@gmail.com`.

Acknowledgments

I would like to take this opportunity to thank a few people whose ideas, inspirations, and diligence have contributed significantly to this book. First and foremost, I thank Steve Anglin for providing me with the opportunity to author this book. We started with a completely different idea way back in September 2007. Later it was Steve who came up with the idea to merge the Spring Framework and Java EE design patterns.

I am indebted to Prosenjit Bhattacharyya and Tom Welsh for the hours they spent on the technical review. Prosenjit is my old buddy since college days, and his objective feedback (especially for Chapter 7) helped give complete shape to each chapter in this book. I have learned a lot from Tom about writing in general. Tom's guidance proved very important in presenting and elaborating on the topics correctly, in a clear and concise manner.

This section would be incomplete without mentioning Kylie Johnston. Kylie has been the most patient and cooperative project manager. I must admit that this book probably would not have seen the light of day without her. I missed the deadlines for chapter submissions throughout the duration of this project. But Kylie always kept things on track by reminding me about the deadlines time and again yet also ensuring that a high-quality deliverable was produced. I must also thank Kim Wimpsett, Laura Cheu, and Elizabeth Berry for their fabulous work during production.

I am also grateful to my former colleagues at Cognizant Technology Solutions—Suman Ray and Somnath Chakraborty—for guiding and encouraging me to take up a technical career path. The design directive idea discussed in Chapter 7 of this book was introduced by Somnath in 2005 and was an instant hit.

Introduction

This book combines the Java EE design patterns with the Spring Framework. The Java EE design pattern catalog provides an invaluable reference for any Java EE application design and architecture. The Spring Framework, on the other hand, is the de facto standard for Java EE. Spring, with its inherently simple programming model and emphasis on object design best practices, has helped revive and increase the adoption of the Java EE platform.

I have been using the Spring Framework in combination with design patterns to build Java EE applications for a long time now. This book is an effort to document a catalog of frequently used design strategies with the Spring Framework, which is relevant in the context of the latest Java 5 EE specifications. I am sure this book will be a reference for designers and developers who are interested in building enterprise applications with Java EE and the Spring Framework.

Who This Book Is For

This book is primarily meant for Java EE application designers and architects. Experienced developers with knowledge of the Java EE design patterns and the Spring Framework will also find this book immensely useful.

How This Book Is Structured

This book is structured in a very simple way. Chapter 1 starts with an introduction to the fundamental concepts in enterprise application architecture. It analyzes various architectural styles in distributed computing, and it introduces UML as the tool for the visual representation of application design.

Chapter 2 introduces the Spring Framework and its role in building enterprise Java applications. This chapter also highlights the design pattern template that will be used in the next four chapters. Chapter 3 explains the design problems in the presentation tier and presents solutions with the Spring MVC framework. Chapter 4 elaborates on the business tier design patterns. This chapter also shows Spring's support for simplifying EJB development.

Chapter 5 deals with the integration tier design patterns. Chapter 6 takes a look into the often-overlooked areas of security and transaction design strategies. Finally, in Chapter 7, all the concepts presented in earlier chapters are used to develop an order management system.

Prerequisites

This book assumes you are familiar with the Java EE design patterns, the Spring Framework, and the Eclipse IDE.

Downloading the Code

The source code for this book is available to readers at `http://www.apress.com` in the downloads section of this book's home page. Please feel free to visit the Apress website and download all the code there. You can also check for errata and find related titles from Apress.

Contacting the Authors

Feel free to contact the author at `dhrubo.kayal@gmail.com`.

CHAPTER 1

■■■

Introducing Enterprise Java Application Architecture and Design

For a long time, Java Enterprise Edition (Java EE) has been the platform of choice across industries (banking, insurance, retail, hospitality, travel, and telecom, to name a few) for developing and deploying enterprise business applications. This is because Java EE provides a standard-based platform to build robust and highly scalable distributed applications that support everything from core banking operations to airline booking engines. However, developing successful Java EE applications can be a difficult task. The rich set of choices provided by the Java EE platform is daunting at first. The plethora of frameworks, utility libraries, integrated development environments (IDEs), and tool options make it all the more challenging. Hence, selecting appropriate technology is critical when developing Java EE–based software. These choices, backed by sound architectural and design principles, go a long way in building applications that are easy to maintain, reuse, and extend.

This chapter takes a tour of the fundamental aspects of Java EE application architecture and design. They form the foundation on which the entire application is developed.

The journey starts with a review of the evolution of distributed computing and n-tier application architecture. I will then show how the Java EE platform architecture addresses the difficulties in developing distributed applications. You will also learn about the Model-View-Controller (MVC) architectural principle. I'll then combine MVC principles with the Java EE platform to derive multitier Java EE application architecture.

With application architecture in place, I will focus on Java EE application design based on object-oriented principles. I will also explain the use of design patterns to simplify application design and the adoption of best practices. I'll also touch on the Java EE design pattern catalog as documented by Sun's Java BluePrints and subsequently elaborated on in the book *Core J2EE Design Pattern* by Deepak Alur et al (Prentice Hall, 2003). I'll end the chapter with an introduction to Unified Modeling Language (UML) and its role in visually documenting Java EE design and architecture.

Evolution of Distributed Computing

In distributed computing, an application is divided into smaller parts that run simultaneously on different computers. This is also referred to as *network computing* because the smaller parts communicate over the network generally using protocols built on top of TCP/IP or UDP. The smaller application parts are called *tiers*. Each tier provides an independent set of services that can be consumed by the connecting or client tier. The tiers can be further divided into *layers*, which provide granular-level functions. Most applications have three distinct layers:

- The *presentation layer* is responsible for the user interfaces.

- The *business layer* executes the business rules. In the process, it also interacts with the data access layer.

- The *data access layer* is responsible retrieving and manipulating data stored in enterprise information systems (EISs).

The modern state of network computing can be better understood by analyzing the gradual transition of distributed application architecture. In the next few sections, I will examine the transition of distributed architecture with suitable examples.

Single-Tier Architecture

The single-tier architecture dates back to the days of monolithic mainframes connected by dumb terminals. The entire application comprising layers such as user interfaces, business rules, and data was collocated on the same physical host. The users interacted with these systems using terminals or consoles, which had very limited text-based processing capabilities (see Figure 1-1).

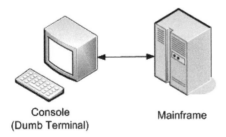

Console
(Dumb Terminal)   Mainframe

Figure 1-1. *Single-tier architecture*

Two-Tier Architecture

In the early 1980s, personal computers (PCs) became very popular. They were less expensive and had more processing power than the dumb terminal counterparts. This paved the way for true distributed, or *client-server*, computing. The client or the PCs now ran the user interface programs. It also supported graphical user interfaces (GUIs), allowing the users to enter data and interact with the mainframe server. The mainframe server now hosted only the business rules and data. Once the data entry was complete, the GUI application could optionally perform validations and then send the data to the server for execution of the business logic. Oracle Forms–based applications are a good example of two-tier architecture. The forms provide the GUI loaded on the PCs, and the business logic (coded as stored procedures) and data remain on the Oracle database server.

Then there was another form of two-tier architecture in which not only the UI but even the business logic resided on the client tier. This kind of application typically connected to a database server to run various queries. These clients are referred to as *thick* or *fat* clients because they had a significant portion of the executable code in the client tier (see Figure 1-2).

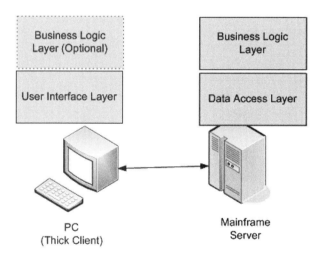

Figure 1-2. *Two-tier architecture*

Three-Tier Architecture

Two-tier thick client applications are easy to develop, but any software upgrade because of changes in user interface or business logic has to be rolled out for all the clients. Luckily, the hardware cost became cheaper and processing power increased significantly on the CPU in the mid-90s. This, coupled with the growth of the Internet and web-based application development trends, resulted in the emergence of three-tier architectures.

In this model, the client PC needs only thin client software such as a browser to display the presentation content coming from the server. The server hosts the presentation, the business logic, and the data access logic. The application data comes from enterprise information systems such as a relational database. In such systems the business logic can be accessed remotely, and hence it is possible to support stand-alone clients via a Java console application. The business layer generally interacts with the information system through the data access layer. Since the entire application resides on the server, this server is also referred to as an *application server* or *middleware* (see Figure 1-3).

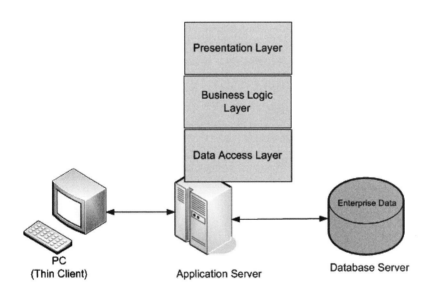

Figure 1-3. *Three-tier application*

N-Tier Architecture

With the widespread growth of Internet bandwidth, enterprises around the world have web-enabled their services. As a result, the application servers are not burdened anymore with the task of the presentation layer. This task is now off-loaded to the specialized web servers that generate presentation content. This content is transferred to the browser on the client tier, which takes care of rendering the user interfaces. The application servers in n-tier architecture host remotely accessible business components. These are accessed by the presentation layer web server over the network using native protocols. Figure 1-4 shows the n-tier application.

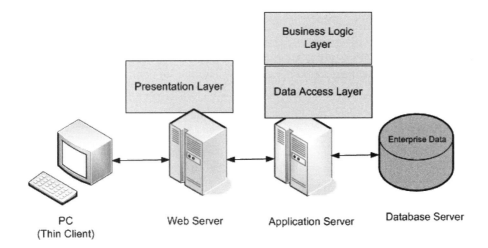

Figure 1-4. *N-tier application*

Java EE Architecture

Developing n-tier distributed applications is a complex and challenging job. Distributing the processing into separate tiers leads to better resource utilization. It also allows allocation of tasks to experts who are best suited to work and develop a particular tier. The web page designers, for example, are more equipped to work with the presentation layer on the web server. The database developers, on the other hand, can concentrate on developing stored procedures and functions. However, keeping these tiers as isolated silos serves no useful purpose. They must be integrated to achieve a bigger enterprise goal. It is imperative that this is done leveraging the most efficient protocol; otherwise, this leads to serious performance degradation.

Besides integration, a distributed application requires various services. It must be able to create, participate, or manage transactions while interacting with disparate information systems. This is an absolute must to ensure the concurrency of enterprise data. Since n-tier applications are accessed over the Internet, it is imperative that they are backed by strong security services to prevent malicious access.

These days, the cost of hardware, like CPU and memory, has gone down drastically. But still there is a limit, for example, to the amount of memory that is supported by the processor. Hence, there is a need to optimally use the system resources. Modern distributed applications are generally built leveraging object-oriented technologies. Therefore, services such as object caches or pools are very handy. These applications frequently interact with relational databases and other information systems such as message-oriented middleware. However, opening connections to these systems is costly because it consumes a lot of process resources and can prove to be a serious deterrent to performance. In these scenarios, a connection pool is immensely useful to improve performance as well as to optimize resource utilization.

Distributed applications typically use middleware servers to leverage the system services such as transaction, security, and pooling. The middleware server API had to be used to access these services. Hence, application code would be muddled with a proprietary API. This lock-in to vendor API wastes lot of development time and makes maintenance extremely difficult, besides limiting portability.

In 1999, Sun Microsystems released the Java EE 2 platform to address the difficulties in the development of distributed multitier enterprise applications. The platform was based on Java Platform, Standard Edition 2, and as a result it had the benefit of "write once, deploy and run anywhere." The platform received tremendous support from the open source community and major commercial vendors such as IBM, Oracle, BEA, and others because it was based on specifications. Anyone could develop the services as long as it conformed to the contract laid down in the specification. The specification and the platform have moved on from there; the platform is currently based on Java Platform, Standard Edition 5, and it is called Java Platform, Enterprise Edition 5. In this book, we will concentrate on this latest version, referred to officially as Java EE 5.

Java EE Container Architecture

The Java EE platform provides the essential system services through a container-based architecture. The container provides the runtime environment for the object-oriented application components written in Java. It provides low-level services such as security, transaction, life-cycle management, object lookup and caching, persistence, and network communication. This allows for the clear separation of roles. The system programmers can take care of developing the low-level services, and the application programmers can focus more on developing the business and presentation logic.

As shown in Figure 1-5, there are two server-side containers:

- The *web container* hosts the presentation components such as Java Server Pages (JSP) and servlets. These components also interact with the EJB container using remoting protocols.

- The *EJB container* manages the execution of Enterprise JavaBeans (EJB) components.

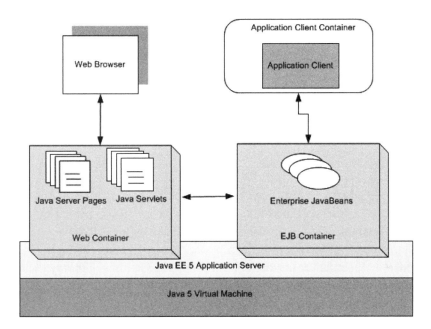

Figure 1-5. *Java EE platform architecture*

On the client side, the application client is a core Java application that connects to the EJB container over the network. The web browser, on the other hand, generally interacts with the web container using the HTTP protocol. The EJB and web containers together form the Java EE application server. The server in turn is hosted on the Java Virtual Machine (JVM).

Different containers provide different sets of low-level services. The web container does not provide transactional support, but the EJB container does. These services can be accessed using standard Java EE APIs such as Java Transaction API (JTA), Java Message Service (JMS), Java Naming and Directory Interface (JNDI), Java Persistence API (JPA), and Java Transaction API (JTA). The greatest benefit, however, is that these services can be applied transparently on the application components by mere configuration. To interpose these services, the application components should be packaged in predefined archive files with specific XML-based deployment descriptors. This effectively helps cut down on development time and simplifies maintenance.

Java EE Application Architecture

The Java EE platform makes the development of distributed n-tier applications easier. The application components can be easily divided based on functions and hosted on different tiers. The components on different tiers generally collaborate using an established architectural principle called MVC.

An MVC Detour

Trygve Reenskaug first described MVC way back in 1979 in a paper called "Applications Programming in Smalltalk-80™: How to use Model-View-Controller." It was primarily devised as a strategy for separating user interface logic from business logic. However, keeping the two isolated does not serve any useful purpose. It also suggests adding a layer of indirection to join and mediate between presentation and business logic layers. This new layer is called the *controller layer*. Thus, in short, MVC divides an application into three distinct but collaborating components:

- The *model* manages the data of the application by applying business rules.

- The *view* is responsible for displaying the application data and presenting the control that allows the users to further interact with the system.

- The *controller* takes care of the mediation between the model and the view.

Figure 1-6 depicts the relationship between the three components. The events triggered by any user action are intercepted by the controller. Depending on the action, the controller invokes the model to apply suitable business rules that modify application data. The controller then selects a view component to present the modified application data to the end user. Thus, you see that MVC provides guidelines for a clean separation of responsibilities in an application. Because of this separation, multiple views and controllers can work with the same model.

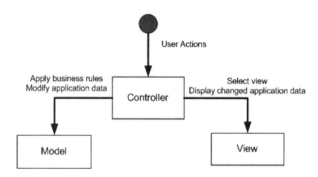

Figure 1-6. *Model-View-Controller*

Java EE Architecture with MVC

The MVC concept can be easily applied to form the basis for Java EE application architecture. Java EE servlet technology is ideally suited as a controller component. Any browser request can be transferred via HTTP to a servlet. A servlet controller can then invoke EJB model components, which encapsulate business rules and also retrieve and modify the application data. The retrieved and/or altered enterprise data can be displayed using JSP. As you'll read later in this book, this is an oversimplified representation of real-life enterprise Java architecture, although it works for a small-scale application. But this has tremendous implications for application development. Risks can be reduced and productivity increased if you have specialists in the different technologies working together. Moreover, one layer can be transparently replaced and new features easily added without adversely affecting others (see Figure 1-7).

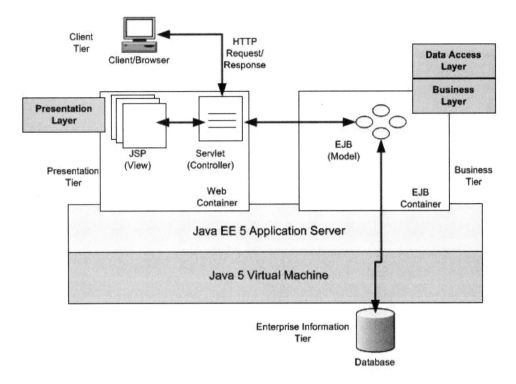

Figure 1-7. *Layered multitier Java EE application architecture based on MVC*

Layers in a Java EE Application

It is evident from Figure 1-7 that layered architecture is an extension of the MVC architecture. In the traditional MVC architecture, the data access or integration layer was
assumed to be part of the business layer. However, in Java EE, it has been reclaimed as a
separate layer. This is because enterprise Java applications integrate and communicate
with a variety of external information system for business data—relational database
management systems (RDBMSs), mainframes, SAP ERP, or Oracle e-business suites, to
name just a few. Therefore, positioning integration services as a separate layer helps the
business layer concentrate on its core function of executing business rules.

The benefits of the loosely coupled layered Java EE architecture are similar to those
of MVC. Since implementation details are encapsulated within individual layers, they can
be easily modified without deep impact on neighboring layers. This makes the application flexible and easy to maintain. Since each layer has its own defined roles and
responsibilities, it is simpler to manage, while still providing important services.

Java EE Application Design

In the past few sections I laid the foundation for exploring Java EE application design in greater detail. However, the design of Java EE software is a huge subject in itself, and many books have been written about it. My intention in this book is to simplify Java EE application design and development by applying patterns and best practices through the Spring Framework. Hence, in keeping with the theme and for the sake of brevity, I will cover only those topics relevant in this context. This will enable me to focus, in the forth-coming chapters, on only those topics that are essential for understanding the subject.

Some developers and designers are of the opinion that Java EE application design is essentially OO design. This is true, but Java EE application design involves a lot more than traditional object design. It requires finding the objects in the problem domain and then determining their relationships and collaboration. The objects in individual layers are assigned responsibilities, and interfaces are laid out for interaction between layers. However, the task doesn't finish here. In fact, it gets more complicated. This is because, unlike traditional object design, Java EE supports distributed object technologies such as EJB for deploying business components. The business components are developed as remotely accessible session Enterprise JavaBeans. JMS and message-driven beans (MDB) make things even complex by allowing distributed asynchronous interaction of objects.

The design of distributed objects is an immensely complicated task even for experi-enced professionals. You need to consider critical issues such as scalability, performance, transactions, and so on, before drafting a final solution. The design decision to use a coarse-grained or fine-grained session EJB facade can have serious impact on the overall performance of a Java EE application. Similarly, the choice of the correct method on which transactions will be imposed can have critical influence on data consistency.

Simplifying Application Design with Patterns

Application design can be immensely simplified by applying Java EE design patterns. Java EE design patterns have been documented in Sun's Java Blueprints (http://java.sun.com/reference/blueprints) and also in the book *Core J2EE Design Pattern* (Prentice Hall, 2003). They are based on fundamental object design patterns, described in the famous book *Design Patterns: Elements of Reusable Object-Oriented Software* (Addison Wesley, 1994). These patterns are also called Gang of Four (GOF) patterns because this book was written by four authors: Eric Gamma, Richard Helm, Ralph Johnson, and John Vlissides. The Java EE patterns catalog also takes into the account the strategies to meet the challenges of remotely accessible distributed objects besides the core object design principles.

Design patterns describe reusable solutions to commonly occurring design problems. They are tested guidelines and best practices accumulated and documented by experienced developers and designers. A pattern has three main characteristics:

- The context is the surrounding condition under which the problem exists.

- The problem is the difficult and uncertain subject area in the domain. It is limited by the context in which it is being considered.

- The solution is the remedy for the problem under consideration.

However, every solution to a problem does not qualify it as a pattern. The problem must be occurring frequently in order to have a reusable solution and to be considered as a pattern. Moreover, patterns must establish a common vocabulary to communicate design solutions to developers and designers. For example, if someone is referring to the GOF Singleton pattern, then all parties involved should understand that you need to design an object that will have only a single instance in the application. To achieve this design pattern, its description is often supplemented by structural and interaction diagrams as well as code snippets. Last but not least, each pattern description generally concludes with a benefit and concern analysis. You will take a detailed look at the constituents of a pattern when I discuss the pattern template in Chapter 2.

The Java EE Design Pattern Catalog

As stated earlier, Java EE has been the dominant enterprise development platform for nearly ten years. Over this period, thousands of successful applications and products have been built using this technology. But some endeavors have failed as well. There are several reasons for such failures, of which the foremost is inadequate design and architecture. This is a critical area because design and architecture is the bridge from requirements to the construction phase. However, Java EE designers and architects have learned their lessons from both failures and successes by drawing up a list of useful design patterns. This Java EE patterns catalog provides time-tested solution guidelines and best practices for object interaction in each layer of a Java EE application.

Just like the platform itself, the Java EE patterns catalog has evolved over time. As discussed earlier, this catalog was first formed as part of Sun's Java BluePrints and later elaborated on in the book *Core J2EE Design Pattern* (Prentice Hall, 2003). Table 1-1 presents the patterns with a brief description of each and its associated layer. I will discuss each of them in greater detail in the subsequent chapters.

Table 1-1. *Java EE Spring Patterns Catalog*

Layer	Pattern Name	Description
Presentation	View Helper	Separates presentation from business logic
	Composite View	Builds a layout-based view from multiple smaller subviews
	Front Controller	Provides a single point of access for presentation tier resources
	Application Controller	Acts as a front controller helper responsible for the coordinations with the page controllers and view components.
	Service to Worker	Executes business logic before control is finally passed to next view
	Dispatcher View	Executes minimal or no business logic to prepare response to the next view
	Page Controller	Manages each user action on a page and executes business logic
	Intercepting filters	Pre- and post-processes a user request
	Context Object	Decouples application controllers from being tied to any specific protocol
Business	Business Delegate	Acts as a bridge to decouple page controller and business logic that can be complex remote distributed object
	Service Locator	Provides handle to business objects
	Session Facade	Exposes coarse-grained interface for entry into business layer for remote clients
	Application Service	Provides business logic implementation as simple Java objects
	Business Interface	Consolidates business methods and applies compile-time checks of EJB methods
Integration	Data Access Object	Separates data access logic from business logic
	Procedure Access Object	Encapsulates access to database stored procedure and functions
	Service Activator (aka Message Facade)	Processes request asynchronously
	Web Service Broker	Encapsulates logic to access external applications exposed as web services standards

Table 1-1 is slightly altered based on the current state of Java EE. The Data Transfer Object pattern, for instance, no longer finds its place in the catalog and therefore is not listed. This pattern was used transfer data across layer and was especially useful if you used remote entity bean persistence components. But with the new Java Persistence API (part of the Java EE 5 platform) and general trend for plain old Java object (POJO) programming models, this pattern is no longer relevant.

This table is far from complete. Certain patterns can be applied across tiers. Security design patterns, for example, can be applied in the presentation layer to restrict access to web resources such as JSPs. Similarly, security patterns can be used to control method invocation on business layer EJB components. Transactional patterns, for example, can be applied at both the business and integration layers. These patterns are classified as *cross-cutting* patterns. I will explore cross-cutting patterns in detail in Chapter 6.

Java EE Architecture and Design with UML

Most modern-day applications are developed iteratively. The system grows gradually as more and more requirements become available. The core of such systems is a high-level design and architecture that evolves through iterations. It is also imperative that design and architecture are documented in both text and visual forms for the benefit of the development and maintenance teams. The visual representation is immensely useful because it helps developers understand runtime interactions and compile-time dependencies.

UML is a graphical language used for modeling and visualizing architecture and detailed design in complex enterprise systems. It is based on a specification developed by Object Management Group (OMG). I will use UML 2.0 notations (which is the latest version) available at `http://www.uml.org/`. However, UML is not limited to architecture and design but can be used in all phases of software development. UML provides a rich set of notation to depict the classes and objects and various relationship and interactions. Modern UML modeling tools such as IBM Rational XDE, Visual Paradigm, Sparx Systems Enterprise Architect, and so on, allow design patterns and best practices to be applied during system design. Moreover, with these tools, the design model can be used to generate significant portions of the application source code.

There are several kinds of UML diagram. But for analysis of Java EE design patterns, I will concentrate primarily on class and sequence diagrams and a simple extension mechanism called *stereotypes*. If you are new to UML or eager to know more, the best UML reference is *UML Distilled Third Edition* by Martin Fowler (Addison Wesley, 2005).

Class Diagram

A class diagram depicts the static relationships that exist among a group of classes and interfaces in the system. The different types of relationships that I will discuss are generalization, aggregation, and inheritance. Figure 1-8 shows the UML notation for a class used to represent the details of an insurance claim. It is represented by a rectangle with three compartments. The first compartment is the name of the class. The second compartment denotes the attributes in the class, and the last one shows the operations defined on these attributes. Note that the + and – signs before the attribute and method names are used to represent the visibility. The + sign denotes public visibility, and the – sign denotes private visibility or that the attribute is not accessible outside this class. Also note that, optionally, you can denote the data type of the attributes, method return type, and parameters.

Figure 1-8. *UML class notation*

Interfaces lay down the contract that implementations must fulfill. In other words, classes that implement an interface provide a guaranteed set of behavior. An interface is represented by the same rectangular box as a class, but with a difference. The top compartment shows the class name augmented by a stereotype <<interface>>. Stereotypes are a mechanism to extend an existing notation. Some UML tools also represent interfaces with a circle with no explicit mention of the methods. Figure 1-9 shows the two different forms.

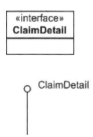

Figure 1-9. *UML interface notations*

Relationships

In the next few sections, I will examine the important relationships that exist between the classes in a software system.

Generalization

The *generalization* relation indicates inheritance between two or more classes. This is a parent-child relationship, in which the child inherits some or all of the attributes and behavior of the parent. It is also possible for the child to override some of the behaviors and attributes. Figure 1-10 shows the generalization relationship.

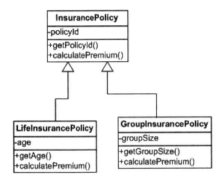

Figure 1-10. *Generalization*

Association

Association shows a general relation between two classes. In an actual class, this is shown with one class holding an instance of the other. An insurance policy always has one or more parties involved, with the most prominent being the policyholder who owns this policy. There can be an agent who helps and guides the policyholder to take this policy. Association often shows named roles, cardinality, and constraints to describe the relation in detail, as shown in Figure 1-11.

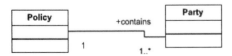

Figure 1-11. *Association*

Aggregation

Aggregation is a form of association in which one element consists of other, smaller constituents. This relationship is depicted by a diamond-shaped white arrowhead. In this
case, if the parent object is deleted, the child object may still continue to exist. Figure 1-12
shows an aggregation relation between an insurance agent and the local insurance office
in which he works. The local insurance office is where insurance agents carry out tasks
such as policy underwriting, depositing premiums for their customers, and various other
functions. So even if the local office is closed down, the agent can report to another
office. Similarly, the agent can de-register from a local office and move to a different
office of the same insurer.

Figure 1-12. *Aggregation*

Composition

Composition is a stronger form of aggregation; as in this case, if the parent is deleted, the
children will also no longer exist. This relationship is depicted by a diamond-shaped solid
arrowhead. Figure 1-13 shows the composition relationship between a party involved in
some policy or claim and their address. If the party is deleted from the system, its address
will also be deleted.

Figure 1-13. *Composition*

Sequence Diagram

A *sequence diagram* is used to model dynamic aspects of the system by depicting the message exchange between the objects in the system over a period of time. A sequence diagram is used to show the sequence of interactions that take place between different objects to fulfill a particular use case. Unlike a class diagram that represents the entire domain model of the application, a sequence diagram can show interaction details of a particular process only.

Object and Messages

In a sequence diagram, an object is shown with its name underlined in a rectangular box. The messages are represented by arrows starting on one object and ending on the other. An object can call a method on itself, which is a self-message and represented by an arrow starting and terminating on the same object, as shown in Figure 1-14.

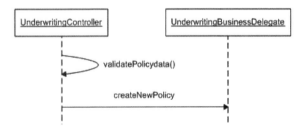

Figure 1-14. *Lifeline in a sequence diagram*

Lifeline

Each object has a *lifeline* represented by a dashed line going downward from the object box (as shown in Figure 1-14). It represents the time axis for the entire sequence diagram with time elapsed measured by moving downward on the lifeline.

Return Values

The messages in a sequence diagram can optionally have a *return value*, as shown in Figure 1-15. The createNewPolicy message, for instance, returns a PolicyDetail object.

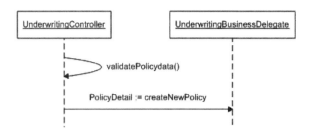

Figure 1-15. *Optional return value in a sequence diagram*

Summary

Developing distributed multitier applications is a daunting task. The Java EE platform looks to simplify this task by defining a container-based architecture. It defines a specification of the runtime environment for the application code and the low-level system services that it should provide. This allows the application developers to focus on writing business logic. The Java EE application architecture is based on the core platform architecture and established MVC principle. With this, you can clearly define specialized component layers in each tier. The web tier, for example, hosts the presentation layer of an application, whereas the business and data access layers generally reside on the application server tier.

Java EE design, on the other hand, is an extended object design. The Java EE design patterns catalog provides guidance and best practices in composing the objects and their interaction within and across the layers and tiers. The design patterns catalog documents the years of experience of designers and developers in delivering successful Java EE applications. The Java EE design and architecture can be documented using UML notations. These are graphical notations that help provide a pictorial view of the static structures and dynamic interactions of the domain objects.

In the next chapter, I'll show how the Spring Framework further simplifies Java EE application design and architecture. If you have experience with the Spring Framework already, you can jump straight to Chapter 3.

■ ■ ■

CHAPTER 2

Simplifying Enterprise Java Applications with the Spring Framework

The first chapter of this book discussed the fundamental principles of Java EE application architecture and design. In this chapter, I will show how these concepts apply to the Spring Framework. I will begin with a brief overview of Spring and its importance as an application framework. Then, I'll cover the building blocks that make up this framework, and in the process you will see the framework in action. After you understand the underlying principles of the Spring Framework, I will discuss its role in enterprise Java application architecture and design. Finally, I will wind up this chapter with the Spring Java design pattern directive that will be used in the next three chapters of this book. If you are interested in running the code in this chapter, then jump to Chapter 7, which provides step-by-step instructions for setting up Eclipse-based Blazon ezJEE Studio with the Spring Framework plug-in. It also shows you how to create the sample project structure required to develop and run these examples.

What Is Spring?

The Spring Framework is an open source application framework initially aimed at the Java platform. It has recently been ported to the .NET platform as well. The idea and code for this framework were first described by Rod Johnson in his book *Expert One-on-One J2EE Design and Development* (Wrox, 2002). This framework was the outcome of Rod's extensive project experience working as an independent software consultant for financial sector customers in the United Kingdom.

The Spring Framework is currently available under the Apache 2.0 open source license. It is a high-quality software product that can be used to build clean, flexible enterprise-class software. This is proven by tests done using Structure101 from Headway Software (`http://www.headwaysoftware.com`). Chris Chedgey, founder and CEO of Headway, reports in this blog (`http://chris.headwaysoftware.com/2006/07/springs_structu.html`) that the Spring Framework code has no package-level dependency cycles "despite its reasonable size of about 70KLOC (estimated from bytecode) divided into 139 packages." This speaks volumes about the sound underlying architecture and design of the Spring Framework. If you're interested in more information, refer to `http://www.` `springframework.org/node/310`.

Why Is Spring So Important?

The Java EE platform was intended to solve the complexities associated with distributed application development. The traditional Java EE platform achieved great success in standardizing low-level middleware services through the various APIs such as EJB, JTA, and JMS. This was possible because both commercial vendors and the open source community came together, realizing the immense potential of the platform based on standard Java. Because the primary focus was on standardizing system services, the fundamental problem of a simplified programming model was overlooked. Hence, in spite of widespread adoption in the late 1990s and early 2000, developing multitier applications on the Java EE platform still required strenuous effort.

The Java EE platform aimed to build applications based on a component model. A *component* is a self-contained piece of code that ideally could be reused in multiple applications. An order component can comprise an entity bean to handle the persistence of order information and a session bean to carry out different workflows on order entities. Theoretically, this has immense potential for reuse. But reality is different, because components developed in one project are seldom utilized again in another project. The Java EE server-specific deployment descriptors also make it difficult to reuse these components. The complexities in the Java EE programming model also leads to a lot of unnecessary code being written, tested, and maintained by development teams. This includes boilerplate code to look up an EJB object on the JNDI tree, retrieve a database connection, prepare and execute database queries, and finally release all database resources. The data transfer objects used to circumvent the limitations of the entity bean API seriously violated the object-oriented principle of encapsulation. Even a midsize project had a significant number of transfer objects to develop and maintain. All these led to a significant drain of resources that should otherwise be used only for developing sound business logic.

EJBs were designed to help ease the development of transactional and distributed applications. Although even the smallest database-driven application requires transaction, it may not need to be distributed. However, overusing EJBs, especially session beans to simplify business logic, leads to the distribution being built into the application component model. Distributed applications are unduly complex and hence consume more CPU cycles for processing. They result in excessive and duplicated code along with metadata. Accessing a distributed application component requires network traversals, and marshalling and unmarshalling of large datasets. The misuses of distributed objects have often led to even a simple application not performing to its desired level.

Java EE encompasses a lot of technologies and APIs that are inherently complex. The entity bean API, for example, required a significant learning curve and in turn provided limited benefits for an application. Since Java EE components run inside the application server containers, they are very difficult to unit test. This prevents test-driven development (TDD).

The difficulties in Java EE application development forced the development community to look for alternatives. Soon there was a rapid proliferation of frameworks built on top of different Java EE APIs. The Apache Struts framework, for example, helps implement MVC principles using the servlet API. The framework implements a servlet-based front controller and allows developers to provide implementation for simple page controllers. Hibernate, on the other hand, emerged to answer the immense pain associated with entity bean development. It provided persistence of POJOs with minimal configuration metadata. These POJOs were not distributed objects like entity beans and hence led to better application performance. Hibernate did not require any container support, thus making it easy to unit test these persistence objects. Then there was HiveMind for developing simple POJO-based business services.

The Spring Framework also started to address the complexity associated with developing Java EE applications. However, unlike the single-tier frameworks such as Struts, Hibernate, or HiveMind, Spring provides a comprehensive multitier framework that can be leveraged in all tiers of an application. It helps structure together the entire application with out-of-the-box components as well as integrates with the best single-tier frameworks. Just like its single-tier counterparts, it provides a simple programming model based on POJOs and makes them easily testable because these components can run outside server containers.

The Spring Inversion of Control (IOC) container (to be discussed in the next section) is the heart of the entire framework. It helps glue together the different parts of the application, thus forming a coherent architecture. Spring MVC components can be used to build a very flexible web tier. The IOC container simplifies the development of business layer with POJOs.

These POJO business components can be made available as distributed objects through the various remoting options available with Spring. They can also be used to develop as well as connect to distributed EJB components. With Spring AOP, it is possible to transparently apply system services such as transactions, security, and instrumentation to POJO components. Spring JDBC and object-relational mapping (ORM) components allow simplified interaction with databases. As an application framework, Spring provides easy standards-based integration with disparate information systems through Java Connector Architecture (JCA) and web services. Last but not least, Spring security is a comprehensive solution to cater to the security requirements of any enterprise application.

Spring Framework's Building Blocks

Spring is an application framework and is divided into several modules or components. Each module provides a specified set of functionality and works more or less independently of the others. Needless to say, these modules can be leveraged to build scalable yet flexible enterprise Java applications. This system is very flexible, because developers can choose to use only the module that is most appropriate in the context of a problem. For example, a developer can just use the Spring DAO module and build the rest of the application with non-Spring components. Moreover, Spring provides integration points to work with other frameworks and APIs. If you think Spring is unsuitable in a particular scenario, you can use alternatives. In case the development team is more proficient in Struts, for example, it can be used instead of Spring MVC while the rest of the application uses Spring components and features such as JDBC and transactions. In the two scenarios described here, the developers need not deploy the entire Spring Framework. They will require only the relevant module (like Spring DAO) along with the Spring IOC container and the Struts libraries.

Figure 2-1 shows the various modules of the Spring Framework.

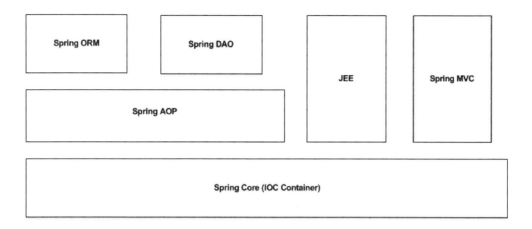

Figure 2-1. *High-level building blocks of the Spring Framework*

Spring Core

The Core module forms the backbone of the entire Spring Framework. All other Spring modules are dependent on this module. It is also called the IOC container and is central to Spring's support for dependency injection (DI).

Inversion of Control

IOC is best described by the term the *Hollywood principle*, which states "Don't call us; we'll call you." (The junior artists often hear this from production managers in Hollywood.) However, this is important in software development as well to control the flow of applications while ensuring high cohesion and low coupling. To better understand, this let us consider a simple case when your application performs some calculations and prints the end result using a logging library like log4j. In this case, the application code is responsible for the flow of control while invoking methods on the log4j API as and when necessary.

IOC, on the other hand, is fundamental to any framework. With IOC, an application object is typically registered with the framework that takes the responsibility of invoking methods on the registered object at an appropriate time or event. The control is inverted because instead of application code invoking the framework API, things happen just the opposite. Thus, in short, IOC is the principle of allowing another object or framework to invoke methods on your application objects on the occurrence of appropriate events.

IOC is not a new concept and has been around for a long time. EJBs, for example, supports IOC. The various EJB components such as session, entity, and message-driven beans lay down specific contracts with the container by implementing the methods defined in different interfaces. The session bean, for example, implements the `ejbActivate` and `ejbPassivate` life-cycle methods defined in the `javax.ejb.SessionBean` interface. However, these methods are never called from other methods of the session bean; rather, the container calls these methods at different times during the life cycle of the bean, thus inverting control. Message-driven beans, for instance, implement the `onMessage` method of the `javax.jms.MessageListener` interface. It is the responsibility of the container to invoke this method on the event of a message arrival.

Dependency Injection

It is common for developers to believe that IOC and DI are the same thing. This is incorrect, and I want to make it clear right at the outset that they are two different yet related concepts. Just as IOC deals with inverting the control flow in an application, DI describes how one object resolves or finds other objects on which it needs to invoke some methods. There are several ways to achieve DI, and one such strategy is IOC. I will explain the different DI strategies one by one in the next few sections.

Direct Instantiation

Direct instantiation is the simplest form of DI. The dependent object is directly instantiated using the new operator, as shown in Listing 2-1.

Listing 2-1. `FormulaOneDriver.java`: *Using Direct Instantiation*

```
public class FormulaOneDriver{
    public Car getCar(){
        Car car = new FerrariCar();
        return car;
    }
}
```

The Formula 1 driver object (`FormulaOneDriver`) needs a car to drive. Hence, it creates an instance of the `Car` object directly and uses it. Direct instantiation increases coupling and scatters object creation code across the application, making it hard to maintain and unit test.

Factory Helper

The factory helper is a common and widely used dependency injection strategy. It is based on the GOF factory method design pattern. The factory method consolidates the use of the new operator and supplies appropriate object instances based on some input. This is shown in Listing 2-2.

Listing 2-2. FormulaOneDriver.java: *Using Factory Helper*

```java
public class FormulaOneDriver{
    public Car getCar(){
        Car car = CarFactory.getInstance("FERARI");
        return car;
    }
}
```

Using a factory promotes an object design best practice called *program to interface* (P2I). This principle states that concrete objects must implement an interface that is used in the caller program rather than the concrete object itself. Therefore, you can easily substitute a different implementation with little impact on client code. In other words, there is no direct dependency on the concrete implementation leading to low coupling. Listing 2-3 shows the Car interface.

Listing 2-3. Car.java

```java
public interface Car{
    public Color getColor();
    //other methods
}
```

The FerrariCar provides a concrete implementation of the Car interface, as shown in Listing 2-4.

Listing 2-4. FerrariCar.java

```java
public class FerrariCar implements Car{
//...implementation of methods defined in Car
// ...implementation of other methods
}
```

This pattern also consolidates object creation in only a handful of factory classes, making it easy to maintain. With a factory helper, it is also possible to make object creation configurable. You can define the concrete implementation that you supply in some properties or XML configuration files, making it swappable on the fly.

Locate in Registry Service

This third method should be familiar with EJB developers. They often need to look up EJB object references on the JNDI registry service. In this case, the EJB objects are already created and registered in JNDI with a specific key. The objects may be located in a remote JVM, but JNDI makes lookup using this key quite similar to Listing 2-2.

All these strategies are commonly called *pull* dependency injection. This is because the dependent object is pulled in by the object that ultimately uses it. I prefer to classify the pull methods as dependency resolution, rather than dependency injection. This is because the true dependency injection happens with IOC and is called *push* DI. In this approach, an external container or application framework creates and passes the dependent object to the object that requires it. The dependent objects are mostly supplied using constructor or setter methods. However, for this the application framework must know which dependent object to provide and which object to notify with the dependent object.

It is interesting to note that EJB containers support not only pull DI (one session bean looking up another session bean, for instance, in the JNDI) but also push DI. This is evident from the setSessionContext(javax.ejb.SessionContext ctx) or setEntityContext (javax.ejb.EntityContext ctx) method where the context object is created, initialized, and passed to the EJB objects by the container. This is called *setter injection*. You can explore different varieties of push DI with examples in a later section when I touch upon the DI features of Spring IOC container.

Benefits of DI

The following are the benefits of DI:

- Dependency injection promotes loose coupling. With a factory helper, for instance, you can remove hard-coded dependencies through P2I. It is possible to configure them outside the application and provide hot-swappable and hot-pluggable implementations.

- It facilitates test-driven development (TDD). Objects can be easily tested because they do not require any particular container to run. They can be tested as long as the dependencies are injected by some mechanism.

- As you will see later with push DI supported by Spring IOC, there is no need for applications to look up objects like EJB remote interfaces.

- DI promotes good object-oriented design and reuse—object composition rather than reuse by inheritance.

Drawbacks of DI

These are the drawbacks of DI:

- The dependencies are generally hard-coded in XML configuration files that are proprietary and nonstandard.

- Wiring instances together can become a hazard if there are too many instances and many dependencies that need to be addressed.

- Dependency on XML-based metadata and excessive use of reflection and bytecode manipulation may impact application performance.

Bean Factory

The `org.springframework.beans.factory.BeanFactory` interface provides the basis for Spring's IOC container or bean factory. It is a sophisticated implementation of the GOF factory method design pattern and creates, caches, wires together, and manages application objects. These objects are affectionately called *beans* because Spring promotes the POJO programming model. Spring provides several out-of-the-box implementations of the bean factory. One such implementation is the `XmlBeanFactory` class. This class allows you to configure the various application classes and their dependencies in XML files. In short, a bean factory like JNDI is a registry of application objects. Listing 2-5 shows a simple Spring bean configuration file.

Listing 2-5. `spring-config.xml`

```
<?xml version="1.0" encoding="UTF-8"?>
<beans xmlns="http://www.springframework.org/schema/beans"
    xmlns:xsi="http://www.w3.org/2001/XMLSchema-instance"
    xsi:schemaLocation="http://www.springframework.org/schema/beans
http://www.springframework.org/schema/beans/spring-beans-2.5.xsd"
    >
```

```
<bean name="carService"
    class="com.apress.simpleapp.service.CatServiceImpl" />

</beans>
```

Now that I have wired the bean in the XML configuration file, it is time to start the IOC container, as shown in Listing 2-6.

Listing 2-6. SpringInitializer.java

```
Resource res = new FileSystemResource("spring-config.xml");
BeanFactory factory = new XmlBeanFactory(res);
```

Because I have the Spring container up and running, it is now possible to retrieve beans from the bean factory that can then be used to perform some useful work in the application.

Listing 2-7 is an example of pull DI with the Spring Framework. The application code uses the Spring bean factory or IOC container to retrieve the car service objects using the specified key. It is also evident from Listing 2-6 that it is possible to support several variants of CarSevice depending on the type of the car. This is because each car is different and provides a different set of features and options. However, it is cumbersome to invoke the getBean method each time you need a bean. It's as good as having the factory method implementation of the pull DI I explained earlier with the example of a Car object.

Listing 2-7. CarServiceLocator.java

```
CarService service = (CarService) factory.getBean("carService");
```

One major goal of Spring is to be unobtrusive and impose minimal dependency on the framework. This is achieved through different forms of push DI supported by the Spring IOC container.

Setter Injection

In this mode of push DI, an object is created in the Spring IOC container by invoking the zero-argument constructor. The dependent object is then passed as a parameter to the setter method. The CarService object needs data access objects (DAO) to execute database operations. The data access objects are injected via setter methods, as shown in Listing 2-8.

Listing 2-8. `CarServiceImpl.java`

```java
public class CarServiceImpl implements CarService{
    private CarDao carDao;

    public void refuel(Car car){
        carDao.updateFuelConsumed(car) ;
    }
    public void setCarDao(CarDao carDao){
        this.carDao = carDao;
    }
}
```

The `CarDao` object is passed by the Spring IOC container using the `setCarDao` method. Now you must wire things up so that Spring knows how to resolve and inject the dependency. You can do this with a simple configuration, as shown in Listing 2-9.

Listing 2-9. `spring-config.xml`: *Setter Injection*

```xml
<?xml version="1.0" encoding="UTF-8"?>
<beans xmlns="http://www.springframework.org/schema/beans"
    xmlns:xsi="http://www.w3.org/2001/XMLSchema-instance"
    xsi:schemaLocation="http://www.springframework.org/schema/beans
http://www.springframework.org/schema/beans/spring-beans-2.5.xsd"
    >

    <bean name="carDao"
        class="com.apress.simpleapp.dao.CatDaoImpl" />

    <bean name="carService"
        class="com.apress.simpleapp.service.CatServiceImpl">

        <property name="carDao"
            ref="carDao" />
    </bean>
</beans>
```

Constructor Injection

In this strategy, the dependent object is passed as part of the constructor call, as shown in Listing 2-10.

Listing 2-10. CarServiceImpl.java *with Constructor Injection*

```
public class CarServiceImpl implements CarService{
    private CarDao carDao;

    public void CarServiceImpl (CarDao carDao){
        this.carDao = carDao;
    }
public void refuel(Car car){
        carDao.updateFuelConsumed(car) ;
    }
}
```

To achieve constructor injection, you need to alter the configuration as well, as depicted in Listing 2-11.

Listing 2-11. spring-config.xml *with Constructor Injection*

```
<?xml version="1.0" encoding="UTF-8"?>
<beans xmlns="http://www.springframework.org/schema/beans"
    xmlns:xsi="http://www.w3.org/2001/XMLSchema-instance"
    xsi:schemaLocation="http://www.springframework.org/schema/beans
http://www.springframework.org/schema/beans/spring-beans-2.5.xsd"
    >

    <bean name="carDao"
        class="com.apress.simpleapp.dao.CatDaoImpl" />

    <bean name="carService"
        class="com.apress.simpleapp.service.CarServiceImpl">
        <constructor-arg>
    <ref bean="carDao"/>
  </constructor-arg>

</beans>
```

Application Contexts

The bean factory is merely an object pool where objects are created and managed by configuration. For small applications, this is sufficient, but enterprise applications demand more. Application context builds on the foundations laid by the bean factory to provide services like the following:

- Support for message resources required for internationalization

- Support for aspect-oriented programming (AOP) and hence declarative transaction, security, and instrumentation support

- Registering event listeners in the bean factory

- Creating application layer–specific context such as `WebApplicationContext` for use in web applications

The Spring application context can be created like a bean factory and without any alteration in the configuration file, as shown in Listing 2-12.

Listing 2-12. `SpringInitializer.java`: *Starting an Application Context*

```
ApplicationContext context = new ➥
ClassPathXmlApplicationContext("spring-config.xml");
```

`ClassPathXmlApplicationContext` looks for a `spring-config.xml` file in the classpath and initializes the application context. Similarly, a servlet listener can be registered to initialize application context in a web application—commonly called *web application context*. The listener looks for the configuration file at a specific location within the web application archive to start the web application context.

So far, I have given a very basic and simplistic introduction to Spring IOC and DI features. For a detailed treatment of the subject, refer to the Spring 2.5 documentation available at `http://static.springframework.org/spring/docs/2.5.x/reference/beans.html`.

Spring AOP

Spring AOP is an important module that provides critical system-level services. It promotes loose coupling and allows cross-cutting concerns (such as business services and transactions) to be separated in a most elegant fashion. It allows these services to be applied transparently through declaration. With Spring AOP, it is possible to write custom aspects and configure them declaratively. Spring AOP supports the creation of aspects through AOP Alliance–compliant interfaces. It also supports AspectJ. Spring AOP is a complicated subject in itself, and a detailed discussion is beyond the scope of this book. I will, however, use AOP topics later in Chapter 6, to describe the transaction and security patterns. So, you may also consider reading a bit about AOP in the book *Foundations of AOP for J2EE Development* (Apress, 2005) and then check out the Spring AOP documentation at `http://static.springframework.org/spring/docs/2.5.x/reference/aop.html`.

Spring DAO

Java EE applications use the JDBC API to connect to and perform operations on relational databases. However, this often results in a lot of common code being written for operations such as the following:

- Retrieving a connection from the connection pool

- Creating a `PreparedStatement` object

- Binding SQL parameters

- Executing the `PreparedStatement` object

- Retrieving data from the `ResultSet` object and populating data container objects

- Releasing all database resources

This kind of boilerplate code seriously hurts reusability. Spring JDBC/DAO makes life very easy by removing the common code in templates. The templates implement the GOF template method design pattern and provide suitable extension points to plug-in custom code. This makes the data access code very clean and prevents nagging problems such as connection leaks, and so on, because the Spring Framework ensures that all database resources are released properly.

Spring ORM

ORM solutions provide easy persistence of POJO objects in relational databases. The Spring ORM module is essentially an extension of the DAO module. Just like the JDBC-based templates, Spring provides ORM templates to work with and integrate most of the leading ORM products such as Hibernate, OpenJPA, TopLink, iBatis, and others. I will cover the best practices and patterns involved with Spring DAO and ORM in Chapter 5.

JEE

The JEE module forms the basis for all of the Spring Framework's interaction with various Java EE technologies such as EJB, JTA, JCA, and JavaMail. As you will read later in this book, just like Spring DAO, the JEE module provides components to simplify the development of and interaction with Java EE technologies such as EJB.

Web MVC

This module helps build highly flexible web applications leveraging the complete benefits of the Spring IOC container. It is based on the MVC architectural pattern and seamlessly integrates with the Servlet API. Spring MVC supports a pluggable architecture and works with a multitude of view technologies such as JSP, FreeMarker, Velocity, and Adobe Flex, to name just a few. If Spring MVC is not the framework of choice, then it is possible to integrate with existing web frameworks such as Struts, Webwork, and JSF and still reap the benefits offered by the core Spring Framework, in other words, IOC and DI.

Building a Layered Application with Spring

Now you are familiar with the roles of various Spring modules and have some idea of their responsibilities. I'll now show how to put these modules together to build a layered web application with the Spring Framework. Figure 2-2 shows the high-level architecture of this application.

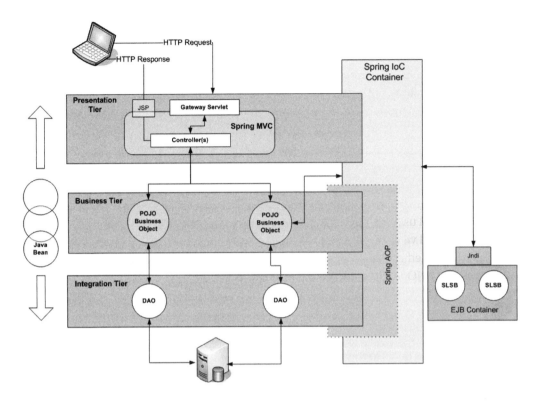

Figure 2-2. *Lightweight application architecture with the Spring Framework*

Figure 2-2 shows a three-tier web application leveraging the different Spring Framework modules. I will dissect each of the tiers to see how these modules are utilized and what different options are available to build a flexible, simple enterprise Spring application.

Presentation Tier

As the name suggests, Spring MVC provides first-class components to build web applications following the MVC pattern. Like any good web framework, Spring MVC helps build the controller layer. It is flexible and supports a variety of components for view management, including core Java EE technologies such as JSP and others such as Extensible Stylesheet Language (XSL) and Portable Document Format (PDF).

As shown in Figure 2-2, the HTTP request from the client's web browser is first intercepted by the controller component. This consists of a gateway servlet that acts as a single entry point into the application. The servlet then delegates successive user requests to respective handlers called *page controllers*. Page controllers are simple Java classes that execute one application use case and invoke the business services. Spring

MVC also contains a view management layer (not shown for simplicity), which is responsible for locating an appropriate view (which may be another JSP). It also binds the data objects returned by the page controllers after invoking the model objects in the business tier and finally dispatches the HTTP response to the client. All the objects that are responsible for view management, controller management, and the page controllers themselves are registered in the underlying Spring IOC container. Thus, all the benefits of this container are available to the Spring MVC module. Note that the gateway servlet is not part of the Spring IOC container; rather, it is managed by the web server.

Spring MVC is a versatile module and supports almost any view and model technology available. If your development team is more confident with Java Server Faces (JSF) or Struts, for example, it is quite possible to integrate these frameworks with Spring MVC. You can very well use template-based view engines such as Velocity and FreeMarker; document-based views such as PDF, Microsoft Word, and Microsoft Excel; and rich user interfaces provided by Adobe Flex. As far as the model is concerned, Spring MVC not only gels well with POJO business components, but it goes equally well with distributed EJB components.

Business Tier

With Spring you can develop business components as plain Java classes without any framework dependency. This is in complete contrast to the EJB programming model, which demands the implementation of several different interfaces along with deployment descriptors, making life complicated for the developer.

The POJO business objects are all configured in the Spring IOC container just like any other bean shown in earlier examples. They are responsible for executing business rules, and in the process they manipulate application data using the data access API available in the integration tier.

The Spring AOP module plays a significant role in the business tier. It can be used to declaratively apply and control transaction and security on the POJO business components.

It is possible to utilize Spring AOP to develop custom aspects that collect audit trail information or instrument method execution time without affecting the existing application code.

It is possible to develop a mixed solution with Spring POJO and EJBs. Spring IOC implements the service locator pattern (to be discussed in Chapter 4) to look up (pull DI) the EJB home interfaces and then injects those objects into the POJO business objects. Note that the system-level services provided by the EJB container are now available to the application. In this scenario, the Spring Framework played the role of an EJB client using a session bean. Spring also helps with EJB implementation through convenient superclasses. We will delve into this in greater detail as part of the Spring business layer patterns in Chapter 4.

It is important to note that Spring MVC is not the only way of connecting to the Spring business tier. It is possible to expose Spring business objects as web services. Similarly, various other remoting options like Spring remoting, Burlap-Hessian, and so on, can be used to connect to Spring components, making them available as remote components. I will explore a few remoting solutions in connection with the integration tier patterns in Chapter 4.

Integration Tier

The integration tier in most applications interacts with the RDBMS using the JDBC API through POJO data access objects. The data access objects provide a consistent API for the business tier objects and wrap the JDBC API. Spring DAO provides templates for simple and flexible data access objects. The data access objects update relational databases as well as retrieve data from them. The retrieved data is wrapped in JavaBean objects and returned to the layers above.

Just like the other two tiers, Spring provides plenty of options even in the integration tier. Spring ORM allows development teams to easily use an object relational bridge solution such as Hibernate or TopLink. The integration tier in a Java EE application is not limited to communicating with relational databases. It can be a requirement to connect to a mainframe or an ERP or CRM system. Just as with the business tier, here too we can leverage the Spring JEE module to connect to these systems and applications using standard technologies such as JCA or web services.

Spring Enterprise Java Design Pattern Directive

In the previous chapter, I have discussed the foundations of Java EE architecture and design. In the process, I mentioned that best practices in design can be collated as design directives or design patterns. These provide a common vocabulary to communicate design ideas among developers and designers. I will now combine the lessons learned in the previous chapter with those from this chapter to formulate the Spring Java EE application design pattern directive. This pattern template or directive will be used in the next four chapters to describe how Java EE design patterns can be best applied using the Spring Framework.

Name

This is the name used to identify a pattern.

Problem

This section describes one or more problems that you are trying to solve. I will use this section to highlight the complexities in devising a solution with existing Java EE technologies.

Forces

This section follows from the previous section and outlines the intent for the pattern and its applicability.

Solution

I will present the detailed solution to solve the problem under consideration. In this section, I will discuss different possible strategies with the Spring Framework. I will also identify various best practices and mention fundamental patterns and object design principles that contribute to the solution. UML class and sequence diagrams will be used extensively along with source code samples to present the solution clearly.

Consequences

Finally, I will wind up the topic with an analysis of the pros and cons of the solutions provided.

Summary

This chapter builds on the foundation laid by Chapter 1. In this chapter, I put the Spring application framework in the context of Java EE application architecture and design. I highlighted the problems associated with Java EE application development. The Spring Framework's multitier components help address these common problems. Besides this, the Spring Framework is an enabler for best practices and effective object design. You probably realize by now that it has two facets—on one hand, it's an IOC container, and on the other hand it's a set of libraries and APIs to help simplify Java EE development. Just like any application, the Spring application framework's core lies in the IOC container. The different modules of the Spring Framework leverage this core framework and help build robust flexible Java EE applications. The modules can be used on demand, making Spring an extremely flexible application development stack.

To give you a sound understanding of Spring Framework, I showed how to put the different modules together to build a multitier Java EE application. In the process, I touched upon the different options available with Spring to design and develop the different tiers with the utmost flexibility. Finally, I presented the design directive that I will use in the next four chapters to explain the different Java EE design patterns. In the next chapter, you will get into real action with the different presentation tier patterns where you will first use this design directive template.

CHAPTER 3

■ ■ ■

Exploring Presentation Tier Design Patterns

Sometime back I joined a team that was developing a product named eInsure for the insurance industry. The goal was to develop a comprehensive online e-business solution encompassing all the major insurance processes such as underwriting, claims management, accounting, customer relationship, re-insurance, and so on. By the time I joined, this application already had a few major releases and was being used in production by two clients. But the development team found it highly cumbersome and effort-intensive to handle any new requirement, enhancement, or change request. This would always lead to unnecessarily long develop-test-fix-release-maintain (DTFRM) cycles. So, I started to investigate and soon made some critical observations about the application.

The main reason for the problem was the source code. The application was huge with nearly 350 JSPs, 30-odd session beans, 600+ POJO helpers, 300+ tables, and an equal number of entity beans. The bulk of the existing source code was generated by a tool that helped convert the legacy product written in Oracle PL/SQL to Java EE. The generated source was based on the enterprise Java component model, but deep down it had fundamental design flaws and bad smells. Code smells generally indicate that something has gone wrong somewhere in your application code. The term was popularized by Kent Beck and Martin Fowler in the book *Refactoring: Improving the Design of Existing Code* (Addison-Wesley, 1999). The data structures used in eInsure mimicked the PL/SQL tables and arrays. As a result, the developers had to first grasp the behavior of legacy code and data structures. As the new code was being added in the same legacy style, there was no scope of any improvement.

The lack of design and OO skills in the eInsure team (most of the team members themselves were making a transition to acquire Java EE technology skills along with the product) added to the woes. There was absolutely no design directive or code documentation. A good software application should have different configuration parameters to control its runtime behavior without having to modify any code. These configuration parameters are generally stored in XML or properties file external to the application.

This configuration information can be modified by system administrators as per the customization needs to alter the runtime behavior of the application. Unfortunately, eInsure had only a small set of configuration parameters, making it vulnerable to code changes.

In this and subsequent chapters, I will discuss in greater detail some of the problems in the application under consideration. I will then provide solutions to these problems by applying the Spring Framework and design patterns and highlighting the best practices. This chapter builds on the foundation laid in Chapters 1 and 2. It shows the first glimpses of how design patterns and the Spring Framework can work in unison to form the backbone of a high-quality software application. In this chapter, I shall focus only on the presentation tier.

Front Controller

Problem

So far, I have been pointing out the negatives of eInsure. Now I will introduce you to a modified version of the source from this application. The source has been cleaned up considerably to concentrate on the problem.

Listing 3-1 shows a simplified version of the JSP that was used to create and modify policy details. It is evident from the JavaScript comments that the request was posted after URL-rewrite. Since the same JSP was used for different underwriting operations, the JavaScript always passed an event code and screen code combination. This was the case with 95 percent of the JSPs in the application.

Listing 3-1. `Policy.jsp`

```
<title>Underwriting</title>
<script>
    function eventValidateAndSubmit (){
        //modify URL
        //submit form
    document.uwr.submit();
    }
</script>
<body onLoad="displayError(<%=request.getAttribute("ERROR_MESSAGE")%>)">
<form name="uwr" action="UnderwritingController.jsp" method="post">
Name of Insured <input type="text" value="" /><br/>
<input type="button" value="Create"
onClick="eventValidateAndSubmit('UWR001','SCR001')"/>
```

```
<input type=" button" value="Update"
onClick=" eventValidateAndSubmit ('UWR002','SCR001')"/>
</form>
```

The controller used this combination of event code and screen code to uniquely identify a block of code to be executed for each user action and subsequent selection of the next view to be rendered. This controller was another JSP and was cluttered with several long-running `if-else` blocks, as shown in Listing 3-2.

Listing 3-2. UnderwritingController.jsp

```
<%
String eventCode = request.getParameter("eventCode");
String screenCode = request.getParameter("screenCode");
String inputPage = request.getParameter("referrer");
Sting userCd = request.getParameter("userCode");
String nextView = "";
try{
        SecurityChecker.getInstance().check(userCd, eventCode);

if(screenCode.equals("SCR001") && eventCode.equals("UWR002")){
        //Look up session bean
        //Create policy by invoking session bean method
        nextView = "Policy.jsp";

}
else if(screenCode.equals("UWR002") && eventCode.equals("SCR001")){
        //similar to above
    nextView = "Policy.jsp";
}
else{
    request.setAttribute("ERROR_MESSAGE",
"You have attempted an unsupported function");
     nextView = "error.jsp";
}
}
catch(AppException appExp){
    request.setAttribute("ERROR_MESSAGE",exp.getMessage());
nextView = inputPage;
}
catch(Throwable exp){
```

```
                    request.setAttribute("ERROR_MESSAGE",exp.getMessage());
nextView = "error.jsp";
}
finally{
//finally redirect to correct view
    RequestDispatcher requestDispatcher = request.getRequestDispatcher(nextView);
requestDispatcher.forward(request,response);
}

%>
```

This controller was inefficient and promoted procedural programming. A new feature would inevitably add another `if-else` block. Now eInsure had thousands of use cases with the underwriting module contributing a significant percentage of them. Hence, the controller was bloated with a large number of `if-else` blocks. This controller showed all the signs of the fat Magic Servlet antipattern (`http://wiki.java.net/bin/view/Javapedia/AntiPattern`) and tried to perform too many tasks. It intercepted the requests, handled all the different service requests, and finally forwarded the response to the browsers.

The controller was very large and soon ran beyond manageable proportions. The development team then created a new controller named `UnderwritingControllerNew.jsp` with a typical clone-and-modify programming style. This new controller too turned bulky in no time, and again the same step was repeated, paving the way for yet another "new" controller. The story was no different for other modules such as accounting, claims, and so on. Each of them had several controllers handling a subset of the features available in that module.

One of the prime goals of OO component-based application development is reusability. But having too many JSP/servlet controllers only promotes procedural programming and minimizes reusability. Also, having multiple points of entry into an application makes it vulnerable to security threats. The copy-paste style of reuse seemed easy but had only short-term benefits. Apparently it saved time, but any application fix had to be rolled out at all duplicated points. Common services such as authorization checks also need to be replicated across all controllers. For bug fixes and maintenance, developers spent hours locating first the correct controller and then the appropriate `if-else` block, as well as comprehending the legacy data structures and code flow. The result was a strenuous development process and unnecessary effort wastage.

It is evident that the JSP controller in Listing 3-2 tries to perform three main tasks:

1. Intercept the incoming request.

2. Invoke the Enterprise JavaBeans components to carry out the business operation in several `if-else` blocks.

3. Finally, select the next view to display and bind the model object returned by the invocation of business methods.

This resembles the MVC architectural pattern discussed earlier. However, the JSP controller component takes on too many responsibilities, thus deviating from the *single responsibility principle* (SRP). SRP states that every class should have one and only one responsibility, and all its functions should be tightly aligned to this responsibility. Adherence to a single concern makes the class robust, and it has limited chances of modification. SRP is explained in greater detail at `http://c2.com/cgi/ wiki?SingleResponsibilityPrinciple`.

You should also consider whether JSP is the appropriate technology to be used as a controller. This is because every technology in the Java EE platform has its own role. JSP was intended to be a dynamic view technology. This allowed the user interface code to be written by developers who were expert in HTML and JavaScript with some knowledge of JSP tags, scriptlets, and implicit objects. These developers need not be seasoned Java programmers, freeing up the latter to focus on writing business and data access logic. Hence, it is recommended that you use JSP as a dynamic view technology and not as a controller.

Forces

- Too many controllers make it difficult to maintain and reuse.

- There should be a single point of entry into the entire application.

- The controller should follow SRP. It should intercept requests and delegate business logic invocation and view selection to pluggable components.

- JSPs should not be used as controllers.

- Extend functionality declaratively around the single entry point.

Solution

Deploy a servlet to act as a single common gateway for all web requests. This servlet is called the *front controller* servlet. Sometimes this pattern is also referred to as Gateway Servlet.

Strategies with the Spring Framework

The Spring MVC framework provides an out-of-the box front controller servlet called `DispatcherServlet`. This central servlet forms the backbone of the Spring MVC framework and is integrated with the Spring IOC container. It is thus possible to get all the benefits offered by the Spring IOC container.

The `DispatcherServlet` intercepts all web requests from the clients and routes them to the appropriate page controllers. The page controllers are simple POJOs responsible for interacting with the business layer components. These are registered in the Spring container and implement the GOF command pattern. The page controllers will be discussed in detail later in this chapter. But in short, the front controller servlet and the page controllers work together to form the core of an event-driven web application. The front controller does not have any `if-else` blocks. All the code in the `if-else` block is moved into page controllers. Hence, the front controller is a generic component that can be reused across applications.

The front controller servlet delegates the responsibility of next-view selection and binding the model object to specialized view managers. This allows the `DispatcherServlet` to concentrate on a single responsibility: intercepting requests and then delegating the rest of the functions to specialized handlers. Thus, the generic front controller helps reduce the number of controllers. A single controller servlet should be sufficient for the entire application. This is possible because the page controllers and view managers can be made accessible to the front controller by simple configuration. However, some designers also prefer to use one front controller per module. It is just a matter of choice, but whatever the case, avoid multiple controllers per module.

Using the Front Controller

I will now show how to put the Spring `DispatcherServlet` to use. I will also discuss how to refactor the bad-smelling JSP in the process. My preference is to use a single controller for the entire application to minimize configuration maintenance overhead. As with all servlets, the first step in using the `DispatcherServlet` is to configure it in the `web.xml` file. The code in Listing 3-3 registers the front controller servlet with the web server.

Listing 3-3. `web.xml`

```
<web-app>
    <servlet>
        <servlet-name>insurance</servlet-name>
            <servlet-class>
org.springframework.web.servlet.DispatcherServlet
            </servlet-class>
            <load-on-startup>1</load-on-startup>
    </servlet>
    <servlet-mapping>
        <servlet-name>insurance</servlet-name>
        <url-pattern>*.do</url-pattern>
    </servlet-mapping>
</web-app>
```

The interesting part in Listing 3-3 is the URL mapping. It shows that this servlet has been configured to handle all requests ending with `.do` in the URL. If you are an experienced Java EE developer and have worked with the Apache Struts framework, you will immediately see its similarity to the `ActionServlet`.

On initialization, the `DispatcherServlet` looks for a configuration file with the naming convention `<servlet-name>-servlet.xml` in the `WEB-INF` folder of the web application. This XML file contains the configuration information about all the beans, including the page controllers and view managers that will be managed by the Spring IOC container. The front controller loads this file to start the Spring web application context and get access to the Spring IOC container. In our case, this file will be named `insurance-servlet.xml`. This is shown in Listing 3-4 with only the page controllers.

Listing 3-4. `insurance-servlet.xml`

```
<?xml version="1.0" encoding="UTF-8"?>

<beans xmlns="http://www.springframework.org/schema/beans"
       xmlns:xsi="http://www.w3.org/2001/XMLSchema-instance"
       xsi:schemaLocation="http://www.springframework.org/schema/beans
       http://www.springframework.org/schema/beans/spring-beans-2.5.xsd">

<bean name="/createPolicy.do"
class="com.apress.insuranceapp.web.CreatePolicyController"/>
<bean name="/updatePolicy.do"
class=" com.apress.insuranceapp.web.UpdatePolicyController"/>
</beans>
```

The `DispatcherServlet` uses the `BeanNameUrlHandlerMapping` class to map an incoming request URL to the appropriate page controller that is going to process that request. The handler mapping bean, however, is not configured in Listing 3-4. This is because Spring assumes this as a sensible default. As we will see later, it is possible to use different logic to map an incoming request to its handler by implementing the `HandlerMapping` interface. I will discuss other `HandlerMapping` implementations provided by the Spring Framework later in this chapter.

With the central request-handling gateway installed, it's time to refactor the JSP described in Listing 3-1 to route all requests to the front controller. This is shown in Listing 3-5.

Listing 3-5. `Policy.jsp`

```
<title>Underwriting</title>
<script>
    function eventSubmit(url){
        document.uwr.action = url;
        document.uwr.submit();
    }
</script>
</head>
<body onLoad="displayError(<%=request.getAttribute("ERROR_MESSAGE")%>)">
<form action="" name="uwr">
    Name of Insured <input type="text" value="" />
    <br/>
    <input type="submit" value="Create" onClick="eventSubmit('createPolicy.do')"/>
    <input type="submit" value="Update" onClick="eventSubmit('updatePolicy.do')"/>
</form>
```

Note that the JSP no longer uses the event code and screen code. Instead, it now uses logical request URLs. When a request for the URL `/createPolicy.do` reaches the front controller, it uses the handler mapping to determine whether a page controller has been registered to process this request. The processing is then delegated to the appropriate page controller if one is registered; otherwise, an error is raised. In this case, the processing is carried out by the `CreatePolicyController`. The simplest controller would implement the `handleRequest` method of the `org.springframework.web.servlet.mvc.Controller` interface. The `handleRequest` method should have most of the code that was in the `if-else` block of the JSP controller. Simply stated, this controller will take care of the code in the `if-else` blocks. After the business components are invoked and page controllers return, the next view is selected with the help of view managers. The simplified sequence diagram in Figure 3-1 shows the interaction between the front controller, the page controller, and the view resolver. I will explain this diagram in greater detail in the subsequent sections.

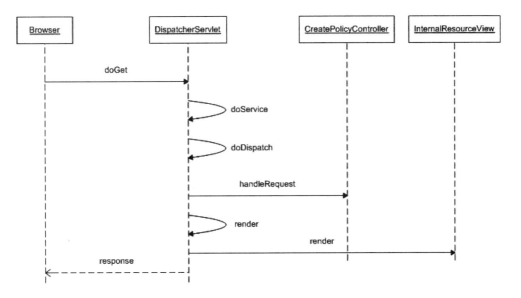

Figure 3-1. *Sequence diagram: front controller request flow*

It is evident from Figure 3-1 that the doDispatch is the most important method in DispatcherServlet. It orchestrates and invokes the page controller and view. The InternalResourceView class is responsible for abstracting a JSP-based view.

Consequences

Benefits

- *Out-of-the-box front controller*: The Spring MVC provides a ready-made front controller that can be used in the application by mere configuration.

- *Centralized control*: The front controller provides a central entry point to consolidate and control the request inflow into the application. This makes it simpler to manage the application.

- *Simplified design*: The front controller now abides by SRP because it is involved only in intercepting requests and delegating to specialized classes.

- *Promotes reusability*: The introduction of the front controller removes the module controllers and immensely improves reusability.

Concerns

- *Single point of failure*: The front controller is also a single point of failure for any application.

Application Controller

Problem

The JSP controller presented while discussing the Front Controller pattern was intended to perform the following tasks related to request processing:

1. Intercept incoming requests.

2. Invoke business components.

3. Identify and redirect to the next view.

The Front Controller design pattern solved the first problem. As with the JSP controller, it is entirely possible to build the two other functions in the front controller. But that would result in a highly inflexible, fat, magic front controller that handles too many responsibilities. As the application grows, it becomes an uphill task to maintain and use such complex and specific front controllers. This was exactly the problem with the JSP-based controller used in the eInsure application.

A new customer wanted to integrate their existing re-insurance product, built on the WebWork 2.0 framework, with eInsure. The integration soon ran into heavy weather because the controller was never designed to cater to this kind of requirement. Another existing client of eInsure demanded a new feature called *policy quotation*. This feature would enable the potential customers of this insurance company to get an approximate value of the premium they needed to pay for a new policy. For this they would use their mobile devices to connect to the system and supply the minimal information required to generate the quote—or tentative premium value.

The monolithic eInsure controller was coded to use only JSP as the view technology. Hence, it was inflexible, and supporting a new view suitable for mobile devices was very difficult.

The new features discussed in the previous two paragraphs can be better managed with a strategy of "divide and conquer." This involves employing pluggable components with the front controller that are specialized to handle specific tasks. Two such important components are the following:

- *Action handler*: The action handler locates and executes the appropriate page controller. The page controllers decouple business logic invocation from the front controller. So, the WebWork 2.0 page controllers can be used with the front controller by implementing WebWork-specific action handler components.

- *View handler*: The view handler finds a view, binds the model returned by the page controller, and prepares the response for the client. The view handler uses logical view names (explained in the next section), thus abstracting the actual view object from the front controller. Using the view handler, it is easy to support multiple view types (HTML, JSP, PDF, Microsoft Excel, and so on). So, the view handler component can be extended to help roll out views for mobile devices.

These components are connected to the front controller via configuration. This enables the front controller to act as a coordinator only. This, along with decoupled action and view management, makes the front controller more robust, reusable, and highly extensible.

Forces

- Remove action and view management functionality from the front controller.

- Deploy pluggable action and view handlers to provide support for different types of page controllers and views.

- Improve the reusability, cohesion, and modularity of the application code.

- The front controller should be generic and as lightweight as possible.

- Promote test-driven development by making it possible to run unit tests outside the web container.

Solution

Use an *application controller* to decouple action and view handling from the front controller.

Strategies with the Spring Framework

The application controller is an important internal component of any Java EE web framework. Since it sits silently behind the gateway servlet and generally suffices to all the requirements of an application, developers are seldom bothered about this component.

In the Struts framework, for instance, the `RequestProcessor` class does the job of an application controller. Internally, the Struts front controller `ActionServlet` delegates the view and action management to this class. It is possible to extend this class to override the default behavior. But Struts developers hardly ever do that.

Spring MVC provides similar support for action-view management orchestrated by the `DispatcherServlet`. As with Struts, no effort is generally required from the developers except, perhaps, some optional configuration. You have already seen this in earlier examples. You have neither written any code nor done any configuration for view or action handling. Yet the request for the resource `createPolicy.do` was handled by the appropriate page controller. This is possible because Spring has sensible defaults for command and view handling. In the next few sections, I will go through the various application controller configuration options available with the Spring Framework. The Spring Framework is highly flexible in that it separates the application controller into two distinct parts to be discussed in the next few sections.

Action Handling

Spring action/command handling can be slightly overwhelming at first because lots of classes are involved. So, we will take it in simple steps. Figure 3-2 shows a simplified view of the action management workflow. I have deliberately left out the view management part for now.

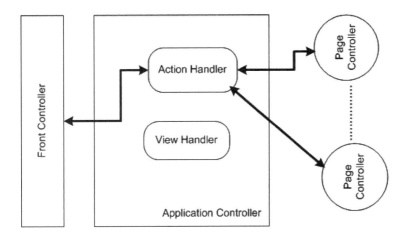

Figure 3-2. *Action-handling workflow*

As shown in Figure 3-2, the front controller interacts with the action handler, which subsequently invokes the page controllers. The class diagram in Figure 3-3 shows the various classes and interfaces that are part of the Spring MVC action handler component.

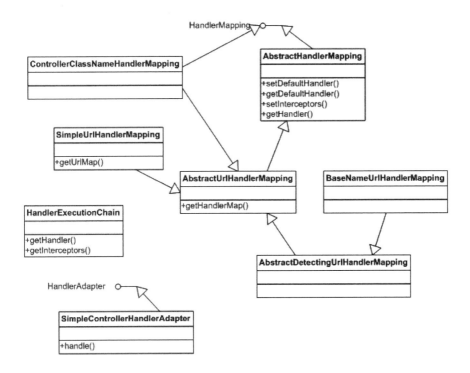

Figure 3-3. *Action handler class diagram*

The HandlerMapping interface is the key to the overall action handler component. On intercepting a request, the dispatcher servlet looks for the appropriate handler mapping object to map between the request and the request-processing object. In other words, a handler mapping provides an abstract way to map the request URL to the eventual handlers or page controllers.

As the name suggests, AbstractHandlerMapping is an abstract handler mapping implementation. It implements the getHandler method of the HandlerMapping interface. This method returns a HandlerExecutionChain, which holds references to the following:

- Single page controller implementations that implement either the Controller interface or the ThrowawayController interface

- An optional set of interceptors implementing the HandlerInterceptor interface

The BeanNameUrlHandlerMapping and SimpleUrlHanderMapping provide two concrete implementations of the HandlerMapping interface that are sufficient for most cases. The BeanNameUrlHandlerMapping is the default handler mapping used by the front controller. If your application needs only this handler mapping, then there is nothing to configure. In some cases, your application may require multiple handler mappings. As I will show in a later section, Spring MVC allows multiple handler mappings to work side by side. In this case, the front controller has to decide the order in which the handler mappings will be invoked. The handler mappings implement the Ordered interface, allowing the front controller to decide the right ordering in the handler mapping chain. The handler mapping with lowest order value has the highest priority.

A handler mapping holds only the reference of a page controller. It does not invoke any method on it. A handler adapter is responsible for invoking methods on a page controller. All handler adapters implement the HandlerAdapter interface. As the name suggests, handler adapters follow the GOF adapter design pattern and have the best knowledge to invoke the appropriate page controller. This opens up another Spring extension point and allows easy integration of page controllers from other frameworks such as WebWork or Struts Action classes. The handle method should be implemented to invoke methods on the page controller. This is exactly what the concrete implementation class SimpleControllerHandlerAdapter does. It is capable of invoking page controllers that implement the Controller interface. In other words, it knows how to invoke the handleRequest method and handle the returned value.

The HandlerExecutionChain also contains an optional set of interceptors. These provide a robust mechanism for declarative processing before and after a request is handled by the page controller. The sequence diagram in Figure 3-4 is an extension of Figure 3-1 and shows the complete message exchange within the action handler part of the Spring MVC application controller component.

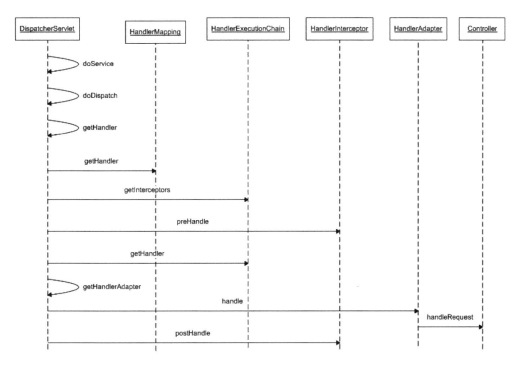

Figure 3-4. *Action handler sequence diagram*

This is a complex interaction diagram, showing the internals of the Spring application controller component. The different steps in this diagram are as follows:

1. The request processing starts off with the doService method. It keeps a copy of the request attributes and delegates to the doDispatch method for further processing.

2. The doDispatch method coordinates and controls the workflow of the application controller.

3. The getHandler method is called on the dispatcher servlet to get hold of the appropriate handler mapping for the given request. There can be a list of handler mappings installed with the Spring MVC runtime. This method checks the list to select the appropriate handler mapping.

4. Once the correct handler mapping for a given request is detected, its getHandler method is invoked to return an instance of HandlerExecutionChain.

5. The doDispatch method looks for an interceptor list that has been configured in the Spring container. However, it is not mandatory to have interceptors for requests; it depends entirely on your requirement.

6. If one or more interceptors have been configured, the `preHandle` method is invoked on each one of them to preprocess a request.

7. The `doDispatch` method gets an instance of a page controller by invoking the `getHandler` method on `HandlerExecutionChain`.

8. Just like handler mappings, there can be multiple handler adapters registered with the Spring MVC framework. The `getHandlerAdapter()` method of the front controller servlet looks up the list of handler adapters to find the one most suitable for executing the selected page controller.

9. Once the handler adapter is found, the request processing is delegated to its `handle()` method.

10. The `handle()` method is responsible for invoking the correct page controller methods and converting the returned value into a type that the Spring MVC framework understands.

11. Finally, any postprocessing task is carried out with the help of the interceptors.

Using Action Handlers

As shown earlier, `HandlerMapping` along with `HandlerAdapter` forms the backbone of the robust and highly flexible Spring action management component. They bring the flexibility of program to interface (P2I), thus allowing different concrete implementations. Both the handler mapping and the handler adapter provide extension points into the Spring MVC framework. Let's say you need to map a page controller based on a value set in a cookie. You can achieve this with a custom handler mapping implementation. Assume that this page controller was developed as part of some homegrown web framework. You can create a handler mapping implementation to invoke appropriate methods on this controller and consume the returned results. Using the customized version is as simple as implementing the interfaces or any of the abstract classes and then configuring it with the Spring container. However, this is not required in most cases. This is because Spring provides several concrete implementations that are sufficient in most cases. I have been explaining a lot of theoretical stuff so far, so I will now show how to put the implementation classes into action.

BeanNameUrlHandlerMapping

This handler mapping is used to map the request URL directly to the bean object or a page controller registered in the Spring IOC container. In other words, the URL is matched with the name of the bean in the application context. Consider a request for the following URL: `http://www.myinsuranceportal.com/insuranceapp/createPolicy.do`. This request is intercepted by the dispatcher or front controller servlet, which would look for a handler mapping registered in the Spring web application context. You can do this as shown in Listing 3-6.

Listing 3-6. `insurance-servlet.xml`

```
<beans>
    <bean name="beanNameUrlHandlerMapping"
            class="org.springframework.web.servlet.➥
handler.BeanNameUrlHandlerMapping"/>

    <bean name="/createPolicy.do" class="com.apress.insuranceapp.➥
web.CreatePolicyController"/>

</beans>
```

However, as stated earlier, this configuration is optional because `BeanNameUrlHandlerMapping` is the default handler. In case no handler mapping is found in the web application context, Spring MVC will create an instance of `BeanNameUrlHandlerMapping`. Now that the handler mapping is detected, the front controller will then look up a bean with the name `/createPolicy.do` in the Spring container. It manages to resolve this as the `CreatePolicyController` command handler bean.

This handler mapping works relative to the servlet mapping and is not dependent on the context path. Hence, changes in context path or servlet mapping will not require a change in the bean configuration in the Spring container. However, it is possible to turn on the use of full path by setting a boolean flag, `alwaysUseFullPath`, as shown in the configuration in Listing 3-7.

Listing 3-7. `insurance-servlet.xml`

```
<beans>

    <bean name="beanNameUrlHandlerMapping" class="org.springframework➥
.web.servlet.handler.BeanNameUrlHandlerMapping">
        <property name="alwaysUseFullPath" value="true" />
    </bean>

</beans>
```

SimpleUrlHandlerMapping

The BeanNameUrlHandlerMapping class does not support wildcards to resolve a request URL to a bean name. Let's assume you want the UpdatePolicyController to handle two requests: /createPolicy.do and /updatePolicy.do. With BeanNameUrlHanderMapping, you will need to configure two <bean /> entries. This is redundant, and configuration can be simplified with Apache Ant–style wildcard path mapping with the SimpleUrlHandlerMapping class. Since this is not the default handler mapping, it has to be explicitly configured in the Spring configuration file, as shown in Listing 3-8.

Listing 3-8. insurance-servlet.xml

```
<beans>

    <bean name="simpleUrlHandlerMapping"
        class="org.springframework.web.servlet.handler.SimpleUrlHandlerMapping">
        <property name="mappings">
            <props>
                <prop key="/*Policy.do">updatePolicyController</prop>
            </props>
        </property>
    </bean>

    <bean name="updatePolicyController" class="com.apress.insuranceapp➥
.web.UpdatePolicyController"/>

</beans>
```

As shown in Listing 3-8, the controllers are configured just like any other bean in the Spring container. The mappings property of the handler mapping is very important. It is wired using a java.util.Properties object. Each key of this object is a URL pattern. The key for the updatePolicyController is the URL pattern: /*Policy.do. It uses the * wildcard. This means any request URL ending with Policy.do will be handled by this page controller.

Note that once this handler mapping is detected by the dispatcher servlet, it no longer needs to create the default bean handler mapping instance.

View Handler

Now it's time to take a closer look at another piece of the application controller puzzle—view management. Figure 3-5 shows the simple application controller workflow with the view handler component.

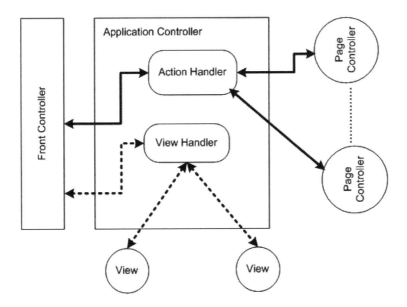

Figure 3-5. *View management workflow*

The role of dispatcher servlet as the coordinator is reemphasized in Figure 3-5. Note that the view handlers are completely decoupled from the action management component.

This is achieved with the `View` and `ViewResolver` interfaces. The `View` interface is an abstraction of any presentation technology available. This makes it possible to integrate and use with Spring MVC any presentation technology, such as an HTML-based JSP or a document-based PDF. Views essentially display the results of business object invocation. They also present controls such as buttons, links, and input boxes for the users to interact with the system. But from the perspective of the application controller and view management, `ViewResolver` is the most important interface. It is responsible for the complete decoupling of view and controllers. Figure 3-6 shows the basic view resolver class diagram.

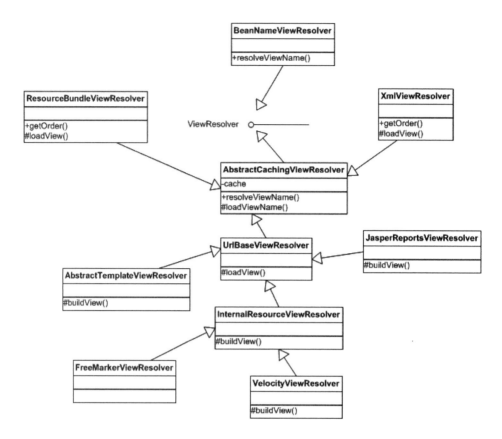

Figure 3-6. *View management class diagram*

The ViewResolver interface defines a single method, resolveViewName, which tries
to resolve a view by name. This method also takes a Locale object as an argument,
which allows implementing classes to support internationalized view lookup. The
BeanNameViewResolver class resolves a view by looking up the current application context
for a bean that has the same name as the view name. AbstractCachingViewResolver provides a convenience base class to implement view resolvers. It caches view objects once
resolved. Like many other classes in the Spring Framework, this class implements the
template pattern, and subclasses implement the abstract method loadView.

The ResourceBundleViewResolver and XmlViewResolver use resource bundles and XML
files to load view definitions. However, this is not the only difference, as I will show you
in the examples later in this chapter. UrlBasedViewResolver is useful because it converts
view names to URLs, without any mapping definition being required explicitly. It can
optionally use a prefix and a suffix. So, a view name of claimdetail and suffix of .jsp will
result in the URL claimdetail.jsp. In short, this class helps map a logical view name to a
physical resource. JasperReportsViewResolver works specifically to map a view name to

a JasperReports-based view. InternalResourceViewResolver, on the other hand, resolves view names to JSP or Apache Tiles–based view components located in the WEB-INF folder. It is the most widely used view resolver. AbstractTemplateViewResolver is the abstract base class used to resolve template-based views. FreeMarkerViewResolver and VelocityViewResolver are two specialized classes to determine views based on FreeMarker and Velocity template engines, respectively. Now that you are familiarized with the important view-handling classes, it's time to turn your attention to the dynamic aspect by exploring the sequence diagram of the view-handling subsystem (see Figure 3-7).

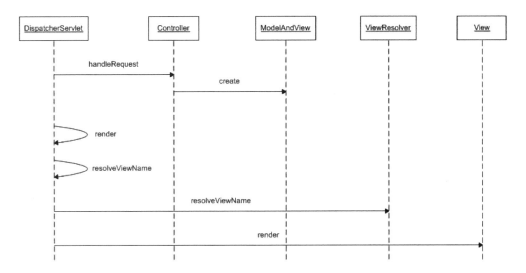

Figure 3-7. *View management sequence diagram*

This is an extension of the workflow discussed in Figure 3-4. The message exchange between the participating objects is as follows:

1. The handler adapter component is responsible for invoking the handleRequest method on the Controller interface.

2. The page controller creates the ModelAndView object and passes it the logical view name and the data to be rendered by the view.

3. The dispatcher servlet then delegates the view-rendering activity to the render method.

4. The render method first tries to locate the appropriate view object by calling the resolveViewName method.

5. The `resolveViewName` method tries to map a given logical view name to a concrete view resource. For this it seeks the help of all the registered `ViewResolver` classes in the application context.

6. When the appropriate view object is resolved, the `render` method is invoked on it to display the model data.

Using View Handlers

In the next section, I will show some of the commonly used concrete view resolvers in action.

ResourceBundleViewResolver

This view resolver implementation has two advantages:

- It allows the logical view name to physical resource mapping to be configured in externalized properties or resource bundle files.

- It adds internationalization support to the view resolution process. If we want to configure a separate set of physical resources for different locales, this class makes that possible.

eInsure had to be rolled out at a leading insurance company that had businesses in Canada and Australia. Hence, eInsure had to support localized views: English in Australia and French in Canada. One solution was to develop two sets of JSPs for presentation, supporting different locales, and let `ResourceBundleViewResolver` find the appropriate view at runtime. To achieve this solution, the eInsure team created two JSPs: `PolicyDetails_en_AU.jsp` and `PolicyDetails_fr_CA.jsp` (Listing 3-9). The first JSP supported the Australian users, while the second catered to the French users in Canada.

Listing 3-9. `PolicyDetails_fr_CA.jsp`

```
<html>
<head>
<title>Underwriting</title>

<script>
    function eventSubmit(url){
        document.policy.action = url;
        document.policy.submit();
```

```
        }
</script>
</head>
<body>

<form name="policy">
    <table>
        <tr>
            <td>Prénom:</td>
            <td><input name="firstName" type="text"/></td>
        </tr>

        <tr>
            <td>Nom de famille:</td>
            <td><input name="lastName" type="text"/></td>

        </tr>

        <tr>
            <td>Age :</td>
            <td><input name="age" type="text"/></td>

        </tr>

        <tr>
            <td colspan="3">
                <input type="button" value="Créer"
            onClick="eventSubmit('createPolicy.do')" />
            </td>
        </tr>
    </table>
</form>

</body>
</html>
```

Next the resource bundle files containing the externalized information to map the logical view names to physical resources were created. Listing 3-10 shows the mapping file for the French Canadian locale. This file is picked up from the classpath and should be placed in the /WEB-INF/classes folder of the web application.

Listing 3-10. `/WEB-INF/classes/insurance-views_fr_CA.properties`

```
policydetails.class=org.springframework.web.servlet.view.JstlView
policydetails.url=/WEB-INF/jsp/PolicyDetails_fr_CA.jsp
```

The base resource bundle file is called `views.properties`. Depending on the locale, the other resources will be named `views_fr_CA.properties` and so on. But this can be changed by configuration. So when a view named `policydetails` is requested, the view resolver creates a new instance of the `JstlView` class. This class represents a JSP-based view that uses the JSP Standard Tag Library. The URL details are then passed to the `JstlView` instance through setter injection. The logical view name is usually supplied by the page controller, as shown in Listing 3-11.

Listing 3-11. `PolicyDetailsController.java`

```java
public class PolicyDetailsController implements Controller {

    public ModelAndView handleRequest(HttpServletRequest request,
HttpServletResponse response)  throws Exception {
        return new ModelAndView("policydetails");
        }
}
```

Finally, the page controller and view resolver should be configured in the Spring application context so that the dispatcher servlet can use them. Listing 3-12 shows the Spring configuration.

Listing 3-12. `insurance-servlet.xml`

```xml
<beans>
     <bean name="/policydetails.do"
class="com.apress.insurance.web.controller.PolicyDetailsController"/>


     <bean id="viewResolver" class="org.springframework.web.servlet.➥
view.ResourceBundleViewResolver">
        <property name="basename" value="insurance-views"></property>
     </bean>

</beans>
```

Note in Listing 3-12 that the base name of the resource bundle has been changed. Hence, in this case the resource bundles that hold the mapping information will be named `insurance-views.properties`, `insurance-views_fr_CA.properties`, and so on. A lot of things happen under the hood because of this configuration. I will summarize them here so you can better understand:

1. A request of `policydetails.do` is intercepted by the dispatcher servlet.

2. The request is handled by the `PolicyDetailsController` page controller. It sets the logical view name that should be used to present the data returned by the business components.

3. The dispatcher servlet invokes the view resolver with the logical view name returned by the controller and the locale information available with the request.

4. The `ResourceBundleViewResolver` first detects the appropriate resource bundle based on the locale.

5. The logical view name is used to detect the appropriate view class configured in the resource bundle. In this is the value of the property `policydetails.class`.

6. Finally, an instance of `JstlView` is created, and the value of the configuration parameter `policydetails.url` is injected into this object and returned to the dispatcher servlet.

The design presented here may be used for an application supporting two locales, but it can have serious side effects. Using a properties file for view management is a cumbersome approach. It can be a nightmare to maintain this application, because we will add n JSPs per locale. In other words, if we support m locales, we will have $m*n$ JSP files. Add to this the view configuration file that is required for each locale. So, effectively we will have $m*(1+n)$ JSP and configuration files to maintain. A better approach is to have a single JSP for all locales. It is backed by m resource bundles for the various locales that the application intends to support. The resource bundles can then be used in the JSP using the View Helper pattern described later. So, in effect we have $(n + 2m)$ files to maintain, which makes things significantly easier.

XmlViewResolver

The `XmlViewResolver` does not support localized view resolution and should replace `ResourceBundleViewResolver` if we intend to implement the solution of one JSP for all locales. So, with `XmlViewResolver`, there is just a single `PolicyDetails.jsp` catering to all the users with the localized labels stored in resource bundles. Most developers find it more convenient to configure the view mapping in an XML file.

To use an XML-based view resolver, configuration information should be moved in XML files from the properties file. This view configuration file should be located in the `WEB-INF` folder and is called `views.xml` by default. As with most parameters in Spring, the location too is configurable. Listing 3-13 shows the `views.xml` file.

Listing 3-13. `/WEB-INF/views.xml`

```
<?xml version="1.0" encoding="UTF-8"?>
<beans xmlns="http://www.springframework.org/schema/beans"
    xmlns:xsi="http://www.w3.org/2001/XMLSchema-instance"
    xsi:schemaLocation="http://www.springframework.org/schema/beans
http://www.springframework.org/schema/beans/spring-beans-2.5.xsd"
    >

    <bean name="policydetails" class="org.springframework.web.➥
servlet.view.JstlView">
        <property name="url" value="/WEB-INF/jsp/PolicyDetails.jsp" />
    </bean>
</beans>
```

Notice that the configuration used is quite similar to the application context configuration. The beans defined in `views.xml` are in fact an extension of the main application context factory. Finally, we need to configure the `XmlViewResolver` in the application context so that it can be used by the front controller servlet. Listing 3-14 shows the modified application context configuration.

Listing 3-14. `insurance-servlet.xml`

```
<?xml version="1.0" encoding="UTF-8"?>
<beans xmlns="http://www.springframework.org/schema/beans"
    xmlns:xsi="http://www.w3.org/2001/XMLSchema-instance"
    xsi:schemaLocation="http://www.springframework.org/schema/beans
http://www.springframework.org/schema/beans/spring-beans-2.5.xsd"
    >

    <bean name="/policydetails.do" class="com.apress.insurance.web.controller.➥
PolicyDetailsController"/>
```

```
        <bean id="viewResolver" class="org.springframework.web.servlet.view.➥
XmlViewResolver" />

</beans>
```

InternalResourceViewResolver

If the application uses only JSPs, then maintaining an external view mapping configuration is not necessary. The `InternalResourceViewResolver` class can determine the physical view in the web application archive given the logical view name. Using this view resolver is just a matter of configuration, as shown in Listing 3-15.

Listing 3-15. `insurance-servlet.xml`

```
<?xml version="1.0" encoding="UTF-8"?>
<beans xmlns="http://www.springframework.org/schema/beans"
    xmlns:xsi="http://www.w3.org/2001/XMLSchema-instance"
    xsi:schemaLocation="http://www.springframework.org/schema/beans
http://www.springframework.org/schema/beans/spring-beans-2.5.xsd"
    >


    <bean name="viewResolver" class="org.springframework.web.servlet.view.➥
InternalResourceViewResolver">
        <property name="viewClass" value="org.springframework.web.servlet.view➥
        .JstlView"></property>
        <property name="prefix" value="/WEB-INF/jsp/"></property>
        <property name="suffix" value=".jsp"></property>
    </bean>
    <bean name="/policydetails.do" class="com.apress.insurance.web.controller➥
.PolicyDetailsController"/>

</beans>
```

Note that the `InternalResourceViewResolver` also returns `JstlView`. It inherits two optional properties—prefix and suffix—from `UrlBasedViewResolver` to completely resolve the physical resource. In this case, the view name `policydetails` will map to a physical resource `/WEB-INF/jsp/policydetails.jps`. This view resolver can also be used with views composed using the Apache Tiles layout framework.

It is possible to chain view resolvers in case a single resolver is insufficient for the application. The view resolver chaining works in a similar way to the handler mapping chain because most of the view resolvers implement the `Ordered` interface.

Consequences

Benefits

- *Enhanced modularity*: Partitioning view and command management into two distinct and decoupled subsystems makes an application modular and robust.

- *Increased reusability*: The application controller makes it possible to reuse the controllers and views.

- *Increased extensibility*: The Spring application controller's various interfaces and abstract base classes with template methods make it easy to extend the framework, supporting a variety of command controllers and views. It is also possible to integrate third-party action-based web frameworks such as WebWork, Struts, and so on, with Spring MVC as well as work with views such as OpenLaszlo and Flex.

Concerns

- *Steep learning curve*: Ideally, the application controller should be a low-level framework concern. For most common needs, you will generally not work with the application controller because Spring has sensible defaults. However, it also throws this component wide open for developers seeking extensibility and flexibility. This adds to the learning curve because you now need to know a lot more about framework internals to support exceptional requirements.

Page Controller

Problem

The JSP-based controller introduced at the beginning of this chapter handled each user action by executing code in `if-else` blocks. Each `if-else` block was responsible primarily for invoking a session bean to carry out a distinct business function. However, this was a most inflexible design and degraded reuse.

I will point out two simple use cases to elaborate on the problem discussed in the previous paragraph. A claimant name can be modified until the claim is finally sanctioned. Such modification involves a simple update operation on the claim record. Now for a slightly tricky situation: consider a case when a lodged claim is rejected because of a lack of evidence. It is easy to think of this as a delete operation. However, it had to be handled as a soft delete by appending an effective end date to the claim record. This was done because a rejected claim could be revived once mandatory information is available. Moreover, it can be used as references for policies taken by the claimant in the future.

The JSP front controller had two distinct if-else blocks to cater to the two scenarios. Two separate blocks of code were unnecessary, because the first case was an update of the name field in the claim record, while the second case required the claim status and effective end date fields to be modified in the same record. Thus, you have two blocks of code where only a single block is really necessary. This is just one example of several such blocks scattered in all the JSP controllers of eInsure. Moreover, as I have already pointed out, JSP is not the appropriate controller to house the user action handlers. For each new feature, a block needs to be added that discouraged OO principles—encapsulation, inheritance, and reusability.

It is easy to consider embedding these blocks in the front controller dispatcher servlet. However, the dispatcher servlet would soon be polluted like the JSP controller, leaving it inflexible and unsuitable for use across applications.

Forces

- Remove the code that invokes business logic in response to user action to reusable components.

- Identify the reusable components based on the request URL instead of hard-coded event and screen code.

- Deploy one reusable component per user action.

Solution

Use a *page controller* to consolidate user action processing.

Strategies with the Spring Framework

I have already introduced Spring page controllers in connection with the Front Controller and Application Controller design patterns. I have also discussed the workflow involved in identifying the appropriate page controller and also configuring them in the Spring registry. However, I left the implementation details until now. In the next few sections, I will explore the page controllers in greater detail.

Using Controller

Listing 3-16 shows the page controller implementation class that I have been referring to and using in the previous examples.

Listing 3-16. CreatePolicyController.java

```java
public class CreatePolicyController implements Controller {

    private UnderwritingBusinessDelegate uwrBusinessDelegate;

    public ModelAndView handleRequest(HttpServletRequest request,
            HttpServletResponse response) throws Exception {

        //transform data from request to a form suitable for use in business layer
        PolicyDetail policyDetail = new PolicyDetail();
        policyDetail.setPolicyId(request.getParameter("policyId"));
        //invoke business component
        this.uwrBusinessDelegate.createPolicy(policyDetail);
        Map model = new HashMap();
        model.put("POLICY_DETAIL", policyDetail);
        //return model and next view
        return new ModelAndView("Success",model);
    }
    public void setUwrBusinessDelegate(
            UnderwritingBusinessDelegate uwrBusinessDelegate) {
        this.uwrBusinessDelegate = uwrBusinessDelegate;
    }
}
```

As shown in Listing 3-16, the `CreatePolicyController` class implements the `Controller` interface provided by the Spring Framework. Hence, it implements the `handleRequest` method of this interface. This method uses the data in the `HttpServletRequest` to populate a simple JavaBean object `PolicyDetail`. It then invokes the business operation to create a new policy. The business logic is invoked using the client-side facade `UnderwritingBusinessDelegate`, which implements the business delegate pattern described in Chapter 4. As shown in Listing 3-17, the business delegate object is injected by the Spring container. Finally, the `ModelAndView` object containing the logical view name and data returned by the business layer is passed to the handler adapter, which invoked this page controller.

Listing 3-17. `Spring-config.xml`

```
<beans xmlns="http://www.springframework.org/schema/beans"
    xmlns:xsi="http://www.w3.org/2001/XMLSchema-instance"
    xsi:schemaLocation="http://www.springframework.org/schema/beans
http://www.springframework.org/schema/beans/spring-beans-2.5.xsd">
    <bean name="/createPolicy.do" class="com.apress.insuranceapp.web.controller➥
.CreatePolicyController">
        <property name="uwrBusinessDelegate" ref="uwrBusinessDelegate"/>
    </bean>

    <bean name="uwrBusinessDelegate" class="com.apress.insuranceapp.business.➥
delegate.UnderwritingBusinessDelegateImpl"/>

</beans>
```

The classes that implement the controller interface must be thread-safe, because they are singleton by default. The controllers have complete access to `HttpServletRequest` and `HttpServletResponse` objects, thus making them dependent on the HTTP protocol. But this also makes these components usable by remoting mechanisms that depend on HTTP. You can use `ThrowawayController` if the target is independent from the servlet API and the controller does not need to be thread-safe.

Using AbstractController

For most cases, the implementation of the `Controller` interface is sufficient. Spring, however, provides several concrete as well as abstract implementations that can be extended depending on the requirement. The class diagram in Figure 3-8 shows one such class.

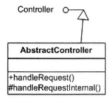

Figure 3-8. *Abstract controller class diagram*

As shown in Figure 3-8, the AbstractController class implements the Controller interface and defines a well-defined workflow that can be used by the subclasses. This class implements the template method design pattern (GOF) to define a fixed workflow with suitable extension hooks to alter the workflow. The sequence diagram shown in Figure 3-9 illustrates the workflow defined by this class.

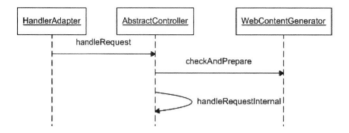

Figure 3-9. *Abstract controller sequence diagram*

The handler adapter invokes the handleRequest method to trigger the workflow. The checkAndPrepare method is then invoked on the superclass WebContentGenerator to perform the following activities:

1. Inspect whether the HTTP method for this request is supported. This can be used to block unwanted HTTP method requests such as DELETE. It can be used for access to some read-only resources such as help pages by supporting GET requests.

2. Check whether an HTTP session is already started. This is can be useful if the application needs some data already stored in the session before carrying out further processing.

3. Set hints for the clients with the cache duration of the final response sent by the dispatcher servlet.

All these tasks can be turned on and off with configuration. The first two tasks will raise a `ServletException` in case of a failure. The extension point here is provided by the abstract `handleRequestInternal` method. All subclasses must implement this template method to provide custom implementation. Thus, `AbstractController` is a convenience base class to simplify page controller implementations.

I will put `AbstractController` into use with a very simple use case. The eInsure application needed to display support and help information to allow the users to comfortably handle the different functions of the application. Listing 3-18 shows the controller for one such scenario.

Listing 3-18. `PolicyQuoteHelpController.java`

```
public class PolicyQuoteHelpController extends AbstractController {


    protected ModelAndView handleRequestInternal(HttpServletRequest request,
            HttpServletResponse response) throws Exception {

        return new ModelAndView("policyquotehelp");
    }
}
```

The `PolicyQuoteHelpController` does not invoke any business logic. Instead, it acts as a read-only controller, just transferring control to the next view. But before doing so, it checks whether the request is by the HTTP `GET` method and a session already exists. Note that these two options are set through configuration, as shown in Listing 3-19.

Listing 3-19. `spring-config.xml`

```
<beans>

    <bean name="/policyquotehelp.do" class="com.apress.insuranceapp.➥
web.controller.PolicyQuoteHelpController">
        <property name="supportedMethods" value="GET"/>
        <property name="requireSession" value="true"/>
    </bean>

</beans>
```

If the two checks mentioned earlier are not required, then the `UrlFilenameView➥` `Controller` class can be combined with view resolvers to implement page controllers that pass only the logical view name. I will cover this kind of controller in greater detail while discussing the Dispatcher View pattern later in this chapter.

Using AbstractCommandController

Most of the use cases in a web application operate by collecting the information supplied in HTML forms and then performing business actions based on this form data. It is possible to get all the form data from the `HttpServletRequest` object primarily using the `getParameter` method. It is a bad practice to pass the request object to the business tier because it would then be tied down to clients of a specific protocol type. Hence, the `getParameter` method can be used to retrieve all required data to populate a JavaBean object. This JavaBean object is passed to the business layer.

Putting the JavaBean creation logic in the controller violates SRP. Any change to the form field may cause a change in the controller. A flexible and clean design would be to create this JavaBean object outside the controller and pass it as a parameter to the controller. This requirement is fulfilled by controllers that implement the `AbstractCommand➥` `Controller` class. The handler adapter populates the POJO object from the `HttpServletRequest` object, which is then passed to the controller. It maps the form field names to the properties of the POJO.

The JSP shown in Listing 3-20 is used to underwrite new policies. It presents a simplified policy underwriting form with only three fields. Listing 3-21 shows the JavaBean class, which is used to populate the form data. Some developers call these classes *command classes*. This name is inappropriate, however, because the page controllers are command objects that implement the command design pattern (GOF). These data holder classes on the server that populate and store values passed through HTML form submission are better called *form beans*.

Listing 3-20. `WEB-INF/jsp/createPolicy.jsp`

```
<html>
<head>
<title>Underwriting</title>
<script>
    function eventSubmit(url){
        document.policy.action = url;
        document.policy.submit();
    }
```

```
</script>
</head>
<body onLoad="displayError(<%=request.getAttribute("ERROR_MESSAGE")%>)">

<form name="policy" method="POST">

    First Name <input type="text" name="firstName" value="" /><br/>
    Last Name <input type="text" name="lastName" value="" /><br/>
    Age <input type="text" name="age" value="" /><br/>

    <input type="button" value="Save" onClick="eventSubmit('saveNewPolicy.do')"/>
</form>
</body>
</html>
```

With Spring MVC, the form bean does not have any life-cycle dependency on the framework, except creation. Also, the form beans do not need to implement any framework-specific interface. Hence, these objects can be safely used in other parts of the application—business tier and integration tier.

Listing 3-21. `PolicyFormBean.java`

```
public class PolicyFormBean implements Serializable {

    private String firstName;
    private String lastName;
    private int age;

    public int getAge() {
        return age;
    }
    public void setAge(int age) {
        this.age = age;
    }
    public String getFirstName() {
        return firstName;
    }
    public void setFirstName(String firstName) {
        this.firstName = firstName;
    }
```

```
    public String getLastName() {
        return lastName;
    }
    public void setLastName(String lastName) {
        this.lastName = lastName;
    }
}
```

Thus, a form bean is a POJO with a get and set method for each field. Note that the field name in this class exactly matches the name attribute of the HTML input elements. Listing 3-22 shows the controller implementation.

Listing 3-22. SaveNewPolicyController.java

```
public class SaveNewPolicyController extends AbstractCommandController {
    private UnderWritingBusinessDelegate uwrBusinessDelegate;

    public SaveNewPolicyController() {
        this.setCommandClass(PolicyFormBean.class);
    }

    public void setUwrBusinessDelegate(
            UnderWritingBusinessDelegate uwrBusinessDelegate) {
        this.uwrBusinessDelegate = uwrBusinessDelegate;
    }

    protected ModelAndView handle(HttpServletRequest request,
            HttpServletResponse res, Object formBean, BindException errors)
            throws Exception {
        PolicyFormBean policyBean = (PolicyFormBean) formBean;
        log.info("First Name--" + policyBean.getFirstName());
        log.info("Last Name--" + policyBean.getLastName());
        log.info("Age --" + policyBean.getAge());

        this.uwrBusinessDelegate.createPolicy(policyBean);

        return new ModelAndView("showPolicydetails","policydetails",policyBean);
    }
}
```

The policy controller now extends the AbstractCommandContoller. The AbstractCommandController workflow was altered by overriding the handle method. Finally, Listing 3-23 shows the Spring configuration file that wires everything up.

Listing 3-23. `insurance-servlet.xml`

```xml
<?xml version="1.0" encoding="UTF-8"?>
<beans xmlns="http://www.springframework.org/schema/beans"
    xmlns:xsi="http://www.w3.org/2001/XMLSchema-instance"
    xsi:schemaLocation="http://www.springframework.org/schema/beans
http://www.springframework.org/schema/beans/spring-beans-2.5.xsd"
    >


    <bean name="simpleUrlHandlerMapping"
        class="org.springframework.web.servlet.handler.SimpleUrlHandlerMapping">
        <property name="mappings">
            <props>
                <prop key="/create*.do">staticViewController</prop>
            </props>
        </property>
    </bean>


    <bean name="beanNameUrlHandlerMapping"
        class="org.springframework.web.servlet.handler.BeanNameUrlHandlerMapping">
        <property name="order" value="1" />
    </bean>

    <bean name="viewResolver"
        class="org.springframework.web.servlet.view.InternalResourceViewResolver">
        <property name="viewClass"
            value="org.springframework.web.servlet.view.JstlView" />
        <property name="prefix" value="/WEB-INF/jsp/" />
        <property name="suffix" value=".jsp" />
    </bean>

    <bean name="staticViewController"
        class="org.springframework.web.servlet.mvc.UrlFilenameViewController" >
    </bean>
```

```
<bean name="/saveNewPolicy.do"
    class="com.apress.insurance.web.controller.SaveNewPolicyController" >
    <property name="uwrBusinessDelegate"
        ref="underwritingBusinessDelegate" />
</bean>

<bean name="underwritingBusinessDelegate"
    class="com.apress.insurance.view.delegate.UnderWritingBusinessDelegate" />
```

```
</beans>
```

The web page that is presented to the end user's browser to create a policy does not require any dynamic data. Hence, I have configured a `UrlFilenameViewController` object to handle this request. It converts a resource name in the URL into a logical view name. So, the request for `createPolicy.do` will result in a symbolic view name: `createPolicy`. The `SimpleUrlHandlerMapping` with wildcard mapping resolves any request starting with `create`, such as `createPolicy.do`, and invokes the `UrlFilenameViewController`, which returns the logical view name. Finally, the view resolver is invoked by the front controller to resolve the logical view name to a physical resource, `/WEB-INF/jsp/createPolicy.jsp`.

In `createPolicy.jsp` (Listing 3-20), whenever the user clicks the Save button, a request is sent to the server for the resource `saveNewPolicy.do`. Now a handler mapping chain has been configured in Listing 3-23. The `BeanNameUrlHandlerMapping` with higher precedence is able to resolve this URL and invokes the `SaveNewPolicyController`. The logical view name returned by this controller is finally resolved to the resource `showPolicydetails.jsp`.

Using SimpleFormController

A typical web application involves displaying a form to collect user input. The users fill in this form and submit the data to the web server for further processing. `SimpleFormController` is widely used to provide page controller implementations because it coordinates and manages the two most important aspects of a form's life cycle—view and submission. As with many other Spring MVC classes, this one also implements the template design pattern and is closed for modification but open for extension at suitable points of the workflow. The workflow can also be altered by setting various configurable properties.

Form Display

I will first look at the form display feature provided by the `SimpleFormController` class. Figure 3-10 shows the workflow of this function.

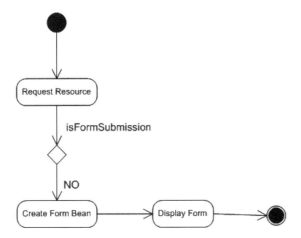

Figure 3-10. *Form display workflow in* `SimpleFormController`

This is an oversimplified workflow, because I want to focus only on areas of interest. You can find a detailed workflow and explanation in the book *Expert Spring MVC and Web Flow* (Apress, 2006). As shown in Figure 3-11, the web browser's request for a resource is eventually delegated to the page controller. The `SimpleFormController` detects that the request has come via HTTP `GET`, so this is not a form submission but a request for form display. It creates an instance of the form bean and makes the form ready to be displayed.

I will now take up the example discussed earlier with `AbstractCommandController` and try to implement it with `SimpleFormController` because the latter offers greater flexibility. As a first step, I will simplify the JSP as shown in Listing 3-24. Note that JavaScript is not used to submit the form anymore. Also notice that the action attribute of the form does not specify a value. This removes any coupling with a particular action URL. Apart from these two changes, the JSP is the same as the one presented in Listing 3-20.

Listing 3-24. `WEB-INF/jsp/createPolicy.jsp`

```
<html>
<head>
<title>Underwriting</title>

</head>

<form action="" method="POST">
```

```
    First Name <input type="text" name="firstName" value="" /><br/>
    Last Name <input type="text" name="lastName" value="" /><br/>
    Age <input type="text" name="age" value="" /><br/>

    <input type="submit" value="Save" />
</form>
</body>
</html>
```

SaveNewPolicyController now extends the SimpleFormController as shown in
Listing 3-25. Note that this version is suitable only for form display.

Listing 3-25. SaveNewPolicyController.java

```java
public class SaveNewPolicyController extends SimpleFormController {

    private UnderWritingBusinessDelegate uwrBusinessDelegate;

    public SaveNewPolicyController() {
        setCommandClass(PolicyFormBean.class);
    }

    public void setUwrBusinessDelegate(
            UnderWritingBusinessDelegate uwrBusinessDelegate) {
        this.uwrBusinessDelegate = uwrBusinessDelegate;
    }
}
```

Finally, I will wire up the beans in the Spring configuration file as shown in
Listing 3-26. This is a very clean configuration. A GET request for /createPolicy.do is intercepted by the SaveNewPolicyController, which considers this as a form display request.
The property formView serves as a logical view name, which is resolved to the physical
view /WEB-INF/jsp/createPolicy.jsp to present the form to the end user.

Listing 3-26. insurance-servlet.xml

```xml
<?xml version="1.0" encoding="UTF-8"?>
<beans xmlns="http://www.springframework.org/schema/beans"
    xmlns:xsi="http://www.w3.org/2001/XMLSchema-instance"
    xsi:schemaLocation="http://www.springframework.org/schema/beans
```

```
http://www.springframework.org/schema/beans/spring-beans-2.5.xsd"
    >

    <bean name="viewResolver"
        class="org.springframework.web.servlet.view.InternalResourceViewResolver">
        <property name="viewClass"
            value="org.springframework.web.servlet.view.JstlView" />
        <property name="prefix" value="/WEB-INF/jsp/" />
        <property name="suffix" value=".jsp" />
    </bean>

    <bean name="/createPolicy.do"
        class="com.apress.insurance.web.controller.SaveNewPolicyController" >
        <property name="uwrBusinessDelegate"
            ref="underwritingBusinessDelegate" />

        <property name="formView"
            value="createPolicy" />

    </bean>

    <bean name="underwritingBusinessDelegate"
        class="com.apress.insurance.view.delegate.UnderWritingBusinessDelegate" />

</beans>
```

Form Submission

The underwriters using the eInsure application would fill up this form and submit it to underwrite new policies. The controller determines this request as a form submission, since the method attribute of the form was set as POST. Now you must be wondering how this form submits to the URL /createPolicy.do again because the action attribute in the form is not specified. This in fact is a trick. If the action attribute is empty, the form will post back to itself, that is, the page that presented the form. This will result in a new POST request reaching the SaveNewPolicyController. Figure 3-11 shows the form submission workflow.

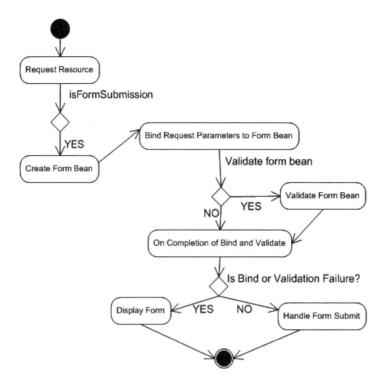

Figure 3-11. *Form submission workflow in* SimpleFormController

To handle form submission, the controller needs to override one of the many template methods. Since the goal is to just invoke a business service in the controller, you can override the simplest method called doSubmitAction. With this method, you do not need to explicitly return any ModelAndView object. The form bean is automatically set in the model object by the framework itself, with the identifier as the command name. If more data has to be passed, then the onSubmit method needs to be overridden. This method allows the creation of a ModelAndView object, which can be used to pass more data than with the default approach.

Listing 3-27 shows the modified controller.

Listing 3-27. SaveNewPolicyController.java

```
public class SaveNewPolicyController extends SimpleFormController {
    private UnderWritingBusinessDelegate uwrBusinessDelegate;

    public SaveNewPolicyController() {
        setCommandClass(PolicyFormBean.class);
    }
```

```
    public void setUwrBusinessDelegate(
            UnderWritingBusinessDelegate uwrBusinessDelegate) {
        this.uwrBusinessDelegate = uwrBusinessDelegate;
    }

    /*

    protected ModelAndView onSubmit(Object formbean) throws Exception {
        PolicyFormBean policyBean = (PolicyFormBean)formbean;
        uwrBusinessDelegate.createPolicy(policyBean);
        return new ModelAndView(this.getSuccessView(),"policydetails",formbean);
    }
*/

}
```

To use the `SimpleFormController`, you have to set a few configuration parameters. The first property is the `commandName` property. This name is used as the key for the form bean object set in the model. The next property you need to consider is `successView`. This specifies a logical view name just like the property `formView`. This view will be used to render a response in case of a successful form submission. Listing 3-28 shows the configuration details.

Note that the command class/form bean has also been configured in `insurance-servlet.xml`. Hence, you don't need to register the form bean in the constructor of the page controller.

Listing 3-28. `insurance-servlet.xml`

```
<?xml version="1.0" encoding="UTF-8"?>
<beans xmlns="http://www.springframework.org/schema/beans"
    xmlns:xsi="http://www.w3.org/2001/XMLSchema-instance"
    xsi:schemaLocation="http://www.springframework.org/schema/beans
http://www.springframework.org/schema/beans/spring-beans-2.5.xsd"
    >

    <bean name="/createPolicy.do"
        class="com.apress.insurance.web.controller.SaveNewPolicyController" >
        <property name="uwrBusinessDelegate"
            ref="underwritingBusinessDelegate" />
```

```
            <property name="formView"
                value="createPolicy" />

            <property name="commandName"
                value="policydetails" />

            <property name="successView"
                value="policydetails" />

            <property name="commandClass"
                value="com.apress.insuranceapp.web.formbean.PolicyFormBean" />

    </bean>
</beans>
```

Finally, Listing 3-29 shows the success view. It uses JSTL tags to retrieve model data.

Listing 3-29. WEB-INF/jsp/policydetails.jsp

```
<%@ taglib prefix="c" uri="http://java.sun.com/jsp/jstl/core" %>
<%@ taglib prefix="fmt" uri="http://java.sun.com/jsp/jstl/fmt" %>

<html>
<head>
<title>Underwriting</title>

</head>
<body>

<form >


    <table>
        <tr>
            <td>First Name:</td>
            <td><c:out value="${policydetails.firstName}"/></td>


        </tr>
```

```
    <tr>
        <td>Last Name:</td>
        <td><c:out value="${policydetails.lastName}"/></td>

    </tr>

    <tr>
        <td>Age :</td>
        <td><c:out value="${policydetails.age}"/></td>

    </tr>

  </table>

</form>

</body>
</html>
```

Form Validation

In the form shown in Listing 3-24, the fields have certain restrictions. The first name and last name fields are mandatory, and age must be an integer. It is possible to check these restrictions using client-side JavaScript. However, most applications these days require cross-browser support, and JavaScript is the most significant obstacle to this. The alternative option is server-side form validation. As shown in Figure 3-12, the `SimpleFormController` supports server-side form validation.

Spring MVC supports two types of validators:

- *Programmatic validators*: These implement the validations with customized logic. These are generally carried out by classes that implement the `Validator` interface. For the sake of simplicity, I will concentrate on this variety only.

- *Declarative validators*: These implement the validations via configuration. Spring MVC integrates with two validation frameworks—Commons Validator and VALANG—to provide this feature. The integration and usage of these two are a huge subject and beyond the scope of this book. For detailed treatment on these two frameworks, refer to *Expert Spring MVC and Web Flow* (Apress, 2006).

The first step to form validation is creating an implementation of the `Validator` interface, as shown in Listing 3-30. The implementation of the supports method is necessary, because it informs the Spring MVC framework whether a validator is applicable for a form bean type. However, the most important is the validate method, which contains the validation logic. For mandatory field validation, Spring provides a helper class with static methods called ValidationUtils. As shown in Listing 3-30, the Errors object reference, the field name that has to be validated, and an error code are passed to the rejectIfEmpty method for validation. If there is a validation failure, the error object is populated with the error message. This message is picked up from a resource bundle based on the supplied error code.

Listing 3-30. PolicyFormbeanValidator.java

```java
public class PolicyFormbeanValidator implements Validator {

public boolean supports(Class clazz) {
                return PolicyFormBean.class.equals(clazz);
        }

    public void validate(Object formBean, Errors errors) {
        PolicyFormBean policybean = (PolicyFormBean) formBean;

        ValidationUtils.rejectIfEmpty(errors, "firstName", "mandatoryfirstname");

    }
}
```

Now that the validator is ready, it must be connected to the controller. This is done by wiring it in the Spring configuration. Apart from this, the resource bundle locator also must be configured. This is shown in the modified Spring configuration in Listing 3-31.

Listing 3-31. insurance-servlet.xml

```xml
<?xml version="1.0" encoding="UTF-8"?>
<beans xmlns="http://www.springframework.org/schema/beans"
    xmlns:xsi="http://www.w3.org/2001/XMLSchema-instance"
    xsi:schemaLocation="http://www.springframework.org/schema/beans
http://www.springframework.org/schema/beans/spring-beans-2.5.xsd"
    >

    <bean name="viewResolver"
        class="org.springframework.web.servlet.view.InternalResourceViewResolver">
        <property name="viewClass"
            value="org.springframework.web.servlet.view.JstlView" />
```

```xml
        <property name="prefix" value="/WEB-INF/jsp/" />
        <property name="suffix" value=".jsp" />
    </bean>
    <bean name="/createPolicy.do"
        class="com.apress.insurance.web.controller.SaveNewPolicyController" >
        <property name="uwrBusinessDelegate"
            ref="underwritingBusinessDelegate" />

        <property name="formView"
            value="createPolicy" />

        <property name="commandName"
            value="policydetails" />

        <property name="successView"
            value="policydetails" />

        <property name="commandClass"
            value="com.apress.insuranceapp.web.formbean.PolicyFormBean" />

        <property name="validator"
            ref="policyUnderwriteValidtor" />

    </bean>

    <bean id="messageSource" class="org.springframework.context.support.➥
ResourceBundleMessageSource">
        <property name="basename" value="messages"/>
    </bean>

    <bean name="policyUnderwriteValidtor"
        class="com.apress.insurance.web.validator.PolicyFormbeanValidator" />

    <bean name="underwritingBusinessDelegate"
        class="com.apress.insurance.view.delegate.UnderWritingBusinessDelegate" />

</beans>
```

The resource bundle file that holds the error messages has a base name of messages. Listing 3-32 shows a sample resource bundle.

Listing 3-32. `WEB-INF/classes/messages_en_US.properties`

```
mandatoryfirstname.policydetails.firstName=First name field is mandatory
mandatoryfirstname.policydetails.mandatorylastname=Last name field is mandatory
mandatoryfirstname.policydetails.mandatoryAge=Age➡
field is mandatory and should be an integer(0-9)
```

Note that the message keys are different from the error keys. This is because the `MessageCodesResolver` implementation converts the error key to append the command name and field name. Finally, we also need to modify the JSP slightly to display validation error messages alongside the corresponding fields. For this purpose, I will use the tag library provided by Spring to simplify the development of JSP-based views. Listing 3-33 shows the modified JSP.

Listing 3-33. `WEB-INF/jsp/createPolicy.jsp`

```jsp
<%@ taglib prefix="form" uri="http://www.springframework.org/tags/form" %>
<%@ taglib prefix="c" uri="http://java.sun.com/jsp/jstl/core" %>
<%@ taglib prefix="fmt" uri="http://java.sun.com/jsp/jstl/fmt" %>

<html>
<head>
<title>Underwriting</title>
<style>
    .error { color: red; }
  </style>
</head>

<form:form action="" method="POST" commandName="policydetails">

    First Name <form:input path="firstName"/>
<form:errors path="firstName" cssClass="error"/><br/>
    Last Name <form:input path="lastName"/>
        <form:errors path="lastName" cssClass="error"/><br/>
    Age <form:input path="age"/> <form:errors path="age" cssClass="error"/><br/>

    <input type="submit" value="Save" />
</form:form>
</body>
</html>
```

Apart from the controllers discussed so far, Spring MVC provides few other controllers (abstract as well as concrete implementations) for specific requirements. Some of these controllers are listed in Table 3-1.They are required occasionally only for a handful of use cases.

Table 3-1. *Occasionally Useful Page Controllers*

File Name	Description
MultiActionController	Some developers think it is useful to group a logical set of actions into a single controller implementation class. All the actions related to a policy creation page—Save, Edit, and so on—can be placed in a single class that extends the MultiActionController. This is useful in reducing concrete implementations of page controllers for a large application. Spring MVC can determine which method to invoke using a class called MethodNameResolver. This class can determine the method name from a parameter set in the HttpServletRequest.
AbstractWizardFormController	Some use cases in an application are best handled by presenting multiple pages, before final action is taken. Such multistep use cases are commonly seen in web applications for the registration or sign-up process. eInsure also deployed a multistep workflow for collecting policy and claim details. Spring MVC provides out-of-the-box support to model use cases of this kind through the AbstractWizardFormController class.

Consequences

Benefits

- *Increased reusability*: The consolidation of use case processing in page controllers enables reuse.

- *Increased extensibility*: With Spring support, it is possible not only to implement custom page controllers but also to integrate with page controllers of other frameworks such as Struts, WebWork, and so on.

- *Life-cycle support*: Without Spring MVC, supporting the form handling life cycle would lead to a lot of custom code, causing effort wastage and difficulties in maintenance. However, with Spring, most of the boilerplate code associated with form life-cycle and command management is provided out of the box.

Concerns

- *Steep learning curve*: With Spring, MVC controller support has a plethora of options. As a result, developers need to know about plenty of interfaces and abstract classes to make the appropriate design decisions.

- *Hard to maintain*: Now the application has one page controller per use case. In a large application, this would lead to a huge set of controller classes, making it difficult to manage and maintain.

Context Object

Problem

eInsure had a product workbench that was used by business analysts and product designers to devise and roll out insurance products. Put simply, an insurance product defines a set of rules used to underwrite a specific class of policies. One of the customers who used eInsure wanted an offline version of the product workbench module. This application would be installed on the laptops used by the business analysts. This would enable them to work out the details of the product even when offline and synchronize with the main database later, before finally releasing the rulesets.

There were two choices for this offline application. One was Java Swing–based desktop software, and the other was the same eInsure application running on an embedded web server with a synchronization facility. Our customer preferred the first solution. Since eInsure was being refactored to use Spring Framework, our initial take was that most of the codebase (except the presentation tier view components) would be reusable. The eInsure team was delighted about having moved to Spring because this Swing application would run easily out of the container.

But soon our high hopes turned to despair when we found that even the page controllers could not be reused. The reason for this was that the presentation tier code was tightly coupled to the HTTP protocol and the servlet API. The page controllers implemented the `Controller` interface and in the process heavily used `HttpServletRequest` and `HttpServletResponse` objects. These objects were used to extract the data from form submission. The result was a set of page controllers that could not be reused outside a web application. The development team was left with no choice but to build the application from scratch, resulting in an unnecessary expenditure of effort.

Forces

- Don't let protocol-specific API usage proliferate deep into a layer. This intrusion pollutes application code by reducing reusability.

- Identify the appropriate context where protocol-specific code is to be used. In this case, the use of protocol-specific code should be limited to the front controller or at most the application controller.

- Increase the reusability of page controllers.

- Make page controllers easily testable components.

Solution

Use a *context object* to encapsulate and share form data without any protocol dependency.

Strategies with the Spring Framework

During the discussion of the Page Controller pattern, I did make attempts to break free from the coupling of protocol-specific code. But since the `SimpleFormController` inherited from controllers that had association with the `HttpServletRequest` and `HttpServletResponse` objects, the runtime dependency remained. Hence, it was not possible to use this controller outside the web container.

Spring MVC, however, provides a controller that is independent of any protocol-specific details. The `ThrowawayController` interface is completely unaware of the servlet-specific API. The implementation classes are similar to JSF managed beans with the properties mapping to the HTML form fields. It also needs to implement the single `execute` method that should be used to invoke business logic. This method is called by the handler adapter only when setting all the properties is successful and there is no data conversion error. Since `ThrowawayController` belongs to a different class hierarchy than other controllers, executing these controllers requires a specific handler adapter called `ThrowawayControllerHandlerAdapter`. However, there is no need to configure this handler adapter explicitly, because it is assumed as the default along with `SimpleControllerHandlerAdapter`.

Listing 3-34 shows the ThrowawayController implementation. For each property it defines a getter/setter combination to map the form fields. The handler adapter extracts the form field values using the servlet API and maps them to the properties of this controller. This makes the controller reusable and free from protocol specifics. It can very well be used with Swing components with an appropriate handler adapter.

Listing 3-34. SaveClaimController.java

```java
public class SaveClaimController implements ThrowawayController {

    private String claimantName;
    private String policyNo;
    private String productCd;

    public ModelAndView execute() throws Exception {
        //Invoke business logic here

        return new ModelAndView("claimDetails");
    }
    public String getClaimantName() {
        return claimantName;
    }

    public void setClaimantName(String claimantName) {
        this.claimantName = claimantName;
    }
    public String getPolicyNo() {
        return policyNo;
    }
    public void setPolicyNo(String policyNo) {
        this.policyNo = policyNo;
    }
    public String getProductCd() {
        return productCd;
    }
    public void setProductCd(String productCd) {
        this.productCd = productCd;
    }
}
```

Listing 3-35 shows the JSP that maps to the throwaway controller shown just now.

Listing 3-35. `WEB-INF/jsp/createClaim.jsp`

```
<html>
<head>
<title>New Claim</title>

</head>

<form action="saveClaim.do" method="POST">

    Claimant Name <input type="text" name="claimantName" value="" /><br/>
    Policy Number <input type="text" name="policyNo" value="" /><br/>
    Product Code<input type="text" name="productCd" value="" /><br/>

    <input type="submit" value="Save" />
</form>
</body>
</html>
```

Finally, the controller needs to be added in the Spring configuration, as shown in Listing 3-36.

Listing 3-36. `insurance-servlet.xml`

```
<?xml version="1.0" encoding="UTF-8"?>
<beans xmlns="http://www.springframework.org/schema/beans"
    xmlns:xsi="http://www.w3.org/2001/XMLSchema-instance"
    xsi:schemaLocation="http://www.springframework.org/schema/beans
http://www.springframework.org/schema/beans/spring-beans-2.5.xsd"
    >
<!- - Other beans - ->

    <bean name="/saveClaim.do"
        class="com.apress.insurance.web.controller.SaveClaimController" />

</beans>
```

Thus, a throwaway controller is a combination of form bean and page controller. Note that its independence from the Servlet API increases reusability and makes this controller easier to unit test. But it has some disadvantages too. Since this is a stateful controller, a new instance should be created for each request. This in turn wastes space on the JVM heap, increasing the need for garbage collection and the resulting pauses. However, with a modern well-tuned JVM, this is not a major problem. This controller is very simple, without any detailed workflow. It does not support validation of form fields. Moreover, since the form fields are now part of this class, it is awkward to pass data from presentation layer to business layer.

The tight coupling of the form bean in the page controller can be solved by a custom solution. To achieve this, I will define a new throwaway controller interface that, like the earlier one, is free from servlet API dependency. This is shown in Listing 3-37.

Listing 3-37. `SimpleFormThrowawayController.java`

```
package com.apress.insurance.web.controller.api;

import org.springframework.web.servlet.ModelAndView;

public interface SimpleFormThrowawayController {
    public ModelAndView execute(Object formBean) throws Exception;
    public Class getFormbeanClass();

}
```

Note that the throwaway controllers now need to implement this new interface, as shown in Listing 3-37. The execute method of this interface needs to be implemented to invoke business logic. It receives an instance of the form bean from the handler adapter. Now I will show an implementation of the new throwaway controller and move the functionality shown in Listing 3-34 to this one.

It is evident from Listing 3-38 that this throwaway controller, being stateless, can have just a single instance in the web application context.

Listing 3-38. `SaveClaimController.java`

```
public class SaveClaimController implements SimpleFormThrowawayController {

    public ModelAndView execute(Object formBean) throws Exception {
        ClaimFormbean formbean = (ClaimFormbean)formBean;
        //Invoke business logic here
        return new ModelAndView("claimDetails");
```

```
    }
    public Class getFormbeanClass() {
        return ClaimFormbean.class;
    }
}
```

Listing 3-39 shows the form bean.

Listing 3-39. ClaimFormbean.java

```
public class ClaimFormbean implements Serializable {
    private String claimantName;
    private String policyNo;
    private String productCd;

    public String getClaimantName() {
        return claimantName;
    }

    public void setClaimantName(String claimantName) {
        this.claimantName = claimantName;
    }

    public String getPolicyNo() {
        return policyNo;
    }

    public void setPolicyNo(String policyNo) {
        this.policyNo = policyNo;
    }

    public String getProductCd() {
        return productCd;
    }

    public void setProductCd(String productCd) {
        this.productCd = productCd;
    }

}
```

To execute this modified workflow, I will need to map the request parameters to the form bean in some component. You already know that the most appropriate component for this is the handler adapter. Listing 3-40 shows the handler adapter that executes the SimpleFormThrowaway controllers.

Listing 3-40. SimpleFormThrowawayControllerHandlerAdapter.java

```java
package com.apress.insurance.web.handleradpter.api;

public class SimpleFormThrowawayControllerHandlerAdapter
    extends ThrowawayControllerHandlerAdapter {

    public boolean supports(Object handler) {
        return (handler instanceof SimpleFormThrowawayController);
    }

    public ModelAndView handle(HttpServletRequest req, HttpServletResponse res,
        Object command) throws Exception {
        SimpleFormThrowawayController throwaway = (SimpleFormThrowawayController)
command;
        Object formBean = throwaway.getFormbeanClass().newInstance();

        ServletRequestDataBinder binder = createBinder(req, formBean);
        binder.bind(req);
        binder.closeNoCatch();

        return throwaway.execute(formBean);
    }

    protected ServletRequestDataBinder createBinder(
        HttpServletRequest request, Object formbean) throws Exception {
        ServletRequestDataBinder binder = new ServletRequestDataBinder(formbean,
                getCommandName());
        initBinder(request, binder);

        return binder;
    }
}
```

Note that the createBinder method is responsible for binding the HTTP parameter values to the properties of the form bean. The handler adapter takes care of all the protocol-specific details. Finally, I will wire up everything in the Spring configuration file. Since this handler adapter is not a default one, I will need to explicitly declare it as part of the configuration information. Because I am using handler adapter chaining, the default handler adapter also has to be explicitly configured. Listing 3-41 shows all of this.

Listing 3-41. `insurance-servlet.xml`

```xml
<?xml version="1.0" encoding="UTF-8"?>
<beans xmlns="http://www.springframework.org/schema/beans"
    xmlns:xsi="http://www.w3.org/2001/XMLSchema-instance"
    xsi:schemaLocation="http://www.springframework.org/schema/beans
http://www.springframework.org/schema/beans/spring-beans-2.5.xsd">

    <bean name="throwawayHandlerAdapter"
        class="com.apress.insurance.web.handleradpter.api.➥
SimpleFormThrowawayControllerHandlerAdapter" />

    <bean name="simpleControllerHandlerAdapter"
        class="org.springframework.web.servlet.mvc.➥
SimpleControllerHandlerAdapter" />

    <bean name="viewResolver"
        class="org.springframework.web.servlet.view.InternalResourceViewResolver">
        <property name="viewClass"
            value="org.springframework.web.servlet.view.JstlView" />
        <property name="prefix" value="/WEB-INF/jsp/" />
        <property name="suffix" value=".jsp" />
    </bean>

    <bean name="/createClaim.do"
        class="com.apress.insurance.web.controller.DisplayNewClaimController" />

    <bean name="/saveClaim.do"
        class="com.apress.insurance.web.controller.SaveClaimController" />

    <bean name="underwritingBusinessDelegate"
        class="com.apress.insurance.view.delegate.UnderWritingBusinessDelegate" />

</beans>
```

In the previous few sections, I have tried to alter and extend the workflow of the throw-away controller. In case you are interested, to further enhance this workflow to add more functionality such as validation, look at extending the `ValidatableThrowawayController` and its corresponding handler adapter `ValidatableThrowawayControllerHandlerAdapter`.

Consequences

Benefits

- *Improved reusability*: Context objects are free from dependencies on any particular protocol.

- *Support variety of clients*: The lack of dependency on any particular protocol makes it easy to support different clients with the same codebase.

- *Easy to test*: Without protocol dependency, the page controllers are easily testable because you can run the tests outside the container and without any servlet-related objects.

Concerns

- *Performance consideration*: Mapping HTML form field values on to form bean properties is done using reflection. This may degrade performance.

- *Hard to maintain*: Using form beans along with page controllers increases the number of classes that have to be maintained.

Intercepting Filter

Problem

The JSP controller presented at the beginning of this chapter performed an authorization check before actually executing an action in the `if-else` block. However, since the eInsure application had multiple controllers, this code was duplicated in all of them. It would be useful if this code were extracted in a common component and applied declaratively, transparent to the controller. This would enhance the application's flexibility. Otherwise, any changes to this common authorization logic would have to be replicated across all the JSP front controllers.

A client who was using eInsure in production submitted some enhancements. They wanted to prevent access to the application beyond the scheduled office hours of 9 a.m. to 6 p.m. This would let them use this downtime to run scheduled batch programs more efficiently. In addition, they wanted to track and analyze the usage pattern of the web site. Last but not least, they wanted a configurable monitor to track the time spent by individual page controllers in fulfilling a request. This would be turned on from time to time to check system performance.

The typical approach in this case would be to create some new components and change some existing ones. But this is risky as new bugs can be added to the existing codebase. A careful analysis of these new requirements reveals that they can best be addressed by applying new reusable components before and after the existing code. It should be possible to configure and apply these components transparently without affecting the existing code. This would save lot of time and effort if existing components had to be altered.

Forces

- You want common processing to be centralized into reusable components.

- The preprocessing and postprocessing components should be loosely coupled to the existing application code.

- Apply common processing declaratively.

Solution

Use an *intercepting filter* to apply reusable processing transparently before and after the actual request execution by the front and page controllers.

Strategies with the Spring Framework

Servlet Filter

It is possible to solve some of the requirements mentioned earlier with filters that are built into the servlet API. All modern web servers provide support for filters—code that is executed before control passes to a target servlet, after control leaves the servlet, or both.

In fact, it is possible to configure a chain of filters to be executed for each request, as shown in Figure 3-12.

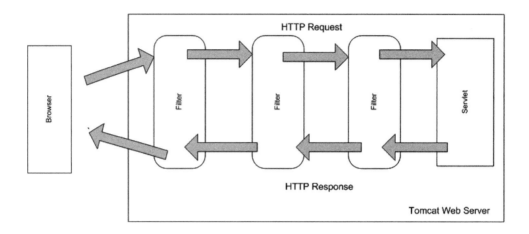

Figure 3-12. *Servlet filter chain*

Filters are pluggable components that provide preprocessing and postprocessing support around a servlet. This technique works with JSPs too, because they are effectively servlets. The filters are configured in web.xml without affecting the existing application code. Listing 3-42 shows the servlet filter used to add time-based access to the production application.

Listing 3-42. TimebasedAccessFilter.java

```
public class TimebasedAccessFilter implements Filter {

    private int startHour;
    private int endHour;

    public void destroy() {}

    public void doFilter(ServletRequest request, ServletResponse response,
        FilterChain chain) throws IOException, ServletException {
int currentHrofDay = Calendar.getInstance().get(Calendar.HOUR_OF_DAY);
        if((startHour <= currentHrofDay) && (currentHrofDay <= endHour)){
            chain.doFilter(request, response);
        }
        else{
```

```
                HttpServletResponse res = (HttpServletResponse)response;
                res.sendRedirect("html/downtimenotice.html");
            }
        }
    public void init(FilterConfig config) throws ServletException {
        startHour = Integer.parseInt(config.getInitParameter("starthour"));
        endHour = Integer.parseInt(config.getInitParameter("endhour"));
    }
}
```

In Listing 3-42 the `doFilter` implements the logic for time-based access to the eIn-sure application. In this case only, the preprocessing of the incoming request is carried out to check whether the scheduled office hour's window has expired for the day. If so, the user is redirected to a downtime notice page. Otherwise, the next filters in the chain (if any) are executed. Finally, the target servlet and page controllers will be executed. Note that the official business hours are configurable. The filter is registered in `web.xml`, as shown in Listing 3-43, along with various parameters and a URL mapping. In this case, this filter intercepts all requests ending with `.do` and heading toward the front controller. This solution is highly reusable and based on Java servlet standards. It can be used even without Spring MVC support because the web container is responsible for managing the filters.

Listing 3-43. `web.xml`

```
<?xml version="1.0" encoding="UTF-8"?>

<web-app version="2.4" xmlns="http://java.sun.com/xml/ns/j2ee"
    xmlns:xsi="http://www.w3.org/2001/XMLSchema-instance"
    xsi:schemaLocation="http://java.sun.com/xml/ns/j2ee
        http://java.sun.com/xml/ns/j2ee/web-app_2_4.xsd">

    <filter>
        <filter-name>timebasedaccess</filter-name>
        <filter-class>
            com.apress.insurance.web.filter.TimebasedAccessFilter
        </filter-class>
        <init-param>
            <param-name>starthour</param-name>
            <param-value>9</param-value>
        </init-param>
        <init-param>
```

```
                <param-name>endhour</param-name>
                <param-value>18</param-value>
            </init-param>
        </filter>
        <filter-mapping>
            <filter-name>timebasedaccess</filter-name>
            <url-pattern>*.do</url-pattern>
        </filter-mapping>


        <servlet>
            <servlet-name>insurance</servlet-name>
            <servlet-class>
                org.springframework.web.servlet.DispatcherServlet
            </servlet-class>
            <load-on-startup>1</load-on-startup>
        </servlet>

        <servlet-mapping>
            <servlet-name>insurance</servlet-name>
            <url-pattern>*.do</url-pattern>
        </servlet-mapping>

        <jsp-config>
            <taglib>
                <taglib-uri>/spring</taglib-uri>
                <taglib-location>
                    /WEB-INF/tld/spring-form.tld
                </taglib-location>
            </taglib>

        </jsp-config>

    </web-app>
```

Using servlet filters, it was possible to deliver the customer's first enhancement without affecting the existing code in any way. However, collecting different information required for usage tracking would require some coding. But you can integrate a simple yet powerful out-of-the-box open source solution called Clickstream from Open-Symphony to achieve this goal. It can be downloaded from http://www.opensymphony.com/clickstream/. Clickstream is also based on filters, providing a highly flexible way to track usage patterns on a web site.

Spring Interceptors

With the two enhancements solved efficiently, it's time to focus on the last requirement. You have guessed it right—filters can be deployed to solve this problem as well. But that would mean the monitoring starts even before the servlet invocation. Though with this solution, the time variation would be negligible; the actual intention was to monitor the total execution time of a use case. So, the best place to apply this processing was around a page controller invocation. This would also make more information available to us (the actual controller class name, and so on) than filters could. Moreover, with servlet filters, you need to code the preprocessing and postprocessing in the same doFilter method, which can be cumbersome. Hence, for this solution, I will resort to the Spring page controller interceptor support shown in Figure 3-13.

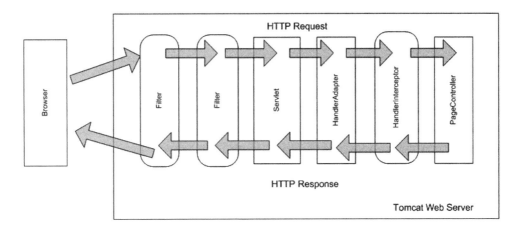

Figure 3-13. *Spring Handler interceptor chain*

While discussing the Application Controller pattern earlier in this chapter, I briefly touched upon the handler interceptors. They implement the HandlerInterceptor interface. As you have come to expect by now, Spring MVC provides some concrete implementations of this interface as well as convenience abstract classes to build on handler interceptor functions, as shown in Figure 3-14.

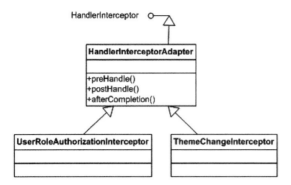

Figure 3-14. *Handler interceptor class diagram*

The convenience abstract base class `HandlerInterceptorAdapter` implements all three methods defined by the `HandlerInterceptor` interface. The `preHandle` method performs preprocessing of a request before it is handled by the page controller. Similarly, `postHandle` is responsible for postprocessing. The `afterCompletion` is a callback method called finally when the view rendering is done. The `UserRoleAuthorizationInterceptor` is a concrete implementation handling authorization checks on the current user based on user role and using the `HttpServletRequest` object's `isUserInRole` method. Finally, the `ThemeChangeInterceptor` is invoked when the current theme (combination of images, style sheets, and so on) of the web site is changed.

I will now try to solve the problem at hand by extending the `HandlerInterceptorAdapter` class. Once the request is intercepted, the current time will be saved as a request attribute as part of preprocessing code. When the page controller returns, the actual time taken will be logged along with any other information required to be monitored. This is shown in Listing 3-44.

Listing 3-44. `ExecutionMonitorInterceptor.java`

```java
public class ExecutiontimeMonitorInterceptor extends HandlerInterceptorAdapter {
    private final Log log = LogFactory.getLog(
ExecutiontimeMonitorInterceptor.class);

    private static final String START_EXECUTION_TIME_KEY = "executionStartTime";

    public void postHandle(HttpServletRequest request, HttpServletResponse response,
 Object handler, ModelAndView modelAndView) throws Exception {
        long executionStartTime = (Long) request.getAttribute(
```

```
START_EXECUTION_TIME_KEY);
        long executionEndTime = System.currentTimeMillis();

        StringBuffer logTxt = new StringBuffer
("Execution completed for request - ");
        logTxt.append(request.getRequestURI());
        logTxt.append(", handler -");
        logTxt.append(handler);
        logTxt.append(", total execution time(ms) -");
        logTxt.append((executionEndTime - executionStartTime));

        log.info(logTxt.toString());

    }

    public boolean preHandle(HttpServletRequest request,
HttpServletResponse response, Object handler) throws Exception {
        request.setAttribute(START_EXECUTION_TIME_KEY, System.currentTimeMillis());
        return true;
    }
}
```

The advantage of using the convenience abstract class is evident in Listing 3-44. I just had to override those methods that are required. Alternatively, using the HandlerInterceptor, I would need to implement three methods, and the callback afterCompletion would be redundant. To use this interceptor, it must be associated with a handler mapping. This is shown in the Spring configuration file (Listing 3-45). Note that I have used the inner bean style of configuration because this bean is relevant only in the context of a handler mapping bean.

Listing 3-45. insurance-servlet.xml

```xml
<?xml version="1.0" encoding="UTF-8"?>
<beans xmlns="http://www.springframework.org/schema/beans"
    xmlns:xsi="http://www.w3.org/2001/XMLSchema-instance"
    xsi:schemaLocation="http://www.springframework.org/schema/beans
http://www.springframework.org/schema/beans/spring-beans-2.5.xsd"
    >
    <! - - Other beans - ->
```

```
    <bean name="beanNamehandlerMapping"
        class="org.springframework.web.servlet.handler.BeanNameUrlHandlerMapping">
        <property name="interceptors">
            <list>
                <bean
                    class="com.apress.insurance.web.controller.interceptor.➥
ExecutiontimeMonitorInterceptor" />
            </list>
        </property>
    </bean>

</beans>
```

This interceptor will now be applied to all the page controllers handled by the
beanNameHandlerMapping.

Consequences

Benefits

- *Improved reusability*: Common code is now centralized in pluggable components,
  enhancing reuse.

- *Increased flexibility*: Generic common components can be applied and removed
  declaratively, improving flexibility.

Concerns

- *Reduced performance*: Unnecessarily long chains of interceptors and filters may
  hurt performance. Also, these components should not perform any long-running
  operation.

View Helper

Problem

The application controller and page controllers combine with the gateway servlet to solve three important concerns of request processing:

- Request interception

- Invoking business components from page controllers

- Resolving the next view to be displayed with the data returned from business layer

However, in all the earlier discussions, I have deliberately bypassed another critical concern—view creation. The data returned by the page controllers, as a result of invoking the business logic, have to be consumed by the view components to provide the final dynamic response.

eInsure primarily used JSP as the view technology. The data returned by the business components was set as request attributes. It was later retrieved, processed, and used in the JSPs using scriptlets. In other words, the dynamic data was combined with the static markup or template text in the JSPs using embedded programming logic. This littering of scriptlets significantly reduced reuse and increased maintenance efforts.

Forces

- Remove the programming logic from the template-based views like JSP.

- Achieve a division of labor between Java developers and web page authors.

- Create reusable components that can be used to combine model data across views.

Solution

Use *view helpers* to adapt model data with the view components in the presentation layer.

Strategies with the Spring Framework

This pattern separates out the logic for retrieving and processing model data from the static markup in the JSPs. It can optionally format data types such as date and currency, depending on the locale. As shown in Figure 3-15, it should be used as a thin layer to adapt model data into views. Note that view helpers should not be responsible for invoking business or data access logic.

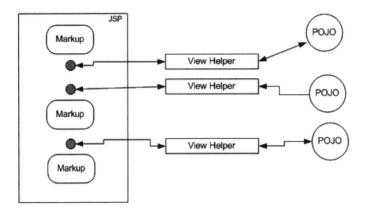

Figure 3-15. *Working of a view helper*

JavaBeans View Helper

This is the simplest form of view helper strategy. JSP provides out-of-the-box tags to support POJO view helpers. Listing 3-46 shows that `policydetails.jsp` is using the `PolicyDetail` POJO as the JavaBean view helper.

Listing 3-46. `policydetails.jsp`

```
<jsp:useBean id="policydetails" scope="request"
class="com.apress.insurance.common.dataholder.PolicyDetail"/>
<html>
<head>
<title>Underwriting</title>

<script>
    function eventSubmit(url){
        document.policy.action = url;
```

```
        document.policy.submit();
    }
</script>
</head>
<body>

<form name="policy">


    <table>
        <tr>
            <td>First Name:</td>
            <td><jsp:getProperty name="policydetails" property="firstName"/></td>


        </tr>

        <tr>
            <td>Last Name:</td>
            <td><jsp:getProperty name="policydetails" property="lastName"/></td>

        </tr>

        <tr>
            <td>Age :</td>
            <td><jsp:getProperty name="policydetails" property="age"/></td>

        </tr>

        <tr>
            <td colspan="3">
                <input type="button" value="Create"
                onClick="eventSubmit('createPolicy.do')" />
                <input type="button" value="Edit"
onClick="eventSubmit('editPolicy.do')" />
            </td>
        </tr>
    </table>
</form>

</body>
</html>
```

The page controller is responsible for invoking the business object, which returns POJOs to be populated in views. Listing 3-47 shows the controller that binds the transfer object in the request scope.

Listing 3-47. `PolicyDetailsController.java`

```java
public class PolicyDetailsController implements Controller {

    //set using setter injection
    private PolicyBusinessDelegate businessDelegate;

    public ModelAndView handleRequest(HttpServletRequest request,
HttpServletResponse response) throws Exception {
        //policy id is part of the request,
        PolicyDetail policyDetail = getBusinessDelegate()
.getPolicyDetails(policyId);
        return new ModelAndView("policydetails","policydetails",policyDetail);
    }
}
```

Finally, Listing 3-48 shows the JavaBean or POJO view helper. This class contains a set of fields and getters/setters for all these fields.

Listing 3-48. `PolicyDetailsController.java`

```java
public class PolicyDetail implements Serializable {

    private long policyId;
    private String firstName;
    private String lastName;
    private int age;

    public long getPolicyId() {
        return policyId;
    }

    public void setPolicyId(long policyId) {
        this.policyId = policyId;
    }
    public int getAge() {
        return age;
```

```
    }
    public void setAge(int age) {
        this.age = age;
    }

    public String getFirstName() {
        return firstName;
    }
    public void setFirstName(String firstName) {
        this.firstName = firstName;
    }

    public String getLastName() {
        return lastName;
    }

    public void setLastName(String lastName) {
        this.lastName = lastName;
    }
}
```

Tag Library View Helper

The JavaBean-based view helper is simple to use. The best part is it works even without any support from the Spring Framework. However, it still mixes programming logic into JSPs. It also does not allow for a component-based view helper. Let us consider a case where you need a pagination display of search results in an HTML table. It would be very convenient if we had a reusable component that displayed paged search results given the search result list. This component can be further extended to support sorting search results on any of the columns.

The JSP pages in eInsure mixed HTML and JavaBeans to display components such as select boxes and drop-down menus. These can best be handled as reusable components. All these components can easily be developed using tag libraries. Tag libraries provide generic reusable components that cater to different requirements handled until now using JavaBeans helpers or scriptlets. Besides, efficient third-party component-based tag libraries are available to ease the development of flexible and robust view components.

Using JSTL Tags

The JSP Standard Tag Library (JSTL) provides a simple yet powerful tag library that encapsulates common functions required by any JSP-based view. The JSTL Expression

Language (EL) makes it simpler to access JavaBean properties. The conditional and itera-
tor tags provide consistent syntax to access data from collection objects such as List, Map,
and arrays. Another important feature of JSTL is the support for i18n with locale-sensitive
messages and formatting tags. Listing 3-49 shows JSTL tags in action, iterating through a
policy search result returned as a list of PolicyDetail objects.

Listing 3-49. policydetails.jsp

```
<%@ taglib prefix="c" uri="http://java.sun.com/jsp/jstl/core" %>
<%@ taglib prefix="fmt" uri="http://java.sun.com/jsp/jstl/fmt" %>

<html>
<head>
<title>Underwriting</title>

</head>
<body>

<form name="policysearch" action="policysearch.do">
    <%-- The search criteria inputs are not shown for simplicity --%>

    <table>
        <tr>
            <td>Policy Id</td>
            <td>First Name</td>
            <td>Last Name</td>
            <td>Age</td>

        </tr>
        <c:forEach var="policyDtl" items="${policyDtlList}" >
        <tr>

            <td><c:out value="${policyDtl.policyId}"/></td>
            <td><c:out value="${policyDtl.firstName}"/></td>
            <td><c:out value="${policyDtl.lastName}"/></td>
            <td><c:out value="${policyDtl.age}"/></td>

        </tr>
        </c:forEach>
        <tr>
```

```
            <td colspan="3">
                <input type="submit" value="Search" />

            </td>
        </tr>
    </table>
</form:form>

</body>
</html>
```

Listing 3-50 shows the controller that invokes the business components to retrieve the search results and then prepares the list to be retrieved and used by the JSTL tags. To use the JSTL tags, you must put jstl.jar and standard.jar in the WEB-INF/lib folder.

Listing 3-50. PolicySearchController.java

```
public class PolicySearchController implements Controller {

    private UnderWritingBusinessDelegate businessDelegate;

    public ModelAndView handleRequest(HttpServletRequest request,
HttpServletResponse response)
            throws Exception {

        List policyList = getBusinessDelegate().listPolicyByProduct(productCd);

        return new ModelAndView("policysearch","policyDtlList",policyList);
    }

}
```

Using Spring Tags

JSTL tags help encapsulate common tasks that allow the static view to be interposed with dynamic model data. But it does not support component-based views. Spring form tags provide this functionality to an extent. You have already used Spring form tags to display input text fields and validation error messages in Listing 3-33. I will now add one more field in the JSP used to underwrite policies. Underwriting a policy requires mandatory product code information. So, in the createPolicy.jsp file, I will add a new drop-down control that will enable the underwriters to select a product code. This is shown in Listing 3-51.

Listing 3-51. `WEB-INF/jsp/createPolicy.jsp`

```jsp
<%@ taglib prefix="form" uri="http://www.springframework.org/tags/form" %>
<%@ taglib prefix="c" uri="http://java.sun.com/jsp/jstl/core" %>
<%@ taglib prefix="fmt" uri="http://java.sun.com/jsp/jstl/fmt" %>

<html>
<head>
<title>Underwriting</title>
<style>
    .error { color: red; }
  </style>
</head>

<form:form action="" method="POST" commandName="policydetails">

    First Name <form:input path="firstName"/> <form:errors path="firstName"
cssClass="error"/><br/>
    Last Name <form:input path="lastName"/> <form:errors path="lastName"
cssClass="error"/><br/>
    Age <form:input path="age"/> <form:errors path="age" cssClass="error"/><br/>
    Product Code <form:select path="productCodeList" items="${productCodeList}"/>
 <form:errors path="productCodeList" cssClass="error"/><br/>
    <input type="submit" value="Save" />
</form:form>
</body>
</html>
```

A list of product code is prepopulated and cached at application startup. It is retrieved and supplied in the form bean by the controller (see in Listing 3-52) by overriding the `formBackingObject` method.

Listing 3-52. `SaveNewPolicyController.java`

```java
public class SaveNewPolicyController extends SimpleFormController {

    private UnderWritingBusinessDelegate uwrBusinessDelegate;

    protected void doSubmitAction(Object formbean) throws Exception {
        PolicyFormBean policyBean = (PolicyFormBean)formbean;
        uwrBusinessDelegate.createPolicy(policyBean);
    }
```

```
    protected Object formBackingObject(HttpServletRequest req) throws Exception {
        PolicyFormBean policyBean = (PolicyFormBean)super.formBackingObject(req);

        List productList = (List) req.getSession(false).getServletContext()
.getAttribute("productCodeList");

        policyBean.setProductCodeList(productList);

        return policyBean;
    }
}
```

Since I have added a field in the form presented by the JSP, a new field has to be added to the form bean class. Listing 3-53 shows the modified version of the form bean.

Listing 3-53. `PolicyFormBean.java`

```
public class PolicyFormBean implements Serializable {

    private String firstName;
    private String lastName;
    private int age;

    private List productCodeList;


    public int getAge() {
        return age;
    }

    public void setAge(int age) {
        this.age = age;
    }

    public String getFirstName() {
        return firstName;
    }

    public void setFirstName(String firstName) {
        this.firstName = firstName;
    }
```

```java
    public String getLastName() {
        return lastName;
    }

    public void setLastName(String lastName) {
        this.lastName = lastName;
    }

    public List getProductCodeList() {
        return productCodeList;
    }

    public void setProductCodeList(List productCodeList) {
        this.productCodeList = productCodeList;
    }
}
```

Using Third-Party Tag Library

Spring tags and JSTL are complementary tag libraries providing a rich set of reusable features. Although Spring tags provide decent component support for common HTML controls, at times you will need more complex controls, such as the pagination table mentioned earlier. In such scenarios, third-party tag libraries can be used along with Spring to ease development. Displaytag, for example, is an open source tag library supporting complex pagination and sorting components. It is available for download and use from `http://displaytag.sourceforge.net/11/`.

Consequences

Benefits

- *Ease maintenance*: View helpers remove scriptlet pollution and thus clean up view code and improve application maintainability.

- *Clear role separation*: The task of application development can now be clearly divided between hard-core Java programmers and web authors.

- *Save development time*: Since mostly third party view helper tag libraries are used, it can speed up development because you just need to integrate these components.

Concerns

- *Steep learning curve*: Since this pattern mostly involves using third-party libraries, care must be taken that we do not mix in too many of them. That would add to the learning curve and increase the maintenance overhead.

Composite View

Problem

Developing and maintaining view components can be a daunting task. It requires not only adaptation between static templates and dynamic data but also building views with smaller reusable subviews. This promotes the reusability of views and allows them to be managed and maintained easily.

Each view is composed of three elements:

- *Components*: UI controls such as buttons, text boxes, and so on

- *Container*: A collection of components

- *Layout*: Responsible for positioning and sizing the different components in a container

Typically applications tend not to identify these critical elements. eInsure, for example, never identified components or view containers even though the application had a fixed layout (Figure 3-16). JSPs were included in this layout using standard include mechanisms. This achieved some flexibility, but even greater flexibility and reuse are possible if the views are composed with subviews containing components and containers embedded with layout.

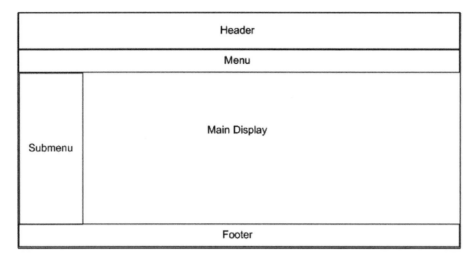

Figure 3-16. *eInsure primary layout*

Forces

- Compose a bigger view using reusable subviews for header, footer, menu, and navigation.

- Identify and compose reusable components and containers.

- Place components and containers in appropriate layouts so that they can be changed in a flexible way.

Solution

Use a *composite view* to group and deploy a pluggable and dynamic set of subview components with the appropriate layout.

Strategies with the Spring Framework

The composite view pattern is a combination of two well-known GOF design patterns: Composite and Strategy. The layouts provide a strategy for forming bigger view components comprised of smaller composite subviews. You have already seen components and a container with respect to the View Helper pattern described earlier. I modified the JSP to support a reusable input text box and select controls, embedded in a form container.

However, I did not focus on the layout aspect, which glues everything together. Let us consider a case where you want to display an important notice at the top of every page. If you are not using subviews with layout, you would have to replicate the notice in each and every JSP file. However, with layout, you can just change the JSP, which comprises the header, and revert back when this notice is no longer relevant.

eInsure typically used a table to configure the layout and used JSP includes to dynamically include subviews to compose the main view. Although this solution works, it's a very naïve approach requiring lot of custom code to make this a flexible and pluggable view framework. Spring provides integration with two view layout frameworks to ease the development and maintenance of composite views.

Using SiteMesh

SiteMesh is an open source web page layout framework from OpenSymphony. It can be downloaded from `http://www.opensymphony.com/sitemesh/`. The greatest advantage of using SiteMesh is that it is not intrusive. Because it is based on servlet filters, using it is just a matter of configuration, and it will work even without Spring MVC. Being based on filters, it implements the GOF Decorator design pattern. It modifies the response from the front controller servlet to inject content before sending the final response to the browser.

The first step in using SiteMesh is to create a JSP file with the desired layout, as shown in Listing 3-54.

Listing 3-54. `WEB-INF/decorators/primaryLayout.jsp`

```
<%@ taglib uri="sitemesh-decorator" prefix="decorator" %>
<%@ taglib uri="sitemesh-page" prefix="page" %>

<html>
    <head>
        <title>
            eInsure - <decorator:title default="Welcome!" />
        </title>
        <decorator:head />
    </head>

    <body>
    <table width="100%">
        <tr id="header">
            <h3>eInsure - rel 3.0.1 </h3>
        </tr>
```

```
        <tr id="body">
            <decorator:body />
        </tr>

        <tr id="footer">
            <h3>eInsure - All rights reserved </h3>
        </tr>

    </table>

</html>
```

Note that I have used a SiteMesh-specific tag library to create the layout. The
`decorator:title` tag picks up the title information from the response sent by the front
controller. Similarly, the `decorator:head` and `decorator:body` tags include the information
in the `head` and `body` tags of the original response and put them in the layout. The header
and footer information is consolidated at a common place in the layout. To use this layout framework and the different tags, you must include SiteMesh filter and tag definition
in the `web.xml` file, as shown in Listing 3-55.

Listing 3-55. `web.xml`

```
<?xml version="1.0" encoding="UTF-8"?>

<web-app version="2.4" xmlns="http://java.sun.com/xml/ns/j2ee"
    xmlns:xsi="http://www.w3.org/2001/XMLSchema-instance"
    xsi:schemaLocation="http://java.sun.com/xml/ns/j2ee
        http://java.sun.com/xml/ns/j2ee/web-app_2_4.xsd">


    <!-- Start of SiteMesh filter config -->
    <filter>
        <filter-name>sitemesh</filter-name>
        <filter-class>
            com.opensymphony.module.sitemesh.filter.PageFilter
        </filter-class>
    </filter>
    <filter-mapping>
        <filter-name>sitemesh</filter-name>
        <url-pattern>*.do</url-pattern>
    </filter-mapping>
```

```
    <!-- End of SiteMesh filter config -->


    <servlet>
        <servlet-name>insurance</servlet-name>
        <servlet-class>
            org.springframework.web.servlet.DispatcherServlet
        </servlet-class>
        <load-on-startup>1</load-on-startup>
    </servlet>

    <servlet-mapping>
        <servlet-name>insurance</servlet-name>
        <url-pattern>*.do</url-pattern>
    </servlet-mapping>

    <jsp-config>
        <taglib>
            <taglib-uri>/spring</taglib-uri>
            <taglib-location>
                /WEB-INF/tld/spring-form.tld
            </taglib-location>
        </taglib>

<!-- Start of SiteMesh tag config -->

<taglib>
            <taglib-uri>sitemesh-page</taglib-uri>
            <taglib-location>
                /WEB-INF/tld/sitemesh-page.tld
            </taglib-location>
        </taglib>
        <taglib>
            <taglib-uri>sitemesh-decorator</taglib-uri>
            <taglib-location>
                /WEB-INF/tld/sitemesh-decorator.tld
            </taglib-location>
        </taglib>

<!-- End of SiteMesh tag config -->
```

```
    </jsp-config>

</web-app>
```

As a final step, I will include the layouts in the decorator configuration for the filter to work. Listing 3-56 shows the decorator configuration.

Listing 3-56. `WEB-INF/decorators.xml`

```
<decorators defaultdir="/WEB-INF/decorators">
    <decorator name="primaryLayout" page="primaryLayout.jsp">
        <pattern>*</pattern>
    </decorator>

</decorators>
```

The `decorators.xml` is the externalized class that manages the layout. The page attribute in the `decorator` tag defines the layout to be applied for the request patterns. The `primaryLayout` will be applied to all the requests as evident from the `pattern` tag. So, when a request for `/createPolicy.do` is handled by the front controller and the response is handed over to the SiteMesh filter, it performs the following activities to manipulate and generate the final response:

- Extract the content of the `title` tag, and apply it in the primary layout.

- Extract the `head` tag, and use it in the primary layout.

- Extract the content from the `body` tag, and use it in primary layout.

Using Apache Tiles

Spring MVC also provides integration with the Apache Tiles framework. Just like SiteMesh, Tiles is a flexible and highly extensible framework that earlier worked primarily with the Struts web framework. As of Tiles 2, it works independently as a flexible, feature-rich layout framework. Both SiteMesh and Tiles 2 are powerful layout frameworks, and the choice of which one to use is basically a matter of taste and expertise. The following link in the Spring documentation provides a step-by-step guide to integrating Spring and Tiles 2:

`http://static.springframework.org/spring/docs/2.5.x/reference/view.html#view-tiles`

Consequences

Benefits

- *Improved flexibility*: The application now consists of smaller view components such as controls and containers embedded in layouts. This makes the view easily configurable, and changes to the application look and feel, as well as component positioning, can be rolled out quickly and efficiently.

- *Improved reuse*: With this pattern, the same subview can be used to compose multiple composite views.

Concerns

- *Performance*: When composing a view, using multiple subviews can impact performance. Hence, you should be judicious in keeping the subviews to an acceptable number.

Dispatcher View

Problem

eInsure had a sign-in page that presented a simple UI to accept a username and password. This screen also had a button control that, on being clicked, triggered the authentication action. Hence, the presentation of this sign-in page did not require any business logic invocation. There were many other pages similar to this. There were several pages to display the input criteria that can be supplied before triggering a search for the policy, claim, and so on. Then we had lookup pages for various codes used in the system. All the values used for lookup were loaded from the database at startup and cached on the server. This was possible because the static data never changed when the application was up and running. Also, the action to load the UI pages to create a policy or claim required only user information that was cached in the session. Last but not least, almost each page had a link to open a help page. The static HTML-based help pages provided context-sensitive help to guide the users on how to use the different features (buttons, menus, text boxes, and so on) in that particular page.

All these cases required no business logic invocation. Although all these are simple scenarios, our application based on a JSP front controller was not able to handle the situation in a simple fashion. Different developers created these pages and merrily added `if-else` blocks to handle their cases. The simplest approach would be to handle the request for these static contents directly, bypassing the page controllers. But this breaks the overall uniform application structure. Also, it might be useful to secure these resources so that no unauthorized access (such as directly typing the URL in the browser address bar) is allowed.

Forces

- The application has a lot of static views that require no business logic processing.

- The semistatic views are presented from cached data.

- The purely static and semistatic views need to be handled consistently as other dynamic views.

Solution

Use a *dispatcher view* to handle the processing of a static or semistatic view.

Strategies with the Spring Framework

Dispatcher View is actually a best practice to combine the other presentation tier patterns. It employs dispatchers to delegate to the view. In this case, the dispatcher is a combination of a controller and view resolver.

There can be two variants of this pattern for static and semistatic views. The semistatic views use cached data and hence need view helper support. I will start with the pure static resources. Figure 3-17 shows the static structure of the Dispatcher View pattern.

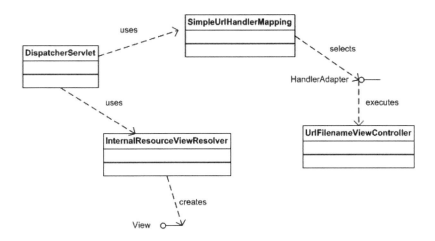

Figure 3-17. *Dispatcher view class diagram*

You have encountered most of the classes and interfaces before, except `UrlFilenameViewController`. This is a concrete controller implementation and converts the requested URL path into a logical view name. For example, a request for `/PolicyCreateHelp.do` will be transformed to the view name `PolicyCreateHelp`. The `InternalResourceViewResolver` then picks up this view name to resolve it to the actual resource—`PolicyCreateHelp.jsp`. Using this controller is just a matter of configuration, as shown in Listing 3-57.

As a first step to implementing this pattern, we create the `PolicyCreateHelp.jsp` file in the `/WEB-INF/jsp/help` folder. It is not advisable to use static HTML files to serve the help contents. This because in the future you may need to support internationalized help. Besides, FreeMarker or Velocity templates can be used to keep the actual content externalized separately from the JSP, making it easy to maintain and change. The final step in using the dispatcher view is setting up the Spring configuration file, as shown Listing 3-57.

Listing 3-57. `insurance-servlet.xml`

```
<?xml version="1.0" encoding="UTF-8"?>
<beans xmlns="http://www.springframework.org/schema/beans"
    xmlns:xsi="http://www.w3.org/2001/XMLSchema-instance"
    xsi:schemaLocation="http://www.springframework.org/schema/beans
http://www.springframework.org/schema/beans/spring-beans-2.5.xsd"
    >
```

```xml
<bean name="simpleUrlHandlerMapping"
    class="org.springframework.web.servlet.handler.SimpleUrlHandlerMapping">
    <property name="mappings">
        <props>
            <prop key="/*Help.do">urlFilenameViewController</prop>
        </props>
    </property>
    <property name="order" value="2" />
</bean>

<bean name="beanNameUrlHandlerMapping"
class="org.springframework.web.servlet.handler.BeanNameUrlHandlerMapping">
    <property name="order" value="1" />
</bean>

<bean name="viewResolver"
    class="org.springframework.web.servlet.view.InternalResourceViewResolver">
    <property name="viewClass"
        value="org.springframework.web.servlet.view.JstlView" />
    <property name="prefix" value="/WEB-INF/jsp/" />
    <property name="suffix" value=".jsp" />
</bean>

<bean name="urlFilenameViewController"
    class="org.springframework.web.servlet.mvc.UrlFilenameViewController" >
        <property name="prefix" value="help/" />
</bean>
<bean name="/policydetails.do"
    class="com.apress.insurance.web.controller.PolicyDetailsController" />

<bean name="underwritingBusinessDelegate"
    class="com.apress.insurance.view.delegate.UnderWritingBusinessDelegate" />

<bean name="/policysearch.do"
    class="com.apress.insurance.web.controller.PolicySearchController">
    <property name="businessDelegate"
        ref="underwritingBusinessDelegate" />
</bean>
</beans>
```

A lot is happening under the hood in Listing 3-57. Note that a common view resolver caters to both dynamic and static resources. You can also see the handler mapping chain. The `BeanNameUrlHandlerMapping` having higher precedence is selected first. Now a request for a dynamic resource such as `/policysearch.do` is resolved by this handler mapping. It looks for a bean with the name `/policydetails.do` in the application context and delegates the processing to it. `BeanNameUrlHandlerMapping`, however, fails to handle the request for the URL `ClaimCreateHelp.do`. Hence, the next handler mapping in the chain, `SimpleUrlHandlerMapping`, is picked up to resolve this URL to a controller. This handler mapping succeeds in detecting the controller. It uses wildcards to resolve the incoming URLs that end in `Help.do` to an instance of `UrlFilenameViewController`. Hence, `UrlFilenameViewController` handles all requests for static requests without any invocation of business logic. This concrete controller implementation will convert the request URL to a logical view name—`ClaimCreateHelp`. It will then use the prefix to finally return `/help/ClaimCreateHelp`. Finally, the view resolver looks for the file `/help/ClaimCreateHelp.jsp` in the folder `/WEB-INF/jsp` and returns the static physical resource. The simplified workflow is shown in the sequence diagram in Figure 3-18.

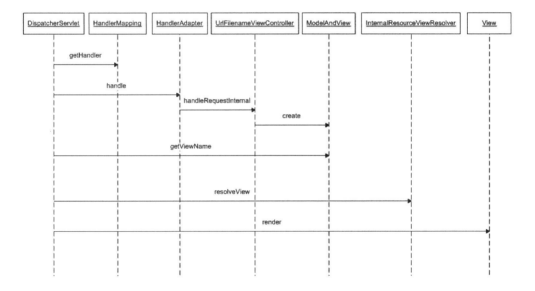

Figure 3-18. *Dispatcher view sequence diagram*

The semistatic views have their data already cached in some form. To use this data, you can use view helpers. To underwrite insurance policies, you must select a product. The active products in the system are cached in the `ServletContext` object at application startup. The physical resource `ProductLoV.jsp` is stored in the `/WEB-INF/jsp/lookup` folder and is shown in Listing 3-58. This JSP retrieves the list of active products from the servlet context and displays them.

Listing 3-58. ProductLoV.jsp

```
<%@ taglib prefix="c" uri="http://java.sun.com/jsp/jstl/core" %>
<%@ taglib prefix="fmt" uri="http://java.sun.com/jsp/jstl/fmt" %>

<html>
<head>
<title>LoV - Product</title>
</head>
<body>
    <table>
        <tr>
            <td>Product Id</td>
            <td>Product Name</td>
        </tr>
        <c:forEach var="productDtl" items="${applicationScope.productDtlList}" >
        <tr>
            <td><c:out value="${productDtl.productId}"/></td>
            <td><c:out value="${productDtl.productName}"/></td>
        </tr>
        </c:forEach>

    </table>

</body>
</html>
```

As shown in Listing 3-58, we are using a JSTL-based view helper to retrieve and present the data stored in application scope. applicationScope is an implicit object available with the JSTL Expression Language, and it gives a handle to the servlet context. In Listing 3-58, it looks for an attribute with the key productDtlList in the servlet context. To use this semistatic view, you need to slightly alter the configuration, as shown in Listing 3-59. Note that the SimpleUrlHandlerMapping has been configured to handle UrlFilenameViewController.

Listing 3-59. `ProductLoV.jsp`

```xml
<?xml version="1.0" encoding="UTF-8"?>
<beans xmlns="http://www.springframework.org/schema/beans"
    xmlns:xsi="http://www.w3.org/2001/XMLSchema-instance"
    xsi:schemaLocation="http://www.springframework.org/schema/beans
http://www.springframework.org/schema/beans/spring-beans-2.5.xsd"
    >

<!-- other beans as above -->
<bean name="staticViewController"
        class="org.springframework.web.servlet.mvc.UrlFilenameViewController" >
            <property name="prefix" value="help/" />
    </bean>

    <bean name="semiStaticViewController"
        class="org.springframework.web.servlet.mvc.UrlFilenameViewController" >
            <property name="prefix" value="lookup/" />
    </bean>


<bean
        class="org.springframework.web.servlet.handler.SimpleUrlHandlerMapping">
        <property name="mappings">
            <props>
                <prop key="/*Help.do">staticViewController</prop>
                <prop key="/*LoV.do">semiStaticViewController</prop>
            </props>
        </property>
    </bean>

</beans>
```

Consequences

Benefits

- *Foster best practice*: This lays down clear guidelines for combining presentation tier patterns.

- *Easy to implement*: It is easy to implement this solution in Spring because we hardly need to write any code; everything is glued together using configuration.

Concerns

- *Overcomplex solution*: Dispatching to a static or semistatic view is a simple task. But still there is dependency on layering and various framework-specific components to maintain a consistent application architecture. This is a complex solution to a simple task.

Service to Worker

Problem

The Dispatcher View pattern sets the guidelines for dispatching control to a static view. In the case of eInsure, these constituted only a handful of use cases. A vast majority of the use cases, however, required a dynamic view prepared from dynamic data.

However, since this product was migrated from legacy PL/SQL it had data access code being invoked from page controllers. Since the product was implemented at several clients and required quick turnarounds, developers would resort to quick fixes. They would mix business logic with data access in page controllers, leading to a poorly designed solution.

Forces

- The application primarily needs to handle a dynamic view generated using dynamic data.

- Business or data access code are mixed in action handlers.

- The business logic and data access code should be placed in separate layers.

Solution

Use *server to worker* to coordinate request processing workflow by invoking components in different layers.

Strategies with the Spring Framework

Just like Dispatcher View, Server to Worker is essentially a guideline for building layered Java EE applications. It is similar to the MVC architectural pattern and proposes that the application must be divided into distinct layers corresponding to specific roles in a request-processing workflow.

Server to Worker effectively is an extension of the Dispatcher View pattern. Just like Dispatcher View, it allows the organization of patterns in the presentation tier, with two differences. On one hand, it allows working with a dynamic view. On the other hand, it invokes business logic before passing control to view. The business logic must be accessed to retrieve the data required for the dynamic view. Server to Worker paves the way for connecting presentation and business layers. The bridge between the two layers is provided by the Business Delegate pattern, which we will explore in the next chapter. The page controllers typically do not directly invoke methods on the actual business objects. Rather, it invokes methods on the bridge or presentation tier proxy called the *business delegate object*. As shown earlier in listings, the business delegate is injected into the controller by the Spring container. The sequence diagram (Figure 3-19) shows the complete workflow of a Server to Worker pattern.

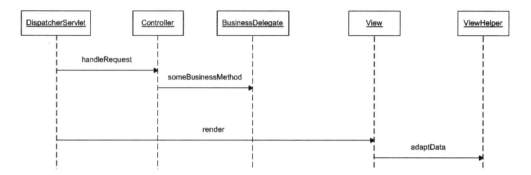

Figure 3-19. *Service to worker sequence diagram*

Consequences

Benefits

- *Foster best practice*: This lays down clear guidelines for combining presentation tier patterns. It also provides the directive to connect business components from page controllers only.

- *Easy to implement*: It is easy to implement this solution in Spring because everything is glued together using configuration once most of the custom components are ready. Spring also provides extensive support for building these custom components quickly and easily.

- *Role separation*: With the guidelines set clearly, the task of application development can be distributed among page authors working on the view and application developers concentrating on page controllers and business components.

Concerns

- *Performance concern*: Too many layers and too much delegation can degrade performance. So, designers must be careful when deciding the layers and components to use.

Summary

In this chapter, I have extensively explored various presentation tier patterns. We started off at one end of the spectrum and finished at the other end, setting the stage for business layer patterns in Chapter 4. The Front Controller pattern intercepted all requests and delegated to the action handlers in the Application Controller pattern. The action handlers work with the Context Object and Page Controller patterns to invoke business logic. Once the page controller selects the logical view and returns the data retrieved from business logic invocation, control is passed back to the application controller. The application controller uses view management components to resolve the appropriate physical view and binds the application data. The View Helper pattern assists in adapting the application data in the views and builds composite views to send the final response for end user display. The working of the front controller and page controllers can be decorated with the Intercepting Filter pattern and handler interceptors. The Dispatcher View pattern provides the guidelines to combine all the presentation tier patterns to delegate efficiently to static views. Finally, the Service to Worker pattern paves the way for interaction with the business layer using the Business Delegate pattern.

Exploring Business Tier Design Patterns

Insurance applications, like most financial solutions, have complex business rules. eInsure was no different. It had implemented very complex mathematical and statistical formulas to derive the values for policy premiums, claim settlement amounts, and several other properties. The eInsure application's business tier was built with EJB technology. The application heavily used both stateless session beans and entity beans. eInsure also employed message-driven beans for asynchronous processing. In this chapter, I will concentrate on session and message-driven beans. The entity beans are integration tier components, which too are available remotely and provide persistence support. With the current EJB 3.0 specification, entity beans are a thing of the past. Hence, in this book, I will not discuss them in detail.

In this chapter, I will explore some of the key design patterns that can be applied to build a flexible yet simple business tier with the Spring Framework. I will start with the Service Locator pattern, which consolidates the boilerplate code required to look up EJB components registered in the JNDI. Then I will look into the Business Delegate pattern, which provides a client-side proxy of the business objects. Business Delegate and Service Locator work together to effectively connect the presentation tier with the business tier. I will cover the business tier in depth and concentrate on showing how to build remotely accessible business logic using the EJB session facade. You will also see the benefits of POJO business tier components in association with the application service and EJB command object patterns. I will finish this chapter with a discussion of the Business Interface pattern, which enforces certain compile-time checks on the session beans as well as simplifies the Business Delegate pattern.

Service Locator

Problem

The EJB session beans and message-driven beans are used to implement business workflows. These components on deployment are registered on the JNDI tree of the application server. The JNDI provides a directory service, which external clients can use to discover and look up objects by name. Hence, the JNDI makes EJBs accessible to remote clients. Besides EJBs, JMS queues, topics, connection factories, and JDBC, data sources are also bound in the JNDI. Listing 4-1 shows the JNDI lookup code used by the magic JSP controller of the eInsure application.

Listing 4-1. UnderwritingController.jsp

```
<%!
    final String JNDI_URL = "t3://localhost:7001";
    public UnderwritingHome getEJBHome() {
        UnderwritingHome home    = null;
        try{
                Hashtable h = new Hashtable();
                h.put(Context.INITIAL_CONTEXT_FACTORY,"");
                h.put(Context.INITIAL_CONTEXT_FACTORY,
            "weblogic.jndi.WLInitialContextFactory");
                h.put(Context.PROVIDER_URL, JNDI_URL);
            Context ctx = new InitialContext(h);
            Object homeObj = ctx.lookup("uwrbusinessslsb");
            home = (UnderwritingHome)PortableRemoteObject.narrow(homeObj,
            UnderwritingHome.class);
        }
        catch(Exception e){
            e.printStackTrace();
            home = null;
        }
          return home;
    }
%>


<%
    String eventCode = request.getParameter("eventCode");
```

```
    String screenCode = request.getParameter("screenCode");
    String inputPage = request.getParameter("referrer");
    String userCd = request.getParameter("userCode");
    String nextView = null;


    try{
        boolean userHasPrivilege = SecurityChecker.getInstance().isAuthorized(
userCd, eventCode);

        if(userHasPrivilege){
            if(eventCode.equals("UWR001") && screenCode.equals("SCR001")){
                nextView = "Policy.jsp";

                UnderwritingHome home = getEJBHome();
                Underwriting remote = home.create();
                remote.underwriteNewPolicy("GAP","Dhrubo",1);
            }
            else if(screenCode.equals("UWR002") && eventCode.equals("SCR001")){
                //lookup session bean
                //perform business operation
            }
        }
        else{
            request.setAttribute("ERROR_MESSAGE",
"You do not have privilege for this operation");
            nextView = inputPage;
        }
    }//try
    catch(Throwable exp){
        request.setAttribute("ERROR_MESSAGE",exp.getMessage());
        nextView = "error.jsp";
    }
    finally{
    //    finally redirect to correct view
        RequestDispatcher requestDispatcher =
request.getRequestDispatcher(nextView);
        requestDispatcher.forward(request,response);
    }
%>
```

Listing 4-1 shows the `getEJBHome` method, which is used to look up the EJB home interface using the JNDI API. This method was invoked in each `if-else` block that required interaction with business components. The lookup method was repeated in all the JSP controllers, thus degrading reuse. The legacy was perpetuated by the copy-and-paste style of reuse. No one in the development team bothered to refactor and move the JNDI object lookup to a generic reusable component ready to work with any server. This point was emphasized as the team faced lot of problems to deploy the product on IBM WebSphere for a new customer. It is clear from Listing 4-1 that the JNDI lookup used proprietary classes such as `weblogic.jndi.WLInitialContextFactory`. This in turn makes the application tightly coupled to a vendor implementation, in this case the BEA WebLogic application server. This adds to the agonies of porting to another Java EE application server.

With this design, each JSP controller was capable of supporting only a single session bean. This also ensured that the session bean would grow to an unmanageable size as more and more underwriting use cases were implemented. The end result was an application with inefficient design and architecture.

Note that the `getEJBHome` method used a static URL to connect to the JNDI service. This was done on the assumption that JSPs and EJBs were collocated in the same JVM. Although there is nothing wrong with this system architecture (it is actually common in midsize applications), this raises a serious question. If the JSPs and EJBs will be collocated, then do you really need EJBs? The tasks of developing and maintaining EJBs are difficult. Hence, unless your application needs the system services offered by an EJB container such as remoting, security, transaction, object pooling, failover, and so on, you will be better served by POJO business components.

To fully benefit from the advantages offered by EJB components, large-scale complex applications like eInsure should use distributed deployment architecture in production. In such deployment scenarios, the presentation tier components such as JSPs will reside in a web container like Apache Tomcat or Jetty. The presentation components access the EJB business objects deployed on an application server such as BEA WebLogic or Red Hat JBoss. The application servers run on a separate box and possibly in a different environment. In short, the presentation and business tier components are generally deployed on JVMs running on different machines. Hence, the distributed deployment of eInsure would require that the static URL is edited in all the JSP controllers.

I am not finished with the drawbacks in Listing 4-1. You may have already observed that this code created a new instance of the `InitialContext` object for each business service lookup. This is a costly operation. A JNDI lookup primarily searches for and retrieves an object proxy from another JVM on the network. Hence, a JNDI lookup is a likely cause of performance bottlenecks in an enterprise Java application.

Forces

- Consolidate EJB, JMS, or data source object lookup into a reusable component that encapsulates the complexities of interaction with the JNDI API.

- The JNDI lookup should be independent of vendor API classes and interfaces. In fact, it should be possible to switch between different servers merely by changing configuration parameters.

- The service lookup code should be flexible enough to support different types of business objects: EJBs, POJO, or even web services.

- Address the performance concerns associated with JNDI lookup.

Solution

Use a *service locator* to encapsulate JNDI object lookup and eliminate any performance overhead.

Strategies with the Spring Framework

As I explained in Chapter 3, page controllers are the most appropriate components to start interaction with the business tier. They do so by invoking methods on POJO business delegate objects. The business delegates provide the client-side interface for the business tier and are responsible for accessing the remote EJB objects. They, in turn, rely on the service locator to retrieve the EJB home object. Figure 4-1 shows this interaction.

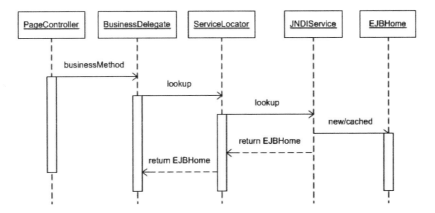

Figure 4-1. *Sequence diagram: service locator interaction*

The Spring Framework provides a comprehensive set of classes for retrieving JNDI bound objects from all different application servers. The JndiObjectFactoryBean is the most widely used service locator class in the Spring Framework. It is a factory bean and hence implements the FactoryBean interface. A factory bean is an object factory within the Spring bean factory. Hence, a factory bean is treated differently from a normal bean by the Spring IOC container. It is configured in the same manner as an ordinary bean, but Spring will not return a new instance of JndiObjectFactoryBean. Instead, the object it exposes for injection is always the one that it creates or retrieves. In the case of JndiObjectFactoryBean, this is made possible by the getObject method that returns the object retrieved from the JNDI. Thus, this service locator implementation can be used to look up and inject any kind of JNDI object. Since JndiObjectFactoryBean inherits from the JndiAccessor class, it easy to configure various JNDI-related properties. Figure 4-2 shows the Spring JNDI class diagram.

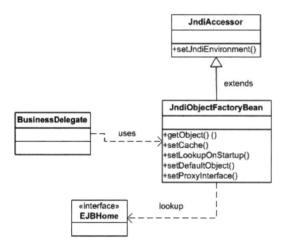

Figure 4-2. *Class diagram: Service locator*

Remote EJB 2.*x* Lookup

I will now put the JndiObjectFactoryBean to use. In Listing 3-27, I combined the page controller with the business delegate but deliberately did not show the code for the sake of simplicity. Listing 4-2 shows the business delegate implementation class. I will cover business delegates in detail later in this chapter. So, the sole intention of this business delegate listing here is to highlight how it is related to the service locator. As shown in Listing 4-2, the business delegate is completely decoupled from the service locator. The JndiObjectFactoryBean service locator works transparently with the Spring container to inject the EJB home object. Although it is possible to inject as many session beans as you want in this business delegate, the best practice is to have one EJB per business delegate.

Listing 4-2. `UnderwritingBusinessDelegate.java`

```java
public class UnderWritingBusinessDelegate {
    private UnderwritingHome underWritingHome;
    public void createPolicy(PolicyFormBean policyBean) {
        try {
            Underwriting bean = this.underWritingHome.create();
            bean.underwriteNewPolicy(policyBean.getProductCode(),
        policyBean.getFirstName(), policyBean.getAge());
        } catch (RemoteException e) {
            throw new RuntimeException(e);
        } catch (CreateException e) {
            throw new RuntimeException(e);
        }
    }
    public UnderwritingHome getUnderWritingHome() {
        return underWritingHome;
    }
    public void setUnderWritingHome(UnderwritingHome underWritingHome) {
        this.underWritingHome = underWritingHome;
    }
}
```

The service locator can be turned on by configuration, as shown in Listing 4-3. Applications should use a single instance of a `JndiObjectFactoryBean` per JNDI object.

Listing 4-3. `insurance-servlet.xml`

```xml
<?xml version="1.0" encoding="UTF-8"?>
<beans xmlns="http://www.springframework.org/schema/beans"
    xmlns:xsi="http://www.w3.org/2001/XMLSchema-instance"
    xsi:schemaLocation="http://www.springframework.org/schema/beans
http://www.springframework.org/schema/beans/spring-beans-2.5.xsd">
```

```
<bean name="underwritingBusinessDelegate"
    class="com.apress.insurance.view.delegate.UnderWritingBusinessDelegate">
    <property name="underWritingHome" ref="uwrSlsbHome" />
</bean>

<bean name="uwrSlsbHome"
    class="org.springframework.jndi.JndiObjectFactoryBean">
    <property name="jndiName" value="uwrbusinessslsb" />
    <property name="jndiEnvironment">
        <props>
            <prop key="java.naming.factory.initial">
                weblogic.jndi.WLInitialContextFactory
            </prop>
            <prop key="java.naming.provider.url">
                t3://localhost:7001
            </prop>
        </props>
    </property>
</bean>
</beans>
```

You can use Spring's property placeholder feature to further externalize the configuration. In this strategy, you replace the values of the different properties with placeholders. Then you move the values to an external properties file. It is easy to change the environment-specific values in the properties file and still keep the Spring XML configuration unaffected. For a detailed treatment of Spring's property placeholder support, you can refer to `http://static.springframework.org/spring/docs/2.5.x/reference/beans.html#beans-factory-placeholderconfigurer`.

So, with the Spring Framework, it is possible to set up a configurable service locator in no time.

Now to support a different application server, you just need to alter the configuration file. The code shown in Listing 4-4 makes it possible to look up the same EJB deployed on a JBoss server.

Listing 4-4. `insurance-servlet.xml` *for JBoss*

```
<?xml version="1.0" encoding="UTF-8"?>
<beans xmlns="http://www.springframework.org/schema/beans"
    xmlns:xsi="http://www.w3.org/2001/XMLSchema-instance"
    xsi:schemaLocation="http://www.springframework.org/schema/beans
```

```
http://www.springframework.org/schema/beans/spring-beans-2.5.xsd"
    >

    <!- -  Other beans - ->

    <bean name="uwrSlsbHome"
        class="org.springframework.jndi.JndiObjectFactoryBean">
        <property name="jndiName" value="uwrbusinessslsb" />

        <property name="jndiEnvironment">
            <props>
                <prop key="java.naming.factory.initial">
            org.jnp.interfaces.NamingContextFactory
                </prop>
                <prop key="java.naming.provider.url"> jnp://localhost:1099</prop>
<prop key=" java.naming.factory.url.pkgs">org.jboss.naming.client</prop>

            </props>
        </property>
    </bean>
</beans>
```

Local EJB 2.*x* Lookup

EJB 2.0 introduced local enterprise bean components collocated in the same JVM with other Java EE components. This improved performance by eliminating the network trip required to look up an object on the JNDI tree. This also simplified EJB object lookup to a great extent. A local stateless session bean can also be accessed using the JndiObjectFactoryBean just by configuration, as shown in Listing 4-5.

Listing 4-5. insurance-servlet.xml: *Local EJB*

```
<?xml version="1.0" encoding="UTF-8"?>
<beans xmlns="http://www.springframework.org/schema/beans"
    xmlns:xsi="http://www.w3.org/2001/XMLSchema-instance"
    xsi:schemaLocation="http://www.springframework.org/schema/beans
http://www.springframework.org/schema/beans/spring-beans-2.5.xsd"
    >
```

```
<!- -  Other beans - ->

<bean name="underwritingBusinessDelegate"
    class="com.apress.insurance.view.delegate.UnderWritingBusinessDelegate">
        <property name="uwrLocalHome" ref="uwrSlsbLocalHome" />

</bean>
<bean name="uwrSlsbLocalHome"
    class="org.springframework.jndi.JndiObjectFactoryBean">
    <property name="jndiName" value="UnderwritingBeanLocal" />
            </bean>
</beans>
```

Note that with local EJBs the various properties related to JNDI lookup are
redundant.

EJB 3 Lookup

With EJB 3 you can turn a POJO into a session bean by using Java EE standard annota-
tions. You are no longer burdened with the home interface and XML deployment
descriptors. All these have immensely simplified EJB development. The changes in EJB 3,
however, have not changed how the Spring service locator works. You can still use the
JndiObjectFactoryBean as a service locator by configuration. As shown in Listing 4-6, it is
used to look up two different session beans.

Listing 4-6. `insurance-servlet.xml`: *EJB 3 Lookup*

```
<?xml version="1.0" encoding="UTF-8"?>
<beans xmlns="http://www.springframework.org/schema/beans"
    xmlns:xsi="http://www.w3.org/2001/XMLSchema-instance"
    xsi:schemaLocation="http://www.springframework.org/schema/beans
http://www.springframework.org/schema/beans/spring-beans-2.5.xsd"
    >

    <!- -  Other beans - ->

<!- - Remote EJB 3 SLSB - ->
    <bean id="uwrRemoteService"
        class="org.springframework.jndi.JndiObjectFactoryBean">
        <property name="jndiName" value="UwrRemoteServiceBean/Remote" />
```

```
        <property name="jndiEnvironment">
            <props>
                <prop key="java.naming.factory.initial">
org.jnp.interfaces.NamingContextFactory
</prop>
                <prop key="java.naming.provider.url"> jnp://localhost:1099</prop>
<prop key=" java.naming.factory.url.pkgs">org.jboss.naming.client</prop>

            </props>
        </property>
    </bean>


<!- - Local EJB 3 SLSB - ->
    <bean id="uwrLocalService"
        class="org.springframework.jndi.JndiObjectFactoryBean">
        <property name="jndiName" value=" UwrLocalServiceBean/Local " />
            </bean>
</beans>
```

Lookup of JMS Objects

The service locator is not limited to EJB components; it can be used for any JNDI bound object such as a JMS queue and topic or a JDBC data source. It can also be used with web services.

Listing 4-7 looks up a local JMS queue and topic configured in JBoss. The listing also shows two ways of using a resource reference while accessing JNDI bound objects. One option is to prefix it directly in the jndiName property; the other is to turn on the resourceRef property, which will automatically prepend the string java:comp/env/: to the JNDI name.

Listing 4-7. insurance-servlet.xml

```
<?xml version="1.0" encoding="UTF-8"?>
<beans xmlns="http://www.springframework.org/schema/beans"
    xmlns:xsi="http://www.w3.org/2001/XMLSchema-instance"
    xsi:schemaLocation="http://www.springframework.org/schema/beans
http://www.springframework.org/schema/beans/spring-beans-2.5.xsd">
```

```
<!- -  Other beans - ->

  <bean id="testTopic"
     class="org.springframework.jndi.JndiObjectFactoryBean">
     <property name="jndiName" value="topic/testTopic" />
  </bean>
  <bean id="testQueue"
     class="org.springframework.jndi.JndiObjectFactoryBean">
     <property name="jndiName" value="queue/testQueue" />
  </bean>
  <bean id="resourceRefOnQueue"
     class="org.springframework.jndi.JndiObjectFactoryBean">
     <property name="jndiName" value="queue/resourceRefOnQueue" />
     <property name="resourceRef" value="true" />
  </bean>
  <bean id="sampleQueue"
     class="org.springframework.jndi.JndiObjectFactoryBean">
     <property name="jndiName" value="java:comp/env/topic/resourceRefOnQueue"
  </bean>
/>
</beans>
```

As shown in Listing 4-7, you can use the JndiObjectFactoryBean to look up JMS objects from the JNDI. In the case of remote JMS objects, you will just need to add the jndiEnvironment property in the same way as the EJB session bean in Listing 4-3.

As already discussed, object retrieval from the JNDI can be detrimental to performance. In highly transactional applications, JNDI objects will be used regularly. So, it is imperative that the clients cache and use these objects. This is exactly what the JndiObjectFactoryBean does by default. It looks up the JNDI tree when the Spring web application context is being initialized and loads the JNDI bound objects. Hence, it is necessary that the EJBs are loaded and registered in the JNDI before the Spring web application starts initialization.

The object caching feature of the service locator is not very important for applications that sparingly use JNDI objects. This will also cause problems if you update your application with hot deployment support from the application servers. Hot deployment allows an entire Java EE application to be reloaded without bringing down the server. This will also refresh the JNDI with new objects. As a result, the service locator cache, if used, will have object references that no longer exist. Hence, any further access to these objects will result in runtime exceptions being raised.

It is possible to look up and load JNDI objects lazily in the Spring IOC container. If JNDI object retrieval at startup and subsequent caching had to be turned off, you must specify the proxy interface. The proxy interface will enable the generation of a proxy object to stand in for the real JNDI object. Hence, the proxy interface must be the same as the JNDI object interface. As shown in Listing 4-8, I have specified the local home interface as the proxy interface. Note that the actual JNDI object will be made available on first use.

Listing 4-8. `insurance-servlet.xml`

```xml
<?xml version="1.0" encoding="UTF-8"?>
<beans xmlns="http://www.springframework.org/schema/beans"
       xmlns:xsi="http://www.w3.org/2001/XMLSchema-instance"
       xsi:schemaLocation="http://www.springframework.org/schema/beans
       http://www.springframework.org/schema/beans/spring-beans-2.5.xsd">
   <!- -  Other beans - ->
   <bean name="underwritingBusinessDelegate"
  class="com.apress.insurance.view.delegate.UnderWritingBusinessDelegate">
       <property name="uwrLocalHome" ref="uwrSlsbLocalHome" />
   </bean>
   <bean id="uwrSlsbLocalHome"
  class="org.springframework.jndi.JndiObjectFactoryBean">
       <property name="jndiName" value="UnderwritingBeanLocal" />
       <property name="cache" value="false" />
       <property name="lookupOnStartup" value="false" />
       <property name="proxyInterface"
value="com.apress.einsure.business.ejbfacade.UnderwritingLocalHome" />
                 </bean>
             </beans>
```

The eInsure application had a large number of session beans carrying out business workflow. But this resulted in lots of redundant metadata information bloating the Spring configuration file. You can minimize the duplication of configuration information by inheriting from an abstract template definition, as shown in Listing 4-9.

Listing 4-9. `insurance-servlet.xml`

```xml
<?xml version="1.0" encoding="UTF-8"?>
<beans xmlns="http://www.springframework.org/schema/beans"
       xmlns:xsi="http://www.w3.org/2001/XMLSchema-instance"
       xsi:schemaLocation="http://www.springframework.org/schema/beans
       http://www.springframework.org/schema/beans/spring-beans-2.5.xsd">
```

```xml
    <bean name="underwritingBusinessDelegate"
          class="com.apress.insurance.view.delegate.UnderWritingBusinessDelegate">
        <property name="uwrLocalHome" ref="uwrSlsbLocalHome" />
    </bean>


    <bean id="lazyJndiObjectFactoryBean" abstract="true"
          class="org.springframework.jndi.JndiObjectFactoryBean">
        <property name="cache" value="false" />
        <property name="lookupOnStartup" value="false" />
    </bean>
    <bean id="uwrSlsbLocalHome" parent="lazyJndiObjectFactoryBean">
        <property name="jndiName" value="UnderwritingBeanLocal" />
        <property name="proxyInterface"
value="com.apress.einsure.business.ejbfacade.UnderwritingLocalHome" />
    </bean>
    <bean id="claimSlsbLocalHome" parent="lazyJndiObjectFactoryBean">
        <property name="jndiName" value="ClaimBeanLocal" />
        <property name="proxyInterface"
value="com.apress.einsure.business.ejbfacade.ClaimLocalHome" />
    </bean>
</beans>
```

Spring 2.*x* introduces the new jee tag, which makes it even simpler to look up JNDI objects.

Listing 4-10 shows how you can use this new tag to look up the stateless session beans. Note that in order to use this tag, you need to modify the configuration file to include the jee namespace and schema location.

Listing 4-10. insurance-servlet.xml

```xml
<?xml version="1.0" encoding="UTF-8"?>
<beans xmlns="http://www.springframework.org/schema/beans"
       xmlns:xsi="http://www.w3.org/2001/XMLSchema-instance"
       xmlns:jee="http://www.springframework.org/schema/jee"
       xsi:schemaLocation="http://www.springframework.org/schema/beans
       http://www.springframework.org/schema/beans/spring-beans-2.5.xsd
       http://www.springframework.org/schema/jee
       http://www.springframework.org/schema/jee/spring-jee-2.5.xsd"
       >
<!- - local ejb lookup - ->
```

```
<jee:jndi-lookup  id="uwrSlsbLocalHome"
        cache="false"
        lookup-on-startup="false"
        jndi-name="UnderwritingBeanLocal"
        proxy-interface="com.apress.einsure.business.➥
ejbfacade.UnderwritingLocalHome"
    />

<jee:jndi-lookup id="uwrSlsbRemoteHome" jndi-name=" UnderwritingBeanRemote ">
    <!-- newline-separated, key-value pairs for the environment  -->
    <jee:environment>
java.naming.factory.initial=org.jnp.interfaces.NamingContextFactory
java.naming.provider.url=jnp://localhost:1099
java.naming.factory.url.pkgs=org.jboss.naming.client
 </jee:environment>
</jee:jndi-lookup>

</beans>
```

Another important aspect of the `JndiObjectFactoryBean` is the support for unit testing. It makes it easy to test components out of the container. You can do this by setting the `defaultObject` property. It is the fallback object, in case the JNDI service or JNDI bound objects are unavailable. Listing 4-11 shows how to use the fallback object.

Listing 4-11. `insurance-servlet.xml`

```
<?xml version="1.0" encoding="UTF-8"?>
<beans xmlns="http://www.springframework.org/schema/beans"
    xmlns:xsi="http://www.w3.org/2001/XMLSchema-instance"
    xsi:schemaLocation="http://www.springframework.org/schema/beans
http://www.springframework.org/schema/beans/spring-beans-2.5.xsd"
    >

    <!- -  Other beans - ->
    <bean name="uwrbusinessPOJO"
class="com.apress.einsure.business.UwrBusinessServiceImpl"

    <bean name="uwrSlsbHome"
        class="org.springframework.jndi.JndiObjectFactoryBean">
        <property name="jndiName" value="uwrbusinessslsb" />
```

```
<property name=" defaultObject" ref="uwrbusinessPOJO" />
        <property name="jndiEnvironment">
            <props>
                <prop key="java.naming.factory.initial">
org.jnp.interfaces.NamingContextFactory
</prop>
                <prop key="java.naming.provider.url"> jnp://localhost:1099</prop>
<prop key=" java.naming.factory.url.pkgs">org.jboss.naming.client</prop>

            </props>
        </property>
    </bean>
</beans>
```

It must be noted that the `JndiObjectFactoryBean` is a convenient way to look up JNDI objects. But the recommended approach is to use a proxy factory bean that effectively combines the service locator with dependency injection. You will learn about this strategy in connection with the Business Delegate pattern.

Consequences

Benefits

- The Service Locator pattern abstracts the complex lookup mechanism associated with service objects. This adds flexibility because the service clients are freed from the lookup code.

- JNDI lookup is achieved by mere configuration with the Spring Framework.

- Performance is improved by the caching behavior of the Spring-based service locator.

- Improved testability of service objects. With Spring, it is now possible to test POJO business components outside the container without any alteration of the application code base.

- It's easy to externalize service locator configuration.

Concerns

- Developers need to know and remember a lot of configuration parameters and options.

Business Delegate

Problem

The page controllers form the boundary classes for the presentation tier in any Java EE application. It is possible for the page controllers to directly invoke the business components. This makes the presentation tier code tightly coupled with the business tier code.

In most cases, the business service components are available as remote objects like stateless session beans (SLSBs). In such cases the page controller also needs to take care of the infrastructure services such as JNDI lookup, handle remote exceptions, and so on. In due course it becomes increasingly difficult to maintain these page controllers because they handle multiple responsibilities.

Forces

- Minimize coupling between the presentation tier and the business tier.

- Hide infrastructure issues from the business service clients.

Solution

Use a *business delegate* to act as an adapter to invoke business objects from the presentation tier.

Strategies with the Spring Framework

Famous computer scientist Butler W. Lampson (who envisioned the modern personal computer at Xerox way back in 1972) once said, "All problems in computer science can be solved by another level of indirection." This principle can be applied to put together a thin layer between page controllers and the EJB business layer. The sole purpose of this layer is to decouple the presentation tier from the business tier. This thin layer is comprised of business delegates.

As you saw in Listing 4-2, the business delegate is a POJO client-side proxy for the business tier. It uses the service locator to access the EJB objects. With the Spring Framework, the service locator works transparently to the business delegate. The EJB objects looked up by the service locator are injected in the business delegate by the Spring IOC container. This EJB object is used to delegate the business logic invocation. So, a business delegate knows how to work with a remoting API such as an EJB. The business delegate also handles exceptions that are raised during EJB method invocation. It will generally convert these exceptions into an application-specific runtime exception.

Another critical responsibility of a business delegate is to provide a consistent API for the page controllers. To achieve this goal, it will apply the object design best practice of program to interface (P2I). Listing 10-12 shows the business delegate interface.

As shown in Listing 4-12, the business delegate replicates the same methods as the actual remote business object.

Listing 4-12. UnderwritingBusinessDelegate.java

```
public interface UnderwritingBusinessDelegate {
    public void underwriteNewPolicy(String productCd,String name,int age);
}
```

Listing 4-13 shows the business delegate implementation class. The business delegate intercepts any exceptions raised by the distributed business objects and transforms them into RuntimeException because in most cases it is not possible to recover from them.

Listing 4-13. UnderwritingBusinessDelegateImpl.java

```
public class UnderwritingBusinessDelegateImpl
implements UnderwritingBusinessDelegate{
    private UnderwritingRemoteHome uwrRemoteHome;
    public UnderwritingRemoteHome getUwrRemoteHome() {
        return uwrRemoteHome;
    }
    public void setUwrRemoteHome(UnderwritingRemoteHome uwrRemoteHome) {
        this.uwrRemoteHome = uwrRemoteHome;
    }
    public void underwriteNewPolicy(String productCd, String name, int age) {
            try {
              UnderwritingRemote bean = this.uwrRemoteHome.create();
              bean.underwriteNewPolicy(productCd, name, age);
```

```
        } catch (CreateException ex) {
            throw new RuntimeException(ex);
        } catch (RemoteException ex) {
            throw new RuntimeException(ex);
        }
    }
}
```

Now everything needs to be wired up in the Spring configuration file shown in List-ing 4-14. Note that the business delegate is injected into the page controller by the Spring container.

Listing 4-14. `insurance-servlet.xml`

```
<?xml version="1.0" encoding="UTF-8"?>
<beans xmlns="http://www.springframework.org/schema/beans"
       xmlns:xsi="http://www.w3.org/2001/XMLSchema-instance"
       xmlns:jee="http://www.springframework.org/schema/jee"
       xsi:schemaLocation="http://www.springframework.org/schema/beans
       http://www.springframework.org/schema/beans/spring-beans-2.5.xsd
       http://www.springframework.org/schema/jee
       http://www.springframework.org/schema/jee/spring-jee-2.5.xsd">
    <!--other beans - -->
<bean name="/createPolicy.do"
    class="com.apress.insuranceapp.web.controller.CreatePolicyController">
    <property name="uwrBusinessDelegate" ref="uwrBusinessDelegate"/>
</bean>

    <bean name="uwrBusinessDelegate"
        class="com.apress.insurance.view.delegate.➡
UnderWritingBusinessDelegateImpl">
        <property name="uwrRemoteHome" ref="uwrSlsbRemoteHome" />
    </bean>

    <bean id="uwrSlsbRemoteHome" class="org.springframework.jndi.➡
JndiObjectFactoryBean">
        <property name="jndiName" value="UnderwritingBeanRemote" />
        <property name="jndiEnvironment">
            <props>
                <prop key="java.naming.factory.initial">
                    org.jnp.interfaces.NamingContextFactory
```

```
            </prop>
            <prop key="java.naming.provider.url">
                jnp://localhost:1099
            </prop>
            <prop key="java.naming.factory.url.pkgs">
                org.jboss.naming.client
            </prop>
        </props>
    </property>
 </bean>
</beans>
```

The program to interface principle adds flexibility to the Business Delegate design. It may happen that you decide to switch from EJBs to an alternative remoting option such as Burlap-Hessian or web services. In such a scenario you need a new implementation of the business delegate. But the page controllers (which are clients of business delegates) will remain unaffected because they use business delegate interfaces. Finally, you will need to wire this bean in the Spring configuration to replace the EJB.

Consequences

Benefits

- The intermediate business delegate layer decouples the business layer from the presentation layer. As a result, you have a more flexible and maintainable presentation tier.

- The business delegate exposes a uniform API to the presentation tier to access business logic. It also handles exceptions and converts them into types that the presentation tier understands.

- With Spring dependency injection support, the development and use of the POJO business delegate are immensely simplified.

Concerns

- The business delegate introduces an extra layer that increases the number of classes in the application. This may be a cause of concern during maintenance.

- If the remote business object interfaces change, the business delegate should take care of this. In an ideal situation, the page controllers will be unaware of such internal changes in the business delegate. However, such a thing seldom happens, and page controllers too are affected by business object changes.

Session Facade

Problem

The eInsure application used SLSBs to deploy remotely accessible business logic. These SLSBs were accessed from the JSP controllers as shown in Listing 4-1. However, as I have already highlighted, business objects should be accessed from the business delegate. Soon, eInsure code was refactored, and the Business Delegate pattern was put in use. But the business service access code that moved from the JSP controller to the business delegate continued to have the original problems. One such problem was the invocation of multiple remote business methods in response to a user action. The use case "underwrite new policy" in eInsure could be divided into four subtasks: saving policy details, querying the product workbench to retrieve the default risk and cover list, associating these risks and cover list to the policy, and finally creating accounting records that will be used later to track premium payments. Hence, to fulfill this use case, the business delegate would invoke the four remote business methods.

The approach described in the previous paragraph had immediate side effects. The fine-grained remote business method invocation from the business delegate increased network round-trips. This also required large data sets to be marshaled and unmarshaled over the network for each method call. The end result was the degradation of application performance. The whole thing was accentuated by the fact that in eInsure the SLSBs relied on entity beans for persistence. Each of the subtasks used at least two entity beans to save and retrieve data from the RDBMS. Since entity beans were remotely accessible persistence components and required data marshaling and unmarshaling, they also added to the network clog.

Invoking multiple session bean methods from the business delegate per user action increased the chances of business logic spilling over into the client tier. It also increased the possibility of client-side transaction management that the EJB component model should have eliminated. Since multiple session bean methods were involved, it created a lot difficulty in setting the appropriate transaction attribute while using declarative container-managed transaction (CMT) support. Using entity beans that themselves were transactional components did not help the cause either. It was difficult to decide whether to handle transactions in session beans or in entity beans.

Forces

- Consolidate business workflow in remotely accessible components.

- Expose coarse-grained business interfaces to access entity beans in one network call.

- Prevent business logic and system-level services such as transaction management from spilling over into the business tier's clients.

- Improve performance by consolidating business methods.

Solution

Expose a remotely accessible *session facade*, which will encapsulate business logic while exposing a coarse-grained API to the clients.

Strategies with the Spring Framework

A session facade is an application of the GOF facade pattern to an EJB session bean. The facade pattern presents a unified interface for a group of interfaces in the subsystem. In other words, a facade is a higher-level interface that makes it easier to use the subsystem. In the context of EJBs, this means the session beans act as a facade and expose only a single business method per user action. This method in turn invokes private session bean methods. Another option is to consolidate the entire business logic in one session facade method. This method then provides coarse-grained access to the business tier. Because only a single method of the remote business object carries out the workflow pertaining to a use case, it is easy to apply a container-managed transaction on this method. Later in this chapter I will explain a flexible and cleaner solution in connection with the Application Service pattern.

EJB 2.0 introduced local EJBs with the aim of limiting network trips and thus enhancing performance. A remote stateless session bean implementing business workflow can be combined with local entity beans to complete a particular use case in just one network trip.

Writing a stateless session bean is a tedious activity even with modern integrated development environments. Each EJB 2.*x* or 1.*x* SLSB requires at least three Java files to be created. You need two Java files for the home and remote interfaces, while the third one is for the bean implementation class. Apart from this, you have two XML deployment descriptors: the standard `ejb-jar.xml` and the other vendor-specific XML that supplies runtime metadata. In the next few sections, I will try to simplify the development of the session facade with Spring EJB support classes.

The first step to building a session bean is to create the home interface, as shown in Listing 4-15.

Listing 4-15. `UnderwritingRemoteHome.java`

```
public interface UnderwritingRemoteHome extends EJBHome {

    UnderwritingRemote create()  throws CreateException, RemoteException;

}
```

The home interface is responsible for managing the life cycle of the remote EJB object. In this case, the create method of the home interface acts as a factory responsible for creating the remote objects. The remote object implements the remote interface as shown in Listing 4-16.

Listing 4-16. `UnderwritingRemote.java`

```
public interface UnderwritingRemote extends EJBObject {
    public void underwriteNewPolicy(String productCd,String name,int age)
throws RemoteException;
}
```

The remote interface defines all the business methods that will be exposed by the SLSB to its clients. The bean implementation class is responsible for providing implementation for the business methods defined in the remote interface. Spring provides convenience base classes to simplify the development of the bean implementation class. So, it is important to understand these classes before I get down into the implementation details.

As you see in Figure 4-3, the `AbstractEnterpriseBean` class forms the core of the Spring EJB support classes. This class can be subclassed to support different forms of EJBs such as session beans, message-driven beans, and so on. However, in most cases, you will not need to do that because Spring already provides the appropriate subclasses. The `AbstractEnterpriseBean` class helps create and load a Spring bean factory and makes it available to the EJB.

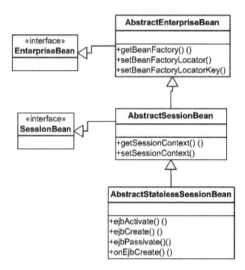

Figure 4-3. *Class diagram: Spring stateless session bean support*

The `AbstractEnterpriseBean` is generic, and Spring provides a specialized `AbstractSessionBean` class to develop session bean components. This class implements the `SessionBean` interface and takes on the responsibility of saving the `SessionContext` object injected by the EJB container. However, it should not be extended for supporting SLSBs. Instead, your bean implementation should inherit from the more specialized `AbstractStatelessSessionBean`. This class implements all the EJB callback methods. This is very useful because in most cases you would require empty implementation of these callbacks. This feature cleans up the bean implementation classes, promotes reuse, and allows it to focus only on business logic. The subclasses should override the `onEjbCreate` method to carry out any post-initialization after loading the bean factory. Finally, Listing 4-17 shows the bean implementation class.

Listing 4-17. `UnderwritingRemoteBean.java`

```java
public class UnderwritingRemoteBean extends AbstractStatelessSessionBean {

 public void underwriteNewPolicy(String productCd, String name, int age)
throws RemoteException {
        //implement business rule
        //invoke Entity beans

    }
    protected void onEjbCreate() throws CreateException {
        //use for post initialisation tasks
    }
}
```

To register as a session bean and subscribe to the container services, the Java classes must be supplemented with metadata information. The metadata information is provided in the form of XML deployment descriptors. The first deployment descriptor is `ejb-jar.xml`, which describes the bean and system services it requires. In this case, the bean requires transactional services for all its methods, as shown in Listing 4-18.

Listing 4-18. `ejb-jar.xml`

```xml
<?xml version="1.0" encoding="UTF-8"?>
<ejb-jar version="2.1" xmlns="http://java.sun.com/xml/ns/j2ee"
xmlns:xsi="http://www.w3.org/2001/XMLSchema-instance"
xsi:schemaLocation="http://java.sun.com/xml/ns/j2ee
http://java.sun.com/xml/ns/j2ee/ejb-jar_2_1.xsd">
    <enterprise-beans>
        <session>
            <display-name>UnderwritingRemoteSB</display-name>
            <ejb-name>UnderwritingRemoteBean</ejb-name>
            <home>com.apress.einsure.business.➥
ejbfacade.UnderwritingRemoteHome</home>
            <remote>com.apress.einsure.business.➥
ejbfacade.UnderwritingRemote</remote>
            <ejb-class>com.apress.einsure.business.➥
ejbfacade.UnderwritingRemoteBean</ejb-class>
            <session-type>Stateless</session-type>
            <transaction-type>Container</transaction-type>
```

```
            <env-entry>
                <env-entry-name>ejb/BeanFactoryPath</env-entry-name>
                <env-entry-type>java.lang.String</env-entry-type>
                <env-entry-value>
com/apress/einsure/business/ejbfacade/Underwriting-beans.xml
</env-entry-value>
            </env-entry>
        </session>
    </enterprise-beans>
    <assembly-descriptor>
        <container-transaction>
            <method>
                <ejb-name>UnderwritingRemoteBean</ejb-name>
                <method-name>*</method-name>
            </method>
            <trans-attribute>Required</trans-attribute>
        </container-transaction>
    </assembly-descriptor>
</ejb-jar>
```

As I mentioned earlier, with Spring EJB support it is possible to start an application context. The default mechanism is to load an application context from a resource specified as a JNDI environment variable: `java:comp/env/ejb/BeanFactoryPath`. Listing 4-18 highlights this environment variable. This default behavior is provided with the help of the `BeanFactoryLocator` implementation provided by the `ContextJndiBeanFactoryLocator` class. It is also possible to provide a custom `BeanFactoryLocator` implementation and inject it using the `setBeanFactoryLocator` method either in the `setSessionContext` method or in the default constructor of the stateless session bean implementation class.

The default behavior of `ContextJndiBeanFactoryLocator` can have serious performance limitations. Loading and initializing an application context with several beans defined in it can be time-consuming. You can overcome this by using a shared bean factory for all the EJBs. The `ContextSingletonBeanFactoryLocator` class provides this support. However, you need to be careful with a singleton context and limit it only amongst the EJBs in your application. Sharing a common application context amongst all tiers (presentation, business, and integration) may result in lots of class-loading issues.

Listing 4-19 shows the Spring configuration file required to start the SLSB application context. Currently, it does not contain any bean definition. I will put this to effective use later when I discuss the Application Service pattern.

Listing 4-19. Underwriting-beans.xml

```xml
<?xml version="1.0" encoding="UTF-8"?>
<beans xmlns="http://www.springframework.org/schema/beans"
       xmlns:xsi="http://www.w3.org/2001/XMLSchema-instance"
       xsi:schemaLocation="http://www.springframework.org/schema/beans
       http://www.springframework.org/schema/beans/spring-beans-2.5.xsd">

</beans>
```

Finally, to complete the EJB, you also need an application server vendor-specific deployment descriptor, which is used to provide meta-information such as the JNDI name to bind the EJB home object in the JNDI tree. Listing 4-20 shows the JBoss-specific deployment descriptor.

Listing 4-20. jboss.xml

```xml
<?xml version="1.0" encoding="UTF-8"?>
<jboss>
    <enterprise-beans>
            <session>
             <ejb-name>UnderwritingRemoteBean</ejb-name>
             <jndi-name>UnderwritingBeanRemote</jndi-name>
             <local-jndi-name>UnderwritingBeanLocal</local-jndi-name>
          </session>
    </enterprise-beans>
    <resource-managers>
    </resource-managers>
</jboss>
```

The final task is to compile, package, and deploy this EJB in a JBoss 4.*x* application server. The clients can easily look up this EJB using the Service Locator pattern described earlier in this chapter.

Consequences

Benefits

- The session facade exposes a coarse-grained API to the clients of the remote business object.

- It allows Java EE applications to effectively leverage container-managed services such as transaction and security.

- The consolidation of business method invocation into a single coarse-grained call reduces network trips and improves performance.

- The session facade helps to clearly establish the responsibilities of different components in a Java EE application. This also prevents business logic from spilling over to the client tier.

Concerns

- Session facades have steep learning curves with complex concepts.

- Besides different classes and interfaces, a lot of configuration information is required. This adds overhead during maintenance.

Application Service

Problem

The eInsure application's business logic was entirely coded in the session facades. As I explained in connection with session facades, EJB development was a very complex task. You had to work with three Java source files. Then there were two deployment descriptors and a large set of configuration information. EJB development requires seasoned programmers. There are a lot of concepts related to system services, configuration, and server-specific settings that can be managed effectively only with experienced developers.

The container manages the life cycle of the EJB components. These components also subscribe to different container services such as security, transaction, and object pooling. The developers need to have a clear understanding of the concepts and intricacies behind these services and life-cycle stages. This is imperative to write code that will respond correctly to life-cycle state changes. It will also help the developers appropriately set configuration metadata and prevent unexpected results.

Since the entire business logic is now in the SLSB, chances are high that in a large-scale application like eInsure that it will grow quickly to an unmanageable size. The session facade not only intercepts business logic invocation, but also each method in the SLSB is responsible for executing business rules. Hence, it also violated SRP. A simpler option would be to model the session facade like a front controller servlet. It only takes the responsibility of intercepting the business method execution requests. The actual task of business logic execution is delegated to the helper classes.

The session facades run in the EJB container. As a result, they were difficult to unit test. A prospective client of eInsure could not afford commercial application server licenses. Hence, they wanted to deploy this application on open source products. Their team was already using an Apache Tomcat and ObjectWeb JOTM-based platform to run a few applications. Hence, they wanted to leverage the Tomcat web server with the JDBC-based transaction-processing capabilities of the JOTM transaction monitor. However, because the all-important business tier of eInsure was tightly coupled to SLSB, it would be a painful and effort-intensive activity to successfully run eInsure without an EJB container support.

Forces

- Session bean development requires experienced developers with sound knowledge of EJBs and application servers.

- The session facade should act only as a gateway to the business tier and delegate the actual business logic execution to helpers. It should declaratively subscribe to container services.

- Session facades should not grow to an unmanageable proportion.

- Business logic should run outside an EJB container.

- Business logic should be easy to unit test.

Solution

Use an *application service* to concentrate business logic in POJO classes.

Strategies with the Spring Framework

Although it is quite legitimate to put the business logic code in session facades, it is not the best approach. You will be better served by moving the business logic to POJO components and letting the session facade delegate to these POJOs. This will free up the session facade. It can now act as the gateway to the remotely accessible business tier. Since the business logic is now moved to POJO, it is easier to unit test. The POJO application services sit behind the SLSB gateway and so can also leverage robust infrastructure support such as transactions. In other words, all POJO methods that are invoked from the session facade will be part of the same transaction scope. Moving business logic to POJO components also reduces the effort that will be required to run an application like eInsure in a web container.

The first step to writing an application service is to define an interface following the P2I principle. Listing 4-21 shows the UnderwritingApplicationService interface.

Listing 4-21. UnderwritingApplicationService.java

```
package com.apress.einsure.business.api;

public interface UnderwritingApplicationService {
    public void underwriteNewPolicy(String productCd,String name,int age);
}
```

Listing 4-22 shows the application service implementation class. Note that this class does not use entity beans for persistence needs. Instead, it uses lightweight data access objects for persistence. You will learn more about data access objects in Chapter 5.

Listing 4-22. UnderwritingApplicationServiceImpl.java

```
package com.apress.einsure.business.impl;

public class UnderwritingApplicationServiceImpl implements
UnderwritingApplicationService{

    private PolicyDetailDao policyDetailDao;

    public void underwriteNewPolicy(String productCd, String name, int age)  {
        //business validation - is this age allowed for this product

        this.policyDetailDao.savePolicyDetails(productCd, name, age);
```

```
    }

    public PolicyDetailDao getPolicyDetailDao() {
        return policyDetailDao;
    }

    public void setPolicyDetailDao(PolicyDetailDao policyDetailDao) {
        this.policyDetailDao = policyDetailDao;
    }

}
```

The PolicyDetailDao is injected in the application service by the Spring container. The data access object also needs a data source to save data. This is shown in the EJB application context configuration in Listing 4-23.

Listing 4-23. Underwriting-beans.xml

```xml
<?xml version="1.0" encoding="UTF-8"?>
<beans xmlns="http://www.springframework.org/schema/beans"
       xmlns:xsi="http://www.w3.org/2001/XMLSchema-instance"
       xsi:schemaLocation="http://www.springframework.org/schema/beans
       http://www.springframework.org/schema/beans/spring-beans-2.5.xsd">

    <bean id="uwrBusinessService"

class="com.apress.einsure.business.impl.UnderwritingApplicationServiceImpl">
        <property name="policyDetailDao" ref="policyDetailDao"/>

    </bean>

<! - - Data access object - ->
    <bean id="policyDetailDao"
          class="com.apress.einusre.persistence.dao.impl.PolicyDetailDaoImpl"
    >
        <property name="dataSource" ref="datasource"/>
    </bean>
    <!- - Lookup JNDI bound datasource - - >
    <bean id="datasource" class="org.springframework.jndi.JndiObjectFactoryBean">
        <property name="jndiName" value="einsureDatasource" />
        <property name="jndiEnvironment">
```

```
            <props>
                <prop key="java.naming.factory.initial">
                    org.jnp.interfaces.NamingContextFactory
                </prop>

                <prop key="java.naming.provider.url">
                    jnp://localhost:1099
                </prop>
                <prop key="java.naming.factory.url.pkgs">
                    org.jboss.naming.client
                </prop>
            </props>
        </property>

    </bean>

</beans>
```

You will need to alter the session facade (shown earlier in Listing 4-17) to delegate to the application service that implements the business logic. Listing 4-24 shows the modified implementation class. Note that the onEjbCreate method now gets involved in doing something useful. It retrieves the POJO business service object from the Spring application context associated with this EJB. The constant in the business interface supplies the value of the key used to look up the application service bean.

Listing 4-24. UnderwritingRemoteBean.java

```java
public class UnderwritingRemoteBean extends AbstractStatelessSessionBean {

    private final String SERVICE_BEAN_KEY = "uwrAppService";

    private UnderwritingApplicationService uwrAppService;

    public void underwriteNewPolicy(String productCd, String name, int age)
    throws RemoteException {
        //delegate to application service
        uwrAppService.underwriteNewPolicy(productCd, name, age);
    }
```

```
    protected void onEjbCreate() throws CreateException {
        //use for initialisation
        uwrAppService = (UnderwritingApplicationService) this.getBeanFactory().
getBean(SERVICE_BEAN_KEY);

    }

}
```

Note that there is a possibility that an application service will now increase rapidly in size in order to incorporate complex business rules. It is possible to use a single application service per user case just like you do with the page controllers. However, this will create lot of small classes that are hard to maintain. A more balanced solution would be to logically group the application service methods. In the case of eInsure, for example, a particular application service can include the methods to create, update, suspend, reject, and approve a claim.

Consequences

Benefits

- The business logic is now encapsulated in simple POJO components. These services access EJB container services as they are invoked from the session facade.

- POJO components make the application easier to test and run outside the container.

- You get improved performance because the session facade relies now on the POJO application service and data access object combination. It no longer uses entity beans, which increased the network chattiness.

Concerns

- The Application Service pattern adds an extra layer to the application. This increases maintenance and development effort.

Business Interface

Problem

The remote interface of a session facade defines the business methods that are accessible from the client. The bean class, on the other hand, provides implementation for the business methods. However, there is no direct relationship between the two. This results in annoying runtime or deploy-time errors such as missing methods, inconsistent method names, parameter type and count, and exceptions. Since these errors are generally detected only at runtime, you may end up losing a significant amount of effort in the debug-fix-deploy-test cycle. Thus, this decoupling of remote interface and bean implementation makes it impossible to trap errors early, at compile time.

The easiest solution to this problem is to allow the bean class to implement the remote or local interface. However, this is not allowed by the EJB specification. Although not very common, sometimes a session bean method may need to pass its reference to the called method. This is common in Java programming, where you pass the this reference. But things are different in EJB. The EJB clients should always use the remote interface to invoke business methods. This helps the EJB container intercept all business method invocation and register these methods for applying system services such as security and transaction. Now, since the bean class does not implement the remote interface, you are forced get the associated EJBObject/EJBLocalObject from the SessionContext and pass it to the called method. If the bean class had implemented the remote or local interface, then there is a chance of inadvertently passing this reference from the bean class to the calling method. In this case, however, the behavior of the EJB container is not guaranteed, and you may get unexpected results.

There are other problems for the bean class implementing the remote and local interfaces.

The EJBObject and EJBLocalObject interfaces define two different sets of methods. The container is supposed to provide implementations for these methods during deployment. The container-implemented methods are critical to the overall working of the EJBs. These methods take care of low-level concerns such as networking, serialization of parameters and passed values, and coordination with the container for system services. They also proxy business method calls to the actual bean implementation. But in case the bean class implements these methods, it has to provide implementation for these classes, which may ultimately result in an unusable EJB. To compile the bean, the implementation needs to implement the methods defined in these interfaces. This in turn clutters the bean implementation with unnecessary code. Moreover, if the remote interface is implemented by the bean implementation, the clients will have access to the actual bean just by casting the remote interface, which defeats the core goals of the EJB, which are location transparency and distributed business objects.

Forces

- Consolidate business methods in a common interface.

- Enforce compile-time checks to prevent anomalies between the remote interface and the bean implementation.

- Prevent EJB bean implementation classes from implementing remote or local interfaces.

Solution

Implement a *business interface* to consolidate business methods and apply compile-time checks of EJB methods.

Strategies with the Spring Framework

A business interface is a plain Java interface that consolidates the methods that the bean class will implement. The local and remote interfaces also extend the business interface. Thus, this superinterface keeps the method signature and count in sync and allows any differences to be detected at compile time. Further, since the business interface does not extend `EJBObject` or `EJBLocalObject`, the bean class is saved from unnecessary method implementation. I will now show how to put the business interface into action for different types and versions of stateless session beans.

Figure 4-4 shows the class diagram of the business interface for a remote SLSB.

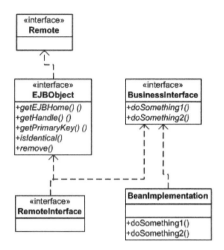

Figure 4-4. *Class diagram: remote business interface*

In the case of the remote SLSB, the business interface methods must declare a `throws` clause for `RemoteException`. Otherwise, the EJB verifier tool that comes with each application server will not allow the deployment of such EJBs. The business interface for the SLSB should ideally be the interface associated with the application service. However, because of this dependency with `RemoteException`, I will create a separate interface as shown in Listing 4-25.

Listing 4-25. `UnderwritingBusinessService.java`

```java
public interface UnderwritingBusinessService {
    public void underwriteNewPolicy(String productCd,String name,int age)
throws RemoteException;
}
```

The remote interface now extends the `UnderwritingBusinessService` and no longer defines any business methods. It is shown in Listing 4-26.

Listing 4-26. `UnderwritingRemote`

```java
public interface UnderwritingRemote extends EJBObject, UnderwritingBusinessService {

}
```

To achieve compile-time consistency, the bean implementation class now implements the business service interface as shown in Listing 4-27. Note that I will continue to
use application services as is.

Listing 4-27. `UnderwritingRemoteBean.java`

```java
public class UnderwritingRemoteBean extends AbstractStatelessSessionBean
implements    UnderwritingBusinessService{

    private final String SERVICE_BEAN_KEY = "uwrAppService";

    private UnderwritingApplicationService uwrAppService;

    public void underwriteNewPolicy(String productCd, String name, int age)
throws RemoteException {
        //delegate business processing to application service
        uwrAppService.underwriteNewPolicy(productCd, name, age);
    }

    protected void onEjbCreate() throws CreateException {
        //use for initialisation
        uwrAppService = (UnderwritingApplicationService)
this.getBeanFactory().getBean(SERVICE_BEAN_KEY);
    }
}
```

Now the compile-time consistency is among the remote interface, and the enterprise
bean class is ensured. Amidst all the changes, the home interface remains unaffected.
The business interface is not limited to providing compile-time checks. It can be used
with the Spring proxy-based service locators to remove the code redundancy associated
with the business delegate. Proxies are like duplicates that stand in for the real object. To
remove the business delegate layer, you will need to alter the page controllers to now
work with the business interface, as shown in Listing 4-28.

Listing 4-28. UnderwritingRemoteBean.java

```java
public class SaveNewPolicyController extends SimpleFormController {

    private UnderwritingBusinessService uwrBusinessService;

        public void setUwrBusinessService(
            UnderwritingBusinessService uwrBusinessService) {
        this.uwrBusinessService = uwrBusinessService;
    }

    protected void doSubmitAction(Object formbean) throws Exception {
        PolicyFormBean policyBean = (PolicyFormBean)formbean;
                uwrBusinessService.underwriteNewPolicy(policyBean.getProductCode()
                        , policyBean.getFirstName(), policyBean.getAge());
        }
    protected Object formBackingObject(HttpServletRequest req) throws Exception {
        PolicyFormBean policyBean = (PolicyFormBean)super.formBackingObject(req);

        return policyBean;
    }
/*

    protected ModelAndView onSubmit(Object formbean) throws Exception {
        PolicyFormBean policyBean = (PolicyFormBean)formbean;
        uwrBusinessDelegate.createPolicy(policyBean);
        return new ModelAndView(this.getSuccessView(),"policydetails",formbean);
    }
*/


}
```

The page controller in Listing 4-28 in fact works with business interface proxies. To inject the business interface proxy, I will use the SimpleRemoteStatelessSessionProxy➡ FactoryBean class. This factory bean performs two tasks. It looks up the EJB home interface and caches it. It also creates a proxy object implementing the business interface. The proxy object is injected into the page controller. The first business method invocation on the proxy will result in the creation of the remote object by invoking the create method on the cached home interface. It will then delegate the business processing to the remote object. This is possible because the remote object also implements the business interface. Listing 4-29 shows the configuration of this service locator and the page controller.

Listing 4-29. `insurance-servlet.xml`

```xml
<?xml version="1.0" encoding="UTF-8"?>
<beans xmlns="http://www.springframework.org/schema/beans"
       xmlns:xsi="http://www.w3.org/2001/XMLSchema-instance"
       xmlns:jee="http://www.springframework.org/schema/jee"
       xsi:schemaLocation="http://www.springframework.org/schema/beans
       http://www.springframework.org/schema/beans/spring-beans-2.5.xsd
       http://www.springframework.org/schema/jee
       http://www.springframework.org/schema/jee/spring-jee-2.5.xsd">

    <bean id="viewResolver"
         class="org.springframework.web.servlet.view.InternalResourceViewResolver">
        <property name="viewClass"
                  value="org.springframework.web.servlet.view.JstlView" />
        <property name="prefix" value="/WEB-INF/jsp/" />
        <property name="suffix" value=".jsp" />
    </bean>
        <bean id="uwrBusinessServiceProxy"
          class="org.springframework.ejb.access.➥
        SimpleRemoteStatelessSessionProxyFactoryBean">
        <property name="jndiName" value="UnderwritingBeanRemote" />
        <property name="businessInterface"
value="com.apress.einsure.business.api.UnderwritingBusinessService" />
        <property name="jndiEnvironment">
            <props>
                <prop key="java.naming.factory.initial">
                    org.jnp.interfaces.NamingContextFactory
                </prop>
                <prop key="java.naming.provider.url">
                    jnp://localhost:1099
                </prop>
                <prop key="java.naming.factory.url.pkgs">
                    org.jboss.naming.client
                </prop>

            </props>
        </property>
    </bean>
    <bean name="/createPolicy.do"
         class="com.apress.insurance.web.controller.SaveNewPolicyController" >
```

```
        <property name="uwrBusinessService"
                  ref="uwrBusinessServiceProxy" />

        <property name="formView"
                  value="createPolicy" />

        <property name="commandName"
                  value="policydetails" />

        <property name="successView"
                  value="policydetails" />

        <property name="commandClass"
                  value="com.apress.insuranceapp.web.formbean.PolicyFormBean" />

    </bean>

</beans>
```

You may be thinking that because the business delegate is no longer there, the page controller will be tightly coupled with the EJBs and need to handle RemoteException. However, this task is handled by the SimpleRemoteStatelessSessionProxyFactoryBean class. It will intercept any RemoteException raised by the EJBs and convert it to Spring's unchecked RemoteAccessException.

Business interfaces work best with local SLSBs as well. In this case, you need not define any extra interface. You can very well use the interface defined by the application service because the local EJBs are not required to throw RemoteException. Another difference is that in the case of local EJBs, you need to use LocalStatelessSessionProxy➥ FactoryBean as the proxy service locator. Listing 4-30 shows the use of this service locator.

Listing 4-30. insurance-servlet.xml

```
<?xml version="1.0" encoding="UTF-8"?>
<beans xmlns="http://www.springframework.org/schema/beans"
       xmlns:xsi="http://www.w3.org/2001/XMLSchema-instance"
       xmlns:jee="http://www.springframework.org/schema/jee"
       xsi:schemaLocation="http://www.springframework.org/schema/beans
       http://www.springframework.org/schema/beans/spring-beans-2.5.xsd
       http://www.springframework.org/schema/jee
       http://www.springframework.org/schema/jee/spring-jee-2.5.xsd">
```

```
    <bean id="viewResolver"
        class="org.springframework.web.servlet.view.InternalResourceViewResolver">
      <property name="viewClass"
                value="org.springframework.web.servlet.view.JstlView" />
      <property name="prefix" value="/WEB-INF/jsp/" />
      <property name="suffix" value=".jsp" />
    </bean>
        <bean id="uwrBusinessServiceProxy"
          class="org.springframework.ejb.access.➡
SimpleRemoteStatelessSessionProxyFactoryBean">
        <property name="jndiName" value="UnderwritingBeanRemote" />
        <property name="businessInterface"
value="com.apress.einsure.business.api.UnderwritingApplicationService" />
        </bean>
    <bean name="/createPolicy.do"
        class="com.apress.insurance.web.controller.SaveNewPolicyController" >
      <property name="uwrBusinessService"
                ref="uwrBusinessServiceProxy" />

      <property name="formView"
                value="createPolicy" />

      <property name="commandName"
                value="policydetails" />

      <property name="successView"
                value="policydetails" />

      <property name="commandClass"
                value="com.apress.insuranceapp.web.formbean.PolicyFormBean" />

    </bean>

</beans>
```

Note that the same proxy service locators can be applied to look up EJB 3 session beans as well.

Consequences

Benefits

- It is now possible to catch differences in remote interfaces and bean implementations during the compilation phase.

- The implementation of business interface ensures consistency.

- The code or layer redundancy associated with the business delegate is removed because the page controllers use the proxy business interface implementations.

- Because the EJBs are now invoked through proxied objects that implement simple Java interfaces, it is easy to remove EJB dependencies and deploy the application in web servers like Apache Tomcat.

Concerns

- The business interface is not reusable across local and remote stateless session beans.

- It increases the number of classes that you already are maintaining for EJBs.

- Performance overhead is added because EJB methods are now invoked by reflection from the proxies.

Summary

In this chapter, you explored different ways of building a flexible business layer combining Spring and EJB—a stateless session bean, to be specific. The Service Locator and Business Delegate patterns are client-side extensions of the business logic exposed as remote objects. The Session Facade pattern provides coarse-grained access to the business logic as well as gives them access to the robust infrastructure support provided by the container. The Application Service pattern describes a simple yet flexible mechanism for encapsulating business logic in POJO components. The Business Interface pattern allows compile-time checks on exposed business methods and reduces dependency on business delegates.

In Chapter 5, I will cover the integration tier patterns. You have already had a short glimpse of an integration tier pattern: the Data Access Object pattern. Integration tier patterns expose a variety of strategies to retrieve data for use by the business components. These patterns also help business objects alter enterprise data. In addition to this, I will explore strategies to expose business tier functionalities for use by external clients.

CHAPTER 5

■■■

Exploring Integration Tier Design Patterns

The integration tier is a boundary tier and interacts with different external systems for data exchange. The integration tier in the eInsure application accessed the relational database for storing, retrieving, and manipulating data related to policies, claims, accounting, customers, and products. eInsure used entity beans for typical create, read, update, and delete (CRUD) operations with the database. The legacy version of eInsure had lots of leftovers in the form of stored procedures. The eInsure application made heavy use of these stored procedures for database-intensive tasks, especially for the batch jobs that ran daily after regular business hours or in certain intervals such as monthly or quarterly.

Users of eInsure required a variety of reports to find out important information about the state of the business. For reporting requirements, the eInsure system connected to an asynchronous reporting subsystem. Last but not least, some of the services provided by eInsure had to be exposed as web services. These services were consumed by third-party external applications.

In this chapter, I will start with the Data Access Object (DAO) pattern for accessing relational databases. I will explore the need for DAO and the strategies to simplify DAO implementation with Spring JDBC support. The Spring JDBC API can also be used to provide OO-style access to stored procedures. I will explain this in detail while describing the Procedure Access Object (PAO) pattern. Also, I will cover asynchronous service access mechanisms in connection with the Service Activator pattern. I will wind up the chapter with the Web Services Broker design strategy, which can be used to expose existing services as web services.

Data Access Object

Problem

The eInsure application relied heavily on entity beans for database operations. Way back in 1999, when entity beans first made their appearance (as part of the EJB 1.*x* specification), they were thought to be a remarkable enterprise component that would completely change enterprise software development, deployment, maintenance, and portability. This thinking was backed by reason. Entity beans provided standard-based, container-managed, distributed, secure, transactional persistence components. They provided transparent and automatic persistence without the client worrying about the underlying data store. But this popularity was only short-lived. As developers, designers, and architects started using entity beans, the problems became apparent. They soon realized that most of the features offered by entity beans, except persistence, were not required in their applications. The distributed nature of entity beans led to fine-grained calls from the clients. This increased network traffic and had an adverse impact on performance. The Session Facade pattern described in Chapter 4 was a solution to tackle this fine-grained entity bean access. The session bean also took care of security and transactional requirements.

With the quickly declining usage, the EJB 2.*x* specification introduced the concept of local interfaces to at least alleviate the problems of network trips. But this still did not address the complexity involved in developing entity beans. Entity bean development required four Java source files comprising the home and remote interfaces, the bean implementation, and a primary key class. Apart from the Java sources, you had two to three deployment descriptors depending on your server vendors. You are already aware of the two deployment descriptors from session beans in Chapter 4. Some application servers used a third deployment descriptor for mapping the database table and column to the bean class and its properties. Because the entity beans ran inside the EJB containers, they were difficult to test. The result was long development cycles and maintenance overhead.

The developers' problems were compounded by the side effects of using entity beans. Because the accessing of getter/setters in entity beans were remote method invocations, the data transfer objects (DTOs) were designed to extract all the data from the entity beans in just a single method call. The DTOs were simple POJOs with getters and setters and implemented the `Serializable` interface. In a large to midsize project that had several DTOs, these classes added to the maintenance problem. A small field change in any DTO often resulted in compilation failures in multiple source files.

The development community had no choice but to move to lightweight persistence solutions provided by ORM frameworks such as Hibernate, Kodo, iBatis, and others. These products focused on the persistence of POJOs with minimal configuration information. This proved to be a telling blow for entity beans, and it finally made way for JPA in the EJB 3.*x* specification. JPA supports POJO persistence with annotation-based configuration. More important, JPA entities run outside the EJB container and are easily testable.

The eInsure development team soon realized that search operations that returned large lists were highly inefficient with entity beans since each object in the search list was itself an entity bean. So, accessing a property in this entity bean resulted in a network trip and in the marshaling and unmarshaling of the data. The team soon switched over to a straight JDBC approach. The JDBC API was being used directly from the session beans to execute SQL queries, as shown in Listing 5-1.

Listing 5-1. UnderwritingRemoteBean.java

```java
public class UnderwritingRemoteBean implements SessionBean{

    public List listPolicyByProductAndAgeLevel(String productCd, int age) throws
      RemoteException {

        String SQL = "SELECT POLICY_ID,PRODUCT_CODE, NAME, AGE FROM T_POLICY_DETAILS
          WHERE PRODUCT_CODE = ? AND AGE > ? ";
        List policyList = new ArrayList();
        Connection conn = null;
        PreparedStatement pstmt = null;
        ResultSet rs = null;

        try{
            pstmt = conn.prepareStatement(SQL);
            pstmt.setString(0, productCd);
            pstmt.setInt(1, age);

            rs = pstmt.executeQuery();

            while(rs.next()){
                policyList.add(new PolicyDetail(rs.getInt("POLICY_ID"),
 rs.getString("NAME")
    ,rs.getString("NAME"),rs.getInt("AGE")));
            }
        }
        catch(SQLException sqlex){
            throw new RuntimeException(sqlex);
        }
        finally{
```

```
            if(rs!=null){
                try {
                    rs.close();
                } catch (SQLException ex) {
                    throw new RuntimeException(ex);
                }
            }
            if(pstmt!=null){
                try {
                    pstmt.close();
                } catch (SQLException ex) {
                    throw new RuntimeException(ex);
                }
            }
            if(conn!=null){
                try {
                    conn.close();
                } catch (SQLException ex) {
                    throw new RuntimeException(ex);
                }
            }
        }
        return policyList;
    }

}
```

The mixed approach to persistence in eInsure (entity beans and straight JDBC) made the business component vulnerable to change. As you can see in Listing 5-1, the direct use of the JDBC API meant a lot of boilerplate code for establishing a connection, preparing SQL statements, setting parameters, executing the SQL, iterating over the result set to prepare a list of Java objects, and finally releasing database resources. This last step is critical and often neglected, causing connection leaks and resource wastage. If the straight JDBC approach were used in all the DAO methods, it would result in significant code duplication.

Forces

- You should prevent the unnecessary mixing of business logic with persistence logic.

- The entity bean is an obsolete technology.

- The business tier required a consistent API to access integration tier components.

- Working directly with the JDBC API leads to a lot of boilerplate code being written, thus degrading reusability and increasing development time.

Solution

Implement a *data access object* (DAO) to encapsulate the data access logic and provide a consistent interface to the business tier components.

Strategies with the Spring Framework

As the name suggests, DAOs are generic objects and theoretically can support any kind of persistence store. The primary goal of these classes is to abstract the underlying data access mechanism from the business services. Since most applications interact with RDBMSs, I will focus only on JDBC-based data access objects.

The Spring JDBC module implements robust object design principles that make it simple to develop JDBC-based DAOs. It takes care of all the boilerplate code generally associated with JDBC API usage and helps provide a consistent API for data access.

Application developers are no longer required to work directly with the JDBC API; instead, they work with a high-level API.

Because eInsure had an affinity for Oracle owing to its legacy, the SQL syntax used in the next few sections will be compatible with Oracle Database. But the general discussion and concepts hold true for any database, and using them merely involves making minor changes in the SQL statements. Listing 5-2 shows the Oracle script to create the `T_POLICY_DETAIL` table and corresponding sequence.

Listing 5-2. `createTbl_T_Policy_Detail.sql`

```
CREATE table "T_POLICY_DETAIL" (
    "POLICY_ID"     NUMBER,
    "PRODUCT_CD"    VARCHAR2(20) NOT NULL,
    "POLICY_HOLDER" VARCHAR2(150) NOT NULL,
```

```
    "AGE"              NUMBER,
    constraint  "T_POLICY_DETAIL_PK" primary key ("POLICY_ID")

CREATE sequence "T_POLICY_DETAIL_SEQ"
/
```

The first step to building DAOs with Spring is to declare interfaces for the DAOs. This follows program to interface (P2I), as described earlier, as an object design best practice. It lays out a contract with the clients that deal with the concrete implementations only through these interfaces. As a result, it is easy to swap or modify implementation classes. Listing 5-3 shows the DAO interface for the policy details.

Listing 5-3. PolicyDetailDao.java

```
package com.apress.einusre.persistence.dao.api;
public interface PolicyDetailDao {
    String SAVE_POLICY_DETAILS_SQL = " insert into T_POLICY_DETAIL
values(T_POLICY_DETAIL_SEQ.nextval,?,?,?)";
    public void savePolicyDetails(String productCd, String name, int age);
}
```

Figure 5-1 shows the Spring JDBC support classes. Spring provides a convenient class called JdbcDaoSupport to ease the development of JDBC-based DAO classes. This class is associated with a data source and supplies the JdbcTemplate object for use in the DAO.

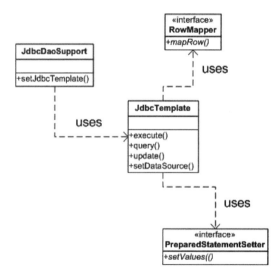

Figure 5-1. *Class diagram: Spring JDBC support classes*

JdbcTemplate is the most important class in the Spring JDBC DAO support. This class implements the GOF Template Method design pattern. The Template Method pattern defines the workflow or algorithm for a specific operation. It allows the subclasses to modify certain steps without changing the algorithm's core structure. JdbcTemplate consolidates all the common repeated code blocks typically associated with JDBC workflow. As I will show later, the workflow defined by JdbcTemplate can be modified at appropriate points to provide customized processing. Listing 5-4 shows the policy detail DAO implementation class.

Listing 5-4. PolicyDetailDaoImpl.java

```
package com.apress.einusre.persistence.dao.impl;
public class PolicyDetailDaoImpl extends JdbcDaoSupport implements PolicyDetailDao{
    public void savePolicyDetails(String productCd,String name,int age) {
        Object args [] = {productCd,name,new Integer(age)};
        this.getJdbcTemplate().update(PolicyDetailDao.
SAVE_POLICY_DETAILS_SQL, args);
    }
}
```

From the simplified code in Listing 5-4, it is clear that JdbcTemplate fosters reuse, and this has resulted in a significant code reduction in the DAO implementation. The tight coupling with the JDBC and collection packages (as in Listing 5-1) has been removed. The leakage of JDBC resource is no longer a problem because JdbcTemplate methods ensure that database resources are released in the proper sequence after they have been used. In addition, you are not forced to handle exceptions while using Spring DAO. The JdbcTemplate class handles the SQLException and rethrows a runtime exception because in most cases it is not possible to recover from these database errors.

The DAO implementation will be injected into the application service used by the session bean. Listing 5-5 shows the application service code.

Listing 5-5. UnderwritingApplicationServiceImpl.java

```
public class UnderwritingApplicationServiceImpl implements
UnderwritingApplicationService{
    private PolicyDetailDao policyDetailDao;
    public void underwriteNewPolicy(String productCd, String name, int age) {
        //business rules - here
        this.policyDetailDao.savePolicyDetails(productCd, name, age);
    }
    public PolicyDetailDao getPolicyDetailDao() {
```

```
            return policyDetailDao;
    }
    public void setPolicyDetailDao(PolicyDetailDao policyDetailDao) {
        this.policyDetailDao = policyDetailDao;
    }
}
```

Note that the session facade invokes the application service, which in turn calls the DAO method. As a result, the DAO method automatically comes into the same transactional scope as the session bean method. So, there is no need for any programmatic transaction handling in the DAO.

The `JdbcDaoSupport` object needs a data source to connect to and execute the SQL query. The data source object is generally registered in the application server's JNDI. The Spring service locator (explained in Chapter 4) will be used to look up the data source from the JNDI and inject it into the `JdbcDaoSupport` object.

Finally, everything needs to be wired up by the configuration in the Spring application context associated with the stateless session bean, as shown in Listing 5-6. I am showing the application service and DAO in the same configuration so that you can understand and visualize the coupling between the two. However, for modularity, it is advised that you put them in separate configuration files.

Listing 5-6. `Underwriting-service.xml`

```
<?xml version="1.0" encoding="UTF-8"?>
<beans xmlns="http://www.springframework.org/schema/beans"
       xmlns:xsi="http://www.w3.org/2001/XMLSchema-instance"
       xsi:schemaLocation="http://www.springframework.org/schema/beans
       http://www.springframework.org/schema/beans/spring-beans-2.5.xsd">

    <bean id="uwrApplicationService"
          class="com.apress.einsure.business.impl.➥
UnderwritingApplicationServiceImpl">
        <property name="policyDetailDao" ref="policyDetailDao"/>
    </bean>

    <bean id="policyDetailDao"
          class="com.apress.einusre.persistence.dao.impl.PolicyDetailDaoImpl"
    >
        <property name="dataSource" ref="datasource"/>
    </bean>
```

```
<bean id="datasource" class="org.springframework.jndi.JndiObjectFactoryBean">
    <property name="jndiName" value="einsureDatasource" />
    <property name="jndiEnvironment">
        <props>
            <prop key="java.naming.factory.initial">
                org.jnp.interfaces.NamingContextFactory
            </prop>

            <prop key="java.naming.provider.url">
                jnp://localhost:1099
            </prop>
            <prop key="java.naming.factory.url.pkgs">
                org.jboss.naming.client
            </prop>
        </props>
    </property>
</bean>
</beans>
```

Using Bind Variables

The SQL query in Listings 5-1 and 5-3 uses positional bind variables denoted by ?, which are static. Any change in the position of the bind variable will lead to a change in the code that sets this variable value. In Listing 5-1, the arguments in the method call `PreparedStatement.setXXX` will be affected. Similarly, in Listing 5-3, the position of the array elements would have to be altered to accommodate the query change.

Spring JDBC provides a convenient solution to this with support for named bind variables denoted by `:variable_name`. To use this feature, you should change the SQL query as shown in Listing 5-7. Note that the signature of the `savePolicyDetails` method has also changed, and it now takes a `Map` object as an argument.

Listing 5-7. `PolicyDao.java`

```
public interface PolicyDetailDao {
    String SAVE_POLICY_DETAILS_SQL = " insert into T_POLICY_DETAIL
values(T_POLICY_DETAIL_SEQ.nextval,
:productCd,:name,:age)";
    public void savePolicyDetails(Map policyDetailMap);
}
```

Because the interface has changed, you will have to change the implementation as well. To support named parameter bind variables, the implementation class inherits from another convenient class called NamedParameterJdbcDaoSupport, as in Listing 5-8.

Listing 5-8. PolicyDaoImpl.java

```
public class PolicyDetailDaoImpl extends NamedParameterJdbcDaoSupport
implements PolicyDetailDao{
    public void savePolicyDetails(Map policyDetailMap) {
        this.getNamedParameterJdbcTemplate().update(SAVE_POLICY_DETAILS_SQL,
 policyDetailMap);
    }
}
```

It is noteworthy that our DAO code has shrunk even further. The Map object is important in this case; the keys of the objects stored in the map must match those of the named bind variables in the SQL. Hence, even if the positions of the parameters or bind variables change in the SQL query string, the code does not break. This is a useful feature, and it is quite feasible to pass a Map from the HttpServletRequest in the page controller all the way down to the DAO. This would save a lot of effort because we no longer need to develop and maintain form beans.

Spring DAO Callbacks

As we already know, JdbcTemplate implements the template design pattern. So, the algorithm implemented by this class can be altered at suitable points by supplying customized logic. In the examples discussed so far, I have allowed the template class to set the JDBC bind variables for us. In some scenarios, you may be interested in controlling the setting of these variables. One such case is when database-specific datatypes such as Oracle's XMLType are used. Listing 5-9 shows the modified DAO implementation class.

Listing 5-9. PolicyDaoImpl.java

```
public class PolicyDetailDaoImpl extends JdbcDaoSupport implements PolicyDetailDao{
    public void savePolicyDetails(String productCd,String name,int age) {
        this.getJdbcTemplate().update(PolicyDetailDao.SAVE_POLICY_DETAILS_SQL,
                new SavePolicyPreparedStatementSetter(productCd,name,age));
    }
}
```

As shown in Listing 5-9, I have used an overloaded version of the update method to supply a prepared statement setter. The `PreparedStatementSetter` is a callback interface used by Spring JDBC to set the bind variables in the SQL being submitted to the database for processing. Note that the `SQLException` thrown by the `setValues` method will be handled and converted to a runtime exception called `DataAccessException` by the framework. Listing 5-10 shows the `PreparedStatementSetter` implementation class.

Listing 5-10. `SavePolicyPreparedStatementSetter.java`

```java
public final class SavePolicyPreparedStatementSetter
implements PreparedStatementSetter{
    private String productCd;
    private String name;
    private int age;
    public SavePolicyPreparedStatementSetter(String productCd,String name,int age){
        this.productCd = productCd;
        this.name = name;
        this.age = age;
    }
    public void setValues(PreparedStatement pstmt) throws SQLException {
        pstmt.setString(0, productCd);
        pstmt.setString(1, productCd);
        pstmt.setInt(2, age);
    }
}
```

I will now take a look at another case where all the policies for a given product code need to be listed. As a first step, I'll add a new method in the existing interface, as shown in Listing 5-11.

Listing 5-11. `PolicyDetailDao.java`

```java
public interface PolicyDetailDao {
//other SQL statements
    String LIST_POLICY_BY_PRODUCT_SQL =
" select * from T_POLICY_DETAIL where PRODUCT_CD = ?";
    //other methods
    public List listPolicyByProductCode(String productCode);
}
```

Listing 5-12 shows the implementation of the new method.

Listing 5-12. PolicyDetailDaoImpl.java

```
public class PolicyDetailDaoImpl extends JdbcDaoSupport implements PolicyDetailDao{
    //other implementation methods
    public List listPolicyByProductCode(String productCode) {
        return this.getJdbcTemplate().queryForList
(PolicyDetailDao.LIST_POLICY_BY_PRODUCT_SQL,
                new Object[]{productCode});
    }
}
```

The queryForList method returns a list of Map objects representing each row of the record fetched. The keys in this map object are the same as the retrieved column names in the result set. This is a convenient solution, but passing and retrieving a Map object would force the code to know the keys in the Map. Hence, you might have lots of constants declared for the keys. But all of this will change if you rename any of the columns, leading to changes in the constant file. A better approach would be to use a callback object to retrieve the data from the result set and return a JavaBean. This callback object must implement the RowMapper interface, as shown in Listing 5-13.

Listing 5-13. ListPolicyByProductRowMapper.java

```
public class ListPolicyByProductRowMapper implements RowMapper{
    public Object mapRow(ResultSet rs, int rowCount) throws SQLException {
        long policyId = rs.getLong(1);
        String productCode = rs.getString(2);
        String name = rs.getString(3);
        int age = rs.getInt(4);
        PolicyDetail policyDetail = new PolicyDetail(policyId,
                productCode,name,age);

        return policyDetail;
    }
}
```

You should observe a few things in this row mapper callback object. The values in a row are accessed using the positional index instead of the column name. This is more effective in terms of performance, but changes in the position of the column in the row will make the code vulnerable to change. You can use column names instead. The data retrieved from the result set row is used to populate a JavaBean. Listing 5-14 shows the JavaBean.

Listing 5-14. `PolicyDetail.java`

```java
public class PolicyDetail implements Serializable {
    private long policyId;
    private String productCd;
    private String name;
    private int age;
    public PolicyDetail() {
    }
    public PolicyDetailTo(long policyId, String productCd, String name, int age) {
        this.policyId = policyId;
        this.productCd = productCd;
        this.name = name;
        this.age = age;
    }
    public int getAge() {
        return age;
    }

    public void setAge(int age) {
        this.age = age;
    }

    public String getName() {
        return name;
    }

    public void setName(String name) {
        this.name = name;
    }

    public long getPolicyId() {
        return policyId;
    }

    public void setPolicyId(long policyId) {
        this.policyId = policyId;
    }
```

```
    public String getProductCd() {
        return productCd;
    }

    public void setProductCd(String productCd) {
        this.productCd = productCd;
    }
}
```

As I mentioned at the start of this chapter, more and more Java EE applications are switching to ORM instead of the straight JDBC approach. Although Spring JDBC simplifies things to a great extent, there are certain scenarios where you are better served by ORM. ORMs are better suited to provide POJO persistence. They provide an OO way to access the RDBMS. ORM is most useful for applications such as eInsure that need to be portable across a variety of databases. The Spring ORM module provides extensive support to integrate with all leading ORM solutions such as Hibernate, TopLink, JPOX, and OpenJPA. In the next few sections, I will take you on a tour of using Hibernate 3 with Spring ORM. For this discussion, I assume you are familiar with Hibernate. If you are new to Hibernate, you can take a look at the product documentation at `http://www.hibernate.org`.

The first step to using Hibernate with Spring ORM is to set up the Hibernate `SessionFactory` with a data source, as shown in Listing 5-15. `SessionFactory` is responsible for creating session objects. You can think of sessions as abstractions of the underlying database connection.

Listing 5-15. `UnderwritingDao-config.xml`

```xml
<?xml version="1.0" encoding="UTF-8"?>
<beans xmlns="http://www.springframework.org/schema/beans"
       xmlns:xsi="http://www.w3.org/2001/XMLSchema-instance"
       xsi:schemaLocation="http://www.springframework.org/schema/beans
http://www.springframework.org/schema/beans/spring-beans-2.5.xsd">

    <bean id="datasource" class="org.springframework.jndi.JndiObjectFactoryBean">
        <property name="jndiName" value="einsureDatasource" />
        <property name="jndiEnvironment">
            <props>
                <prop key="java.naming.factory.initial">
                    org.jnp.interfaces.NamingContextFactory
                </prop>
```

```xml
                <prop key="java.naming.provider.url">
                    jnp://localhost:1099
                </prop>
                <prop key="java.naming.factory.url.pkgs">
                    org.jboss.naming.client
                </prop>

            </props>
        </property>
    </bean>
    <bean id="hibernateSessionFactory"
class="org.springframework.orm.hibernate3.LocalSessionFactoryBean">
        <property name="dataSource" ref="dataSource"/>
        <property name="mappingResources">
            <list>
                <value>policydetail.hbm.xml</value>
            </list>
        </property>
        <property name="hibernateProperties">
            <value>
                hibernate.dialect= org.hibernate.dialect.Oracle9Dialect
            </value>
        </property>
    </bean>
</beans>
```

LocalSessionFactoryBean is a factory bean that creates a Hibernate SessionFactory
from the supplied configuration parameters and data source object. Note that Hibernate
ORM knows all about the PolicyDetail POJO from the mapping resource policydetail.
hbm.xml. Since I intend to support Oracle Database for now, I have configured
Oracle9Dialect. Thus, switching to another database is just a matter of configuration.
You will need to change your data source configuration and the dialect used by
SessionFactory.

It is not advisable to directly expose the ORM persistence API to the business tier
objects. I will use the DAO to wrap the underlying ORM access. Spring ORM provides the
convenience base class HibernateDaoSupport just for this purpose. Listing 5-16 shows the
modified PolicyDetailDaoImpl from Listing 5-12.

Listing 5-16. `PolicyDetailDaoImpl.java`

```
public class PolicyDetailDaoImpl extends HibernateDaoSupport
implements PolicyDetailDao{
    public List listPolicyByProductCode(String productCode) {
        return getHibernateTemplate().find( "from ProductDetail where
productCode = ?", productCode);
    }
  //other methods
}
```

The getHibernateTempate method of HibernateDaoSupport supplies a HibernateTemplate object. This is similar to the JdbcTemplate class. It also implements the GOF Template Method design pattern and carries out the workflow associated with the Hibernate ORM to interact with the RDBMS. It is important to note here that, even if you have changed the underlying ORM persistence implementation, the business tier code will be unaffected. This is because the business tier objects access the DAOs using interfaces. Thus, you have seen the value of P2I.

Consequences

Benefits

- The high-level Spring JDBC API makes it easy to access relational databases.

- Spring JDBC implements the boilerplate low-level code, resource management, and exception handling. The result is a significant reduction in code and hence development effort.

- The use of named parameter support makes application code more robust.

- Spring-based DAOs provide a consistent interface to the business tier for data access.

Concerns

- There is a significant learning curve to start off, even though the API is concise.

Procedure Access Object

Problem

A customer of eInsure had a two-tier thick client lead management application. eInsure had to integrate with this existing two-tier application. The lead management application heavily used legacy stored procedures running on Oracle Database. The stored procedures contained both business logic and persistence logic. It was not possible to reuse the UI, which was built with Visual Basic. Because the integration had to be completed in a short time period, it was not possible to port the business logic to Java components. Moreover, eInsure was not allowed direct access to the database tables of the lead management application.

The legacy version of eInsure had also left behind several stored procedures that were accessed using straight JDBC. But as you saw with DAO, this involves a lot of code redundancy. The mixing of persistence logic with business logic made the business tier a regular candidate for change. The stored procedure can directly subscribe to the transactional services provided by the RDBMS. This makes it difficult for the application server to manage distributed transactions. This often leads to bugs that are hard to detect and fix. Using stored procedures limits portability options. In other words, a lot of code changes are required to support the same application on a different RDBMS.

Forces

- Accessing a stored procedure from a session facade using the JDBC API causes an intermingling of persistence logic with application services.

- Invoking a stored procedure involves lots of low-level programming against the JDBC API.

- Stored procedure access with a low-level JDBC API results in a lot of code duplication.

- Stored procedures make it difficult to apply system services such as transactions.

Solution

Use a *procedure access object* (PAO) to invoke stored procedures without directly interacting with a low-level JDBC API.

Strategies with the Spring Framework

Spring JDBC provides the convenient abstract class StoredProcedure to execute stored procedures. This class, like other support classes in Spring JDBC, implements the GOF Template Design pattern and provides an OO abstraction of a stored procedure. With this class, it is possible to perform stored procedure operations such as setting input and output variables, using database-specific datatypes, and returning cursors. This specific class extends from the SqlCall class, which can be used to model the execution of any stored procedure and function. The root of the SqlCall class is the RdbmsOperation, which can be used to model any database-specific operation such as a SQL query to retrieve results, update or delete records, and invoke stored procedures. Figure 5-2 shows the class diagram of the stored procedure support classes.

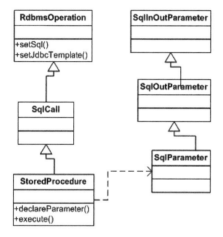

Figure 5-2. *Class diagram: Spring stored procedure support classes*

To explore Spring JDBC's support for stored procedure, I will show the case when lead information has to be saved into the database. Listing 5-17 shows the simplified signature of the stored procedure. This stored procedure is used to create a new lead in the database. It accepts the lead name and country as input and outputs the lead ID, which is the primary key in the database and generated by a sequence.

Listing 5-17. *Stored Procedure Signature*

```
SaveNewLead (:pLeadId OUT NUMBER,:pName IN VARCHAR2,:pCountryCd VARCHAR2)
```

Procedure access objects are similar to data access objects. They wrap the execution of a single stored procedure. Listing 5-18 shows the PAO to save information about a new lead.

Listing 5-18. SaveNewLeadPao.java

```java
public class SaveNewLeadPao extends StoredProcedure{
    public SaveNewLeadPao(){
        declareParameter(new SqlOutParameter("pLeadId", Types.INTEGER));
        declareParameter(new SqlParameter("pName", Types.VARCHAR));
        declareParameter(new SqlParameter("pCountryCd", Types.VARCHAR));
    }
    public Map execute(Map inParamMap){
        return super.execute(inParamMap);
    }
}
```

The declareParameter method needs to be called in the exact order in which the parameters are declared in the stored procedure. The stored procedure abstraction supports input as well as output variables. The procedure execute is triggered by the execute method, which accepts a Map argument. This Map object contains the input values to be passed to the stored procedure. The keys of this Map are the same as the stored procedure input parameter names. The execute method in the SaveNewLeadPao subclass delegates to the superclass execute method. The execute method returns a Map as output. The output map contains results returned from the database. The keys of this map are the same declared output parameter names of the stored procedure.

The application service is the client of the PAO. Everything can be configured in the Spring configuration as in Listing 5-19.

Listing 5-19. underwriting-service.xml

```xml
<?xml version="1.0" encoding="UTF-8"?>
<beans xmlns="http://www.springframework.org/schema/beans"
       xmlns:xsi="http://www.w3.org/2001/XMLSchema-instance"
       xsi:schemaLocation="http://www.springframework.org/schema/beans
       http://www.springframework.org/schema/beans/spring-beans-2.5.xsd"
>

    <bean id="uwrApplicationService"
          class="com.apress.einsure.business.impl.➥
        UnderwritingApplicationServiceImpl">
```

```xml
            <property name="policyDetailDao" ref="policyDetailDao"/>
    </bean>

    <bean id="policyDetailDao"
          class="com.apress.einusre.persistence.dao.impl.PolicyDetailDaoImpl"
    >
            <property name="dataSource" ref="datasource"/>
    </bean>

    <bean id="datasource" class="org.springframework.jndi.JndiObjectFactoryBean">
        <property name="jndiName" value="einsureDatasource" />
        <property name="jndiEnvironment">
            <props>
                <prop key="java.naming.factory.initial">
                    org.jnp.interfaces.NamingContextFactory
                </prop>

                <prop key="java.naming.provider.url">
                    jnp://localhost:1099
                </prop>
                <prop key="java.naming.factory.url.pkgs">
                    org.jboss.naming.client
                </prop>

            </props>
        </property>

    </bean>

     <bean id="leadApplicationService"
           class="com.apress.einsure.business.impl.➥
LeadManagementApplicationServiceImpl">
        <property name="savelLeadPao" ref="savelLeadPao"/>

    </bean>
     <bean id="savelLeadPao"
           class="com.apress.einsure.persistence.pao.SaveNewLeadPao">
        <property name="dataSource" ref="datasource"/>

    </bean>

</beans>
```

Consequences

Benefits

- The high-level API provided by Spring JDBC makes it easy to access legacy stored procedures.

- PAO promotes object orientation and minimizes code redundancy.

- PAO manages the boilerplate low-level code and resource management.

Concerns

- Using legacy stored procedures limits application portability.

- It has difficult-to-manage system services such as transaction, security, and so on.

- Invoking a stored procedure running on a remote database server comes with all the baggage associated with remote procedure calls. So, this can have a possible adverse effect on performance.

Service Activator

Problem

Like most enterprise applications, eInsure also had to support reports. Reports provide valuable insights into the state of the business. In eInsure, for example, there were reports to find out how many policies have been sold per product over a period, how many premium collections over a period of time, the number of new leads in the month of January, and so on. The contents and number of reports varied with the needs of the customer.

eInsure supported two types of reports: scheduled and user generated. The scheduled reports were triggered by schedulers like Unix CRON after certain intervals. An example of a scheduled report is the monthly premium collection report. The user-generated reports were triggered by the users of the eInsure application from their browser. A user would typically select a report, supply the necessary inputs, and start the report generation.

This synchronous report generation strategy was found wanting in some midsize to large companies where eInsure was installed. As these companies used this application to add new products, policies, parties, and claims, the data volume increased at a rapid pace. This led to frustrating user experiences because the synchronous reports mostly timed out with the large data volume. The users were already frustrated because of the blocking nature of the synchronous reports. Most reports generated large data sets, and transferring this data from the database to the application server and subsequently to the client browser clogged the network.

Forces

- Applications need to support long-running use cases.

- It is necessary to execute the business services asynchronously.

- Long-running operations should not block users.

Solution

Use a *service activator* to receive and carry out an asynchronous service request.

Strategies with the Spring Framework

You can solve the blocking problem discussed earlier by allowing the actual report generation service request to be handled asynchronously. JMS message listeners can be applied to process this business request asynchronously. However, a more robust approach would be to use a message-driven bean (MDB). This is because MDBs combine the asynchronous behavior of the message listener with services provided by the EJB container.

Spring provides support for building MDBs as well as sending messages to a JMS queue or topic. Just like stateless session beans, Spring also provides convenient base classes to develop MDBs, as shown in Figure 5-3. The root of the class hierarchy is the AbstractEnterpriseBean class, which can be used to load a Spring application context.

The subclass AbstractMessageDrivenBean is the convenient class for developing MDBs. The setMessageDrivenContext is used to save the MessageDrivenContext object supplied by the EJB container. The subclasses can override the onEjbCreate method for the initializing or loading of any bean from the Spring application context associated with the MDB. The AbstractJmsMessageDrivenBean implements the MessageListener interface, thus making MDBs compatible with JMS messages.

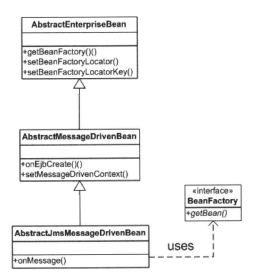

Figure 5-3. *Class diagram: Spring MDB support*

Listing 5-20 shows the MDB used in the eInsure reporting subsystem. MDB development is less cumbersome compared to SLSB because you don't have home and remote interfaces.

Listing 5-20. ReportingMDB.java

```java
public class ReportingMDB extends AbstractJmsMessageDrivenBean {
    protected void onEjbCreate() {
        //initialize application service components from Spring bean factory
    }
    public void onMessage(Message msg) {
        //handle business request here - report generations
    }
}
```

Figure 5-4 shows the message sequence of message flow as the EJB container invokes the MDB. The client that triggered the asynchronous processing returns just after sending the message to the queue. Once the message arrives in a queue, the EJB container delegates the processing to an MDB instance by invoking the onMessage method. This method can be utilized to invoke a POJO service component for report generation.

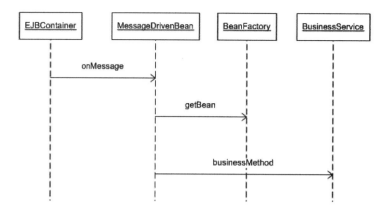

Figure 5-4. *Sequence diagram: Spring MDB execution*

Listing 5-21 shows the deployment descriptor for the MDB.

Listing 5-21. `ejb-jar.xml`

```
<?xml version="1.0" encoding="UTF-8"?>
<ejb-jar version="2.1" xmlns="http://java.sun.com/xml/ns/j2ee"
xmlns:xsi="http://www.w3.org/2001/XMLSchema-instance"
xsi:schemaLocation="http://java.sun.com/xml/ns/j2ee
http://java.sun.com/xml/ns/j2ee/ejb-jar_2_1.xsd">
  <enterprise-beans>
      <message-driven>
          <display-name>ReportingMDB</display-name>
          <ejb-name>ReportingMDB</ejb-name>
          <ejb-class>com.apress.einsure.reports.aysync.activator.ReportingMDB
          </ejb-class>
          <transaction-type>Container</transaction-type>
          <env-entry>
              <env-entry-name>ejb/BeanFactoryPath</env-entry-name>
              <env-entry-type>java.lang.String</env-entry-type>
              <env-entry-value>com/apress/einsure/reports/aysync/activator➥
/Reporting-beans.xml</env-entry-value>
          </env-entry>
          <message-destination-type>javax.jms.Queue</message-destination-type>
          <message-destination-link>reportQ</message-destination-link>
          <activation-config>
              <activation-config-property>
                  <activation-config-property-name>
```

```
acknowledgeMode</activation-config-property-name>
                    <activation-config-property-value>
                Auto-acknowledge</activation-config-property-value>
                </activation-config-property>
                <activation-config-property>
                    <activation-config-property-name>
                destinationType</activation-config-property-name>
                    <activation-config-property-value>
                javax.jms.Queue</activation-config-property-value>
                </activation-config-property>
            </activation-config>
        </message-driven>
        </enterprise-beans>
    <assembly-descriptor>
        <container-transaction>
            <method>
                <ejb-name>ReportingMDB</ejb-name>
                <method-name>*</method-name>
            </method>
            <trans-attribute>Required</trans-attribute>
        </container-transaction>
        <message-destination>
            <display-name>Destination for ReportingMDB</display-name>
            <message-destination-name>reportQ</message-destination-name>
        </message-destination>
        </assembly-descriptor>
    </ejb-jar>
```

To deploy this EJB, you also need a JBoss-specific deployment descriptor declaring the JNDI name of the JMS queue, as shown in Listing 5-22.

Listing 5-22. `jboss.xml`

```
<?xml version="1.0" encoding="UTF-8"?>
<jboss>
  <enterprise-beans>
    <message-driven>
      <ejb-name>ReportingMDB</ejb-name>
      <destination-jndi-name>queue/reportQ</destination-jndi-name>
    </message-driven>
  </enterprise-beans>
</jboss>
```

The `ReportingMDB` has a Spring application context associated with it. It uses the beans registered in this application context to carry out long-running report generation tasks. This Spring application context is configured as shown in Listing 5-23.

Listing 5-23. `Reporting-beans.xml`

```xml
<?xml version="1.0" encoding="UTF-8"?>
<beans xmlns="http://www.springframework.org/schema/beans"
       xmlns:xsi="http://www.w3.org/2001/XMLSchema-instance"
       xsi:schemaLocation="http://www.springframework.org/schema/beans
       http://www.springframework.org/schema/beans/spring-beans-2.5.xsd"
       >

    <bean name="reportServiceProvider"
class="net.sf.reporting.ReportServiceProviderImpl">
    </bean>

</beans>
```

So far, I have explained the server-side Java components and configuration. Now I will focus on the client that triggers the asynchronous report processing. Spring provides the `JmsTemplate` class to simplify the process of sending JMS messages. It is also based on the GOF Template Method design pattern. To use this class, you will need to configure it in the Spring application context and inject the JNDI bound `ConnectionFactory` and `Destination` objects. This is shown in Listing 5-24.

Listing 5-24. `insurance-servlet.xml`

```xml
<?xml version="1.0" encoding="UTF-8"?>
<beans xmlns="http://www.springframework.org/schema/beans"
       xmlns:xsi="http://www.w3.org/2001/XMLSchema-instance"
       xsi:schemaLocation="http://www.springframework.org/schema/beans
       http://www.springframework.org/schema/beans/spring-beans-2.5.xsd">


    <bean id="qConnectionFactory"
        class="org.springframework.jndi.JndiObjectFactoryBean">
        <property name="jndiName" value="ConnectionFactory" />
        <property name="jndiEnvironment">
            <props>
                <prop key="java.naming.factory.initial">
```

```
                    org.jnp.interfaces.NamingContextFactory
                </prop>
                <prop key="java.naming.provider.url">
                    jnp://localhost:1099
                </prop>
                <prop key="java.naming.factory.url.pkgs">
                    org.jboss.naming.client
                </prop>
            </props>
        </property>
    </bean>
    <bean id="qReport" class="org.springframework.jndi.JndiObjectFactoryBean">
        <property name="jndiName" value="queue/reportQ" />
        <property name="jndiEnvironment">
            <props>
                <prop key="java.naming.factory.initial">
                    org.jnp.interfaces.NamingContextFactory
                </prop>
                <prop key="java.naming.provider.url">
                    jnp://localhost:1099
                </prop>
                <prop key="java.naming.factory.url.pkgs">
                    org.jboss.naming.client
                </prop>
            </props>
        </property>
    </bean>

    <bean id="jmsTemplate" class="org.springframework.jms.core.JmsTemplate" >
        <property name="connectionFactory" ref="qConnectionFactory"/>
        <property name="defaultDestination" ref="qReport"/>
    </bean>

    <bean id="reportingDelegate"
class="com.apress.insurance.view.delegate.impl.ReportingDelegateImpl">
        <property name="jmsTemplate" ref="jmsTemplate" />
    </bean>

</beans>
```

The JmsTemplate is finally injected into the ReportingDelegate, which is invoked by the page controller that handles the report generation request. The implementation class ReportingDelegateImpl follows the Business Delegate pattern and handles the JMS-related details, as shown in Listing 5-25.

Listing 5-25. ReportingDelegateImpl.java

```java
public class ReportingDelegateImpl implements ReportingDelegate{
    private JmsTemplate jmsTemplate;

    public long triggerReportGeneration(Map reportDataMap) {
        long reportId = ReportUtil.generateReportId(reportDataMap);
        this.jmsTemplate.send(new ReportMessageCreatorImpl(reportDataMap));
        return reportId;
    }
    public void setJmsTemplate(JmsTemplate jmsTemplate) {
        this.jmsTemplate = jmsTemplate;
    }
}
```

The report ID is passed to the page controller so that it can display this token to the user for future reference. The user can search with this ID to find the status of the report generation that he has triggered. Note that I have also altered the workflow of the JmsTemplate class by passing a custom implementation of the MessageCreator interface in the form of ReportMessageCreatorImpl, as shown in Listing 5-26. This class is responsible for transforming the incoming message into a form compatible with the JMS API.

Listing 5-26. ReportMessageCreatorImpl.java

```java
public class ReportMessageCreatorImpl implements MessageCreator{
    private Map reportData;
    public ReportMessageCreatorImpl(Map reportData){
        this.reportData = reportData;
    }

    public Message createMessage(Session jmsSession) throws JMSException {
        MapMessage message = jmsSession.createMapMessage();
        message.setObject("REPORT_DATA", reportData.get("REPORT_DATA"));
        return message;
    }
}
```

There are different strategies for sending the final response to the user who requested the report. The asynchronous reports in eInsure generally fetched records from the RDBMS based on certain criteria, applied formatting (such as date and currency), and saved this data as files of various formats, including Microsoft Word, PDF, Microsoft Excel, and so on. When the report file generation was complete, the users were informed about it by e-mail.

Message-Driven POJO

With Spring, it is possible to support asynchronous message listeners even without any application server or JMS provider. In fact, it is possible to turn any POJO class into a message listener—a so-called message-driven POJO (MDP)—without any EJB container support. The MDPs are registered in Spring message listener containers. The message listener containers receive messages from a JMS queue and invoke the registered MDPs.

Listing 5-27 shows the MDP. It is independent of any framework-specific interfaces or abstract classes. Since the message listener is a mere POJO, it is not possible for Spring to determine which method to invoke when a message arrives in the queue. The `MessageListenerAdapter` handles this.

Listing 5-27. `ReportMessageListener.java`

```java
public class ReportMessageListener {
    private void processReport(Map reportParams){
        //generate reports
    }
}
```

The message listener container is started when the Spring application container is initialized and started. You will also need to register the message listener. This can be done with the configuration, as shown in Listing 5-28.

Listing 5-28. `insurance-config.xml`

```xml
<?xml version="1.0" encoding="UTF-8"?>
<beans xmlns="http://www.springframework.org/schema/beans"
       xmlns:xsi="http://www.w3.org/2001/XMLSchema-instance"
           xsi:schemaLocation="http://www.springframework.org/schema/beans
       http://www.springframework.org/schema/beans/spring-beans-2.5.xsd
       "
       >
    <!--the other beans -->
```

```
    <bean id="messageListener"
class="com.apress.einsure.report.async.messagelistener.ReportMessageListener" />

<!-- this is the Message Driven POJO (MDP) -->
<bean id="messageListener"
class="org.springframework.jms.listener.adapter.MessageListenerAdapter">
    <constructor-arg>
        <bean class=" com.apress.einsure.report.async.messagelistener.➥
ReportMessageListener "/>
    </constructor-arg>
</bean>


    <!-- and this is the message listener container -->
    <bean id="jmsContainer"
class="org.springframework.jms.listener.DefaultMessageListenerContainer">
        <property name="connectionFactory" ref="qConnectionFactory"/>
        <property name="destination" ref="qReport"/>
        <property name="messageListener" ref="messageListener" />
    </bean>
</beans>
```

Note that in this configuration you have enlisted the message listener adapter with the container. This adapter knows how to execute the message-driven POJO. `DefaultMessageListenerContainer` is the most widely used message listener container.

Consequences

Benefits

- You get robust support for asynchronous service processing both in the application server and in the Spring IOC container.

- The clients that access the asynchronous services are easy to develop.

- Spring-based MDBs form the backbone for JMS-based integration with external systems.

- Since the request is being processed asynchronously, the users are not blocked for long-running tasks.

Concerns

- The Spring MDP is easy to develop and use but is not based on Java EE standard specifications. Using the MDP and Spring message container may not be suitable for large-scale enterprise requirements.

Web Service Broker

Problem

Generating policy quotations was one very important service provided by the eInsure application. This service would accept the bare minimum information: the policy amount, the number of years of coverage (the "term"), the frequency of premiums, and, of course, the insurance product against which the policy is underwritten. Given these inputs, the output would be the tentative premium to be paid by the client.

This service was available in the online eInsure application and was used heavily at the counters by the underwriters and support executives. However, the partners, resellers, and agents of the company using eInsure but without direct access to the application also wanted to use this functionality. There were others like the affiliates who wanted to integrate only this functionality into their utility web sites as widgets. The policy quotation service was accessible remotely through a session facade. However, the actual functionality was implemented as a POJO application service. Most of these external applications were running on PHP, and others were running on the Microsoft .NET platform. It is possible to have a non-Java client for EJB, but this was not within the skill set of the team developing those external applications. In such situations, an alternative is to expose these services in a technology- or platform-independent manner. Web services are a perfect solution. Exposing the policy quote function as a web service would enable any external application to consume it without being inhibited by technology barriers.

Forces

- It is required to expose internal services to external clients.

- The services should be exposed in a technology-neutral way.

- Open standards are preferred for exposing services while integrating with external systems.

Solution

Use a *web service broker* to expose business services to external clients based on open web-based standards.

Strategies with the Spring Framework

Web services generally involve information exchange between two applications using XML messages. These XML messages follow a standard called Simple Object Access Protocol (SOAP). The operations provided by the web service are described in a Web Service Description Language (WSDL) file. The XML SOAP messages can be transported over several network protocols such as HTTP, SMTP, and JMS. However, I will cover only HTTP as the transport protocol.

Web Services with JAX-RPC

JAX-RPC is one of the most popular and simple mechanisms for developing web services in Java. It can be used to create SOAP-based services called *endpoints*. The Spring convenience base class `ServletEndpointSupport` makes it simple to develop endpoints. This class is useful since it provides access to the Spring application context, as well as acts as the first point of contact in a web service. In this section, I will try to expose the policy quotation service utilizing the Spring Framework and the Apache Axis web services framework. Apache Axis provides a full SOAP-based JAX RPC implementation.

The first step in the development of a JAX RPC-based web service with Spring is to define the service interface as in Listing 5-29. In this case, I will use the same `PolicyQuoteApplicationService` implemented by the application service.

Listing 5-29. `PolicyQuoteApplicationService.java`

```
public interface PolicyQuoteApplicationService {
    public String BEAN_KEY = "policyQuoteApplicationService";
    public double calculatePolicyQuote(String productCd,int age,
double sumAssured,int term);
}
```

The next step is to implement the endpoint class as in Listing 5-30. This endpoint will implement the service interface, but the implementation methods delegate to the actual application service.

Listing 5-30. `PolicyQuoteServiceEndpoint.java`

```java
public class PolicyQuoteServiceEndpoint extends ServletEndpointSupport
    implements PolicyQuoteApplicationService{

    private PolicyQuoteApplicationService policyQuoteService;

    protected void onInit() {
        this.policyQuoteService = (PolicyQuoteApplicationService)
        getWebApplicationContext().
getBean(PolicyQuoteApplicationService.BEAN_KEY);
    }

    public double calculatePolicyQuote(String productCd, int age,
 double sumAssured, int term) {
        return policyQuoteService.calculatePolicyQuote(productCd, age,
sumAssured, term);
    }
}
```

The key thing in this listing is that the endpoint class provides access to the Spring application context. The `onInit` method was overridden to get hold of the application service object.

Since I am trying to expose this service over HTTP using SOAP messages, the Axis servlet has to be configured with the web container. This servlet plays a critical role in coordinating web service calls from the external clients and then delivering them to the endpoint. It also takes care of mapping SOAP messages to the appropriate endpoint methods, as well as returning the values from the methods as SOAP responses. It is responsible for creating the WSDL file, which is used by the clients to access the policy quote web service. The Axis servlet is registered with the web container like any other servlet, as shown in Listing 5-31. It is advisable to deploy the web service as a separate web application for modularity and ease of maintenance.

Listing 5-31. `web.xml`

```xml
<?xml version="1.0" encoding="UTF-8"?>
<web-app version="2.4" xmlns="http://java.sun.com/xml/ns/j2ee"
        xmlns:xsi="http://www.w3.org/2001/XMLSchema-instance"
        xsi:schemaLocation="http://java.sun.com/xml/ns/j2ee
http://java.sun.com/xml/ns/j2ee/web-app_2_4.xsd">
```

```
    <listener>
        <listener-class>org.springframework.web.context.➥
ContextLoaderListener</listener-class>
    </listener>


    <servlet>
        <servlet-name>axis</servlet-name>
        <servlet-class>org.apache.axis.transport.http.AxisServlet</servlet-class>
        <!--<load-on-startup>1</load-on-startup>-->
    </servlet>


    <servlet-mapping>
        <servlet-name>axis</servlet-name>
        <url-pattern>/axis/*</url-pattern>
    </servlet-mapping>


    </web-app>
```

The Axis servlet also requires a deployment descriptor to determine the services that should be exposed on the service interface to external clients. Listing 5-32 shows the deployment descriptor.

Listing 5-32. server-config.wsdd

```
<?xml version="1.0" encoding="UTF-8"?>
<deployment xmlns="http://xml.apache.org/axis/wsdd/"
xmlns:java="http://xml.apache.org/axis/wsdd/providers/java">
    <globalConfiguration>
        <parameter name="adminPassword" value="admin"/>
        <parameter name="sendXsiTypes" value="true"/>
        <parameter name="sendMultiRefs" value="true"/>
        <parameter name="sendXMLDeclaration" value="true"/>
        <parameter name="axis.sendMinimizedElements" value="true"/>
        <requestFlow>
            <handler type="java:org.apache.axis.handlers.JWSHandler">
                <parameter name="scope" value="session"/>
            </handler>
            <handler type="java:org.apache.axis.handlers.JWSHandler">
```

```
                    <parameter name="scope" value="request"/>
                    <parameter name="extension" value=".jwr"/>
                </handler>
            </requestFlow>
        </globalConfiguration>
        <handler name="Authenticate"
type="java:org.apache.axis.handlers.SimpleAuthenticationHandler"/>
        <handler name="LocalResponder"
type="java:org.apache.axis.transport.local.LocalResponder"/>
        <handler name="URLMapper" type="java:org.apache.axis.handlers.http.URLMapper"/>
        <service name="AdminService" provider="java:MSG">
            <parameter name="allowedMethods" value="AdminService"/>
            <parameter name="enableRemoteAdmin" value="false"/>
            <parameter name="className" value="org.apache.axis.utils.Admin"/>
            <namespace>http://xml.apache.org/axis/wsdd/</namespace>
        </service>
        <service name="PolicyQuoteService" provider="java:RPC">
            <parameter name="allowedMethods" value="*"/>
            <parameter name="className"
value="com.apress.einsure.business.external.➥
PolicyQuoteServiceEndpoint"/> </service>
        <service name="Version" provider="java:RPC">
            <parameter name="allowedMethods" value="getVersion"/>
            <parameter name="className" value="org.apache.axis.Version"/>
        </service>
        <transport name="http">
            <requestFlow>
                <handler type="URLMapper"/>
                <handler type="java:org.apache.axis.handlers.http.HTTPAuthHandler"/>
            </requestFlow>
        </transport>
        <transport name="local">
            <responseFlow>
                <handler type="LocalResponder"/>
            </responseFlow>
        </transport>
</deployment>
```

The application service now needs to be accessible from the Axis servlet-managed endpoint objects. To achieve this goal, the application services need to be configured in the root web application context started by the context loader listener. This servlet listener loads the beans defined in `WEB-INF/applicationContext.xml` and binds them to the root application context associated with the web application. Listing 5-33 shows this.

Listing 5-33. `applicationContext.xml`

```xml
<?xml version="1.0" encoding="UTF-8"?>
<beans xmlns="http://www.springframework.org/schema/beans"
       xmlns:xsi="http://www.w3.org/2001/XMLSchema-instance"
       xsi:schemaLocation="http://www.springframework.org/schema/beans
       http://www.springframework.org/schema/beans/spring-beans-2.5.xsd"
       >

       <bean name="policyQuoteApplicationService" class="com.apress.einsure.➥
           business.impl.PolicyQuoteApplicationServiceImpl" />

</beans>
```

Finally, Listing 5-34 shows the actual application service implementation class.

Listing 5-34. `PolicyQuoteApplicationServiceImpl.java`

```java
public class PolicyQuoteApplicationServiceImpl implements
PolicyQuoteApplicationService{

    public double calculatePolicyQuote(String productCd, int age,
 double sumAssured, int term) {
        //return calculated policy value
    }

}
```

Now that the server-side components are ready, I will show how to build a sample client to access the web service. As explained in Chapter 4, I will use a business delegate because it is the most appropriate component to deal with remote services. Listing 5-35 shows the business delegate to invoke methods on the remote policy quote service.

Listing 5-35. `PolicyQuoteBusinessDelegateImpl.java`

```java
public class PolicyQuoteBusinessDelegateImpl implements
PolicyQuoteBusinessDelegate {
    private PolicyQuoteApplicationService service;

    public void calculatePolicyQuote(){
        this.service.calculatePolicyQuote("GNLIFE", 12, 1000, 10);
    }

    public PolicyQuoteApplicationService getService() {
        return service;
    }

    public void setService(PolicyQuoteApplicationService service) {
        this.service = service;
    }

}
```

Now you can wire up everything in the Spring configuration file, as shown in Listing 5-36.

Listing 5-36. `springws-config.xml`

```xml
<?xml version="1.0" encoding="UTF-8"?>
<beans xmlns="http://www.springframework.org/schema/beans"
       xmlns:xsi="http://www.w3.org/2001/XMLSchema-instance"
            xsi:schemaLocation="http://www.springframework.org/schema/beans
       http://www.springframework.org/schema/beans/spring-beans-2.5.xsd"
       >


    <bean name="policyQuoteDelegate"
         class="com.xpress.channel.PolicyQuoteBusinessDelegate" >
              <property name="businessService"
                 ref="policyQuoteWebService" />
    </bean>
```

```
    <bean id="policyQuoteWebService"
        class="org.springframework.remoting.jaxrpc.➥
                JaxRpcPortProxyFactoryBean" >
        <property name="serviceInterface"
value="com.apress.einsure.business.api
.PolicyQuoteApplicationService"/>
        <property name="wsdlDocumentUrl" value="http://localhost:7001/
eInsureWeb/axis/PolicyQuoteService?wsdl"/>
        <property name="namespaceUri"
 value="http://localhost:7001/eInsureWeb/axis/PolicyQuoteService"/>
        <property name="serviceName" value="PolicyQuoteService"/>
        <property name="portName" value="PolicyQuoteService"/>
        <property name="serviceFactoryClass"
 value="org.apache.axis.client.ServiceFactory" />
    </bean>

</beans>
```

You can see from Listing 5-36, the Spring Framework uses a factory bean: `JaxRpcPortProxyFactoryBean`. This class finds the web service from the web service registry. It returns a proxy object implementing the business service interface. Finally, I will put the business delegate into action from a stand-alone Java client, as shown in Listing 5-37.

Listing 5-37. `PolicyQuoteClient.java`

```
public class PolicyQuoteClient {
    public static void main(String[] args) throws ServiceException, AxisFault {
            accessViaSpringClient();
    accessViaNonSpringClient();
        }
    }

    public static void accessViaSpringClient() {
        String configFile = "com/xpress/channel/springws-config.xml";
        ApplicationContext ctx = new ClassPathXmlApplicationContext(configFile);
        PolicyQuoteBusinessDelegate delegate = (PolicyQuoteBusinessDelegate)
ctx.getBean("policyQuoteDelegate");
        delegate.execute();
    }
```

```
    public static void accessViaNonSpringClient() {
        try {
            URL url = new URL("http://localhost:7001/eInsureWeb/axis/➥
                PolicyQuoteService");

            Service service = new Service();

            Call call = (Call) service.createCall();
            call.setTargetEndpointAddress(url);
            call.invoke("calculatePolicyQuote", new Object[]{"ff",1,2.5,4});

        } catch (MalformedURLException ex) {
        throw new RuntimeException(ex);
        }
}
```

Remoting with Burlap

Spring provides some alternative remoting strategies for exposing services over HTTP. One such alternative is its support for the Burlap and Hessian remoting protocols from Caucho. Hessian supports binary data exchange over HTTP. I will concentrate on Burlap, which allows simple text and XML-based data transfer. It is just a matter of configuration to export a Spring service for access through the Burlap protocol. To do that, I will need to ensure that the dispatcher servlet handles Burlap remoting. This requires some alteration in the web application configuration file, as shown in Listing 5-38.

Listing 5-38. web.xml

```
<?xml version="1.0" encoding="UTF-8"?>

<web-app version="2.4" xmlns="http://java.sun.com/xml/ns/j2ee"
        xmlns:xsi="http://www.w3.org/2001/XMLSchema-instance"
        xsi:schemaLocation="http://java.sun.com/xml/ns/j2ee
http://java.sun.com/xml/ns/j2ee/web-app_2_4.xsd">

    <servlet>
        <servlet-name>insurance</servlet-name>
        <servlet-class>
            org.springframework.web.servlet.DispatcherServlet
```

```
        </servlet-class>
        <load-on-startup>1</load-on-startup>
    </servlet>


    <servlet-mapping>
        <servlet-name>insurance</servlet-name>
        <url-pattern>*.do</url-pattern>
    </servlet-mapping>


    <servlet-mapping>
        <servlet-name>insurance</servlet-name>
        <url-pattern>/remoting/*</url-pattern>
    </servlet-mapping>

    <welcome-file-list>
        <welcome-file>WEB-INF/jsp/index.jsp</welcome-file>
    </welcome-file-list>


    <jsp-config>
        <taglib>
            <taglib-uri>/spring</taglib-uri>
            <taglib-location>
                /WEB-INF/tld/spring-form.tld
            </taglib-location>
        </taglib>
        <taglib>
            <taglib-uri>sitemesh-page</taglib-uri>
            <taglib-location>
                /WEB-INF/tld/sitemesh-page.tld
            </taglib-location>
        </taglib>
        <taglib>
            <taglib-uri>sitemesh-decorator</taglib-uri>
            <taglib-location>
                /WEB-INF/tld/sitemesh-decorator.tld
            </taglib-location>
        </taglib>
```

```
    </jsp-config>

</web-app>
```

The next step is the most important because we export the POJO-based policy quotation service as a Burlap remote service. Again, this can be done with mere configuration,
as in Listing 5-39. In this case, the `BurlapServiceExporter` acts as the service endpoint.

Listing 5-39. `insurance-servlet.xml`

```
<?xml version="1.0" encoding="UTF-8"?>
<beans xmlns="http://www.springframework.org/schema/beans"
       xmlns:xsi="http://www.w3.org/2001/XMLSchema-instance"

       xsi:schemaLocation="http://www.springframework.org/schema/beans
       http://www.springframework.org/schema/beans/spring-beans-2.5.xsd
       "
       >

    <bean name="policyQuoteServiceImpl"
         class="com.apress.einsure.business.impl.➥
           PolicyQuoteApplicationServiceImpl">
    </bean>

    <bean name="/PolicyQuoteService" class="org.springframework.remoting.caucho.➥
        BurlapServiceExporter">
        <property name="service" ref="policyQuoteServiceImpl"/>
        <property name="serviceInterface" value="com.apress.einsure.business.➥
api.PolicyQuoteApplicationService"/>
    </bean>

</beans>
```

Now that I have exposed the policy quote service using Burlap remoting, it's time to
focus on the client. Once more you will just need to configure a proxy factory bean, and
that's more or less all there is to it, as shown in Listing 5-40.

Listing 5-40. springburlap-config.xml

```xml
<?xml version="1.0" encoding="UTF-8"?>
<beans xmlns="http://www.springframework.org/schema/beans"
       xmlns:xsi="http://www.w3.org/2001/XMLSchema-instance"
       xsi:schemaLocation="http://www.springframework.org/schema/beans
       http://www.springframework.org/schema/beans/spring-beans-2.5.xsd"
       >


    <bean name="policyQuoteDelegate"
class="com.xpress.channel.PolicyQuoteBusinessDelegate" >
        <property name="service"
                  ref="policyQuoteBurlapService" />
    </bean>


    <bean id="policyQuoteBurlapService"
class="org.springframework.remoting.caucho.BurlapProxyFactoryBean">
        <property name="serviceUrl"
value="http://localhost:7001/eInsureWeb/remoting/PolicyQuoteService"/>
        <property name="serviceInterface"
value="com.apress.einsure.business.api.PolicyQuoteApplicationService"/>
    </bean>
</beans>
```

It is important to note that since I have used a proxy object with P2I, the business
delegate does not need to change. Last but not least, Listing 5-41 shows the stand-alone
client.

Listing 5-41. PolicyQuoteBurlapClient.java

```java
public class PolicyQuoteBurlapClient {
    public static void main(String[] args)  {
        accessViaSpringClient();
    }

    public static void accessViaSpringClient() {
        String configFile = "com/xpress/channel/springburlap-config.xml";
        ApplicationContext ctx = new ClassPathXmlApplicationContext(configFile);
        PolicyQuoteBusinessDelegate delegate =
 (PolicyQuoteBusinessDelegate) ctx.getBean("policyQuoteDelegate");
```

```
        delegate.execute();
    }
}
```

Consequences

Benefits

- It is easy to expose existing POJO services through a variety of remoting options.

- It is easy to develop Spring-based clients for remote web services.

- Technology- and platform-independent service access can be accomplished using web services.

- Existing services can now participate in a bigger integration scenario.

Concerns

- Burlap-Hessian is nonstandard with respect to JAX-RPC and JAX-WS.

- Accessing services over the network can have adverse effects on application performance.

- It will be necessary to implement a robust security infrastructure as more and more services become available as remote web services.

Summary

Spring provides a robust high-level API that makes writing data access code very simple. This is possible because the framework takes care of the boilerplate code generally required for direct JDBC. The API also embodies robust object design principles and patterns. Spring JDBC also provides an OO wrapper to access legacy stored procedures through the PAO pattern. Spring ORM module allows integration with ORM solutions. This also needs to wrap with Data Access Object pattern to provide a consistent persistence API to the business tier.

With Spring's convenient support classes, it is possible to support asynchronous processing with a service activator either in an EJB server or in the Spring container. Finally, existing POJO-based Spring services can be exposed as technology-independent remote web service components, primarily by configuration.

Security and transaction are two foremost important requirements in any Java EE application. Unfortunately, not much has been written or discussed about them. In Chapter 6, I will look into the need for security and transaction in a Java EE application and discuss a few related patterns with the Spring framework.

■■■

Exploring Crosscutting Design Patterns

Most enterprise applications should be secured to prevent malicious access. They also require transaction support to maintain data consistency. The Java EE platform containers provide support for both security and transaction. However, these services can be applied in any of the application tiers. Security, for example, can be applied in the presentation tier to prevent unauthorized access of web resources such as Java Server Pages. The EJB business tier components also require protection because they can be accessed by different remote clients. The web services in the integration tier also need secured access. Similarly, transactional services may be used by the business tier or integration tier data access logic depending on application need.

Unfortunately, Sun's Java BluePrints and the book *Core J2EE Design Patterns* by Deepak Alur, Dan Malks, and John Crupi (Prentice Hall, 2003) do not document any design strategy for transaction and security, which are of critical importance to an enterprise application. Therefore, developers and designers often have a dilemma when deciding the appropriate tier for applying these application concerns. As a result, they often end up using a low-level Java EE platform security API or the Java Transaction API in their code. The core application concerns such as presentation and business logic are soon bloated because of mixing transaction and security code. Hence, I decided to dedicate this chapter to discussing design strategies to counter these crosscutting concerns with the Spring Framework.

The Java EE specification and the Java Authorization and Authentication Service (JAAS) API tries to standardize security services. But they are limited in features and unsuitable for the majority of the applications. The server vendors implement container security in a proprietary way, resulting in vendor lock-in and limited portability. JAAS, on the other hand, just provides a standard interface. The container support for JAAS too lacks any consistency. So, development teams generally resort to a custom solution, which consumes a significant portion of their development time. Spring Security, which was earlier known as Acegi Security, is an easy-to-use and flexible security framework that works irrespective of any container. It is based on the Spring IOC container and heavily relies on its DI and AOP features. It provides declarative security to web requests and business methods. It is highly extensible and provides out-of-the-box components that cover almost every custom security need. In this chapter, I will apply Spring Security in the context of some frequently used Java EE security patterns described in the book *Core Security Patterns* by Christopher Steel, Ramesh Nagappan, and Ray Lai (Prentice Hall, 2005).

Unlike with security, the Java EE containers provide robust support for distributed transactions involving a variety of middleware and database servers. The Java EE specification supports both the programmatic and declarative modes of transaction control. The declarative transaction control is highly flexible and can be controlled by configuration. Programmatic transaction management, on the other hand, can be very cumbersome to develop and maintain. In this chapter, I will focus more on transaction strategies primarily based on Spring AOP support and in the process explore some patterns discussed in the book *Java Transaction Design Strategies* by Mark Richards (Lulu.com, 2006).

In this chapter, I will heavily use AOP concepts. I will also call upon the Spring Framework's AOP support for several examples. If you are new to AOP, then get started with the book *Foundations of AOP for J2EE Development* by Renaud Pawlak, Jean-Philippe Retaillé, and Lionel Seinturieris (Apress, 2006). Also, you should read the Spring AOP documentation at `http://static.springframework.org/spring/docs/2.5.x/reference/aop.html`.

Authentication and Authorization Enforcer

Problem

The eInsure application handled sensitive information related to policies purchased by thousands of people. It also managed crucial business intelligence data that was accessible to the senior management of the companies using this product. So, it was important that eInsure allowed only trusted parties to access data to prevent any kind of data loss or tampering.

The common strategy used by an enterprise application to establish trust with external users or systems is known as *authentication*. In the authentication process, the system asks a user one simple question: "Who you are?" The user will respond by supplying a principal (username) and credential (password). The system verifies the principal-credential combination, and if a match is found, the user is allowed to access the system. Note that authentication does not guarantee that the user has access to system resources. It merely unlocks the door to the web resources.

The decision whether an authenticated user has access to a resource is controlled by another process, called *authorization*. Authorization seeks to answer this question: "What can you do?" In other words, it tries to find out the operations that an authenticated user can perform in the system. In a Java EE application, this mainly involves protecting access to web resources such as JSPs. The user's principal is generally associated with one or more roles. Each role in turn is linked to a set of resources or operations.

The eInsure application had a sign-in form for users to supply a username and password combination to get authenticated. The supplied information was checked into the database, and valid users were granted access to carry out different operations.

The database-driven authentication mechanism used in eInsure was rigid. It was placed deep inside the application and cut across all the tiers. In other words, the authentication logic was implemented just like any normal operation such as policy underwriting. In a refactored eInsure system, this would mean the request for authentication would be intercepted by the front controller and passed on to a page controller. This would be followed by the invocation of the business delegate, session facade, and data access objects.

Ideally, authentication and security code should be applied transparently and need not span tiers. eInsure was being implemented by clients who had an existing enterprise-wide security policy and software in place. So, in most cases the database-driven approach did not work. Instead, the application had to adapt itself to the customers' existing security implementation such as Lightweight Directory Access Protocol (LDAP), Single Sign On (SSO), or OpenID. This resulted in a lot of code changes and testing in different tiers to integrate with an alternate authentication implementation.

As shown in Listing 4-1 later in the chapter, the JSP controller used the user information as well as the event code to check whether the user has the privileges to execute a certain action. This check was also placed deep inside the presentation tier. Any changes to the authorization helper methods would lead to changes across all the controllers. Such deeply embedded authorization checks resulted in the mixing of security and presentation concerns. The authorization code in eInsure would query the database for each request to find out whether the user had the privileges to execute the action with the given event code. This database trip for each request had a negative impact on performance. Last but not least, the event code was hard-coded in the view and controller JSPs as well as maintained in the database. Any change to the event code value meant modification in all the JSPs. This often would lead to minor bugs that were very difficult to detect.

Forces

- Only valid users are allowed entry into the application.

- All different entry points into an application should be guarded by authentication.

- All authenticated users should have the appropriate roles/authority to access secure system resources.

- Authentication and authorization mechanisms should be encapsulated as independent components and applied transparently by configuration.

Solution

Implement a pluggable *authentication and authorization enforcer* to verify a user's identity and allow access to secured resources.

Strategies with the Spring Framework

Spring Security implements the Authentication and Authorization Enforcer pattern as a set of two distinct yet very closely linked components. The authentication and authorization enforcer components work together and transparently apply authentication and authorization support both in the presentation tier of the Java EE web application and in the business tier. These components are highly configurable and extensible, as you will see in subsequent sections.

The authentication enforcer's primary responsibility is validating a user's identity. It also checks for authentication whenever any request reaches the web application. If the user is authenticated, it allows the request to pass on to the authorization enforcer. If the authentication fails, the user will be redirected to the sign-on page.

Authentication enforcers are generally pluggable, which helps to quickly adapt to any new authentication mechanism such as OpenID. The core component sits behind protocol-independent interceptors and uses helpers to delegate the actual authentication process. All user actions must go through these interceptors to apply authentication.

Once the authentication core components are done, the authorization enforcer picks up the request. It checks to see whether the user who has initiated this action has enough privileges to access a particular web page or execute a certain method. If the user is trying to access a resource without validating his identity, the authorization enforcer will force him out to the sign-on page or access-denied page. Figure 6-1 shows the basic architecture of the authentication and authorization enforcer.

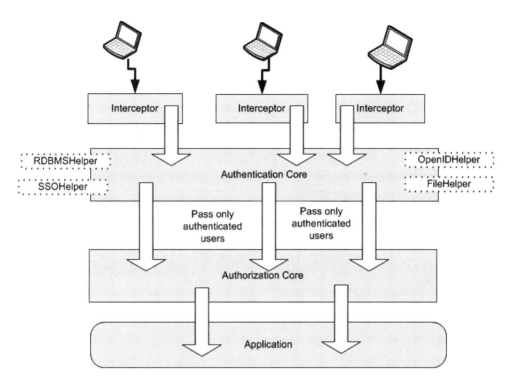

Figure 6-1. *Authentication and authorization enforcer high-level components*

Key Components of Spring Security

The basic architecture of Spring Security is similar to the one described in Figure 6-1. Figure 6-2 shows the high-level components of Spring Security. (The figure shows only those components relevant to this discussion.)

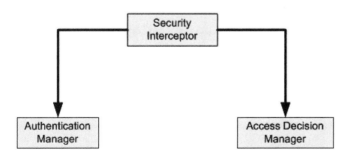

Figure 6-2. *Spring Security high-level components*

The different components of the Spring Security framework are the following:

- The *security interceptor* acts as the gateway that intercepts requests for resources. It delegates security enforcement responsibilities to the core components. If a web resource is being protected, then the Spring Security interceptor is provided in the form of a servlet filter. Method invocation interceptors are implemented as aspects.

- The *authentication manager* verifies a user's identity. It is a pluggable component with a clearly defined service provider interface (SPI). So, it is possible to integrate virtually any authentication mechanism. Spring Security comes with several concrete authentication manager implementations covering most common needs.

- The *access decision manager* is another pluggable component responsible for authorization. It allows authenticated requests to access system resources based on certain roles.

Spring Security is based on the core Spring Framework. So, it has all the benefits of the Spring IOC container available with the security subsystem.

Authentication and Authorization with Spring Security

Spring Security's support for web application security starts with a servlet filter. The filter intercepts incoming web requests and delegates to the authentication manager. To install the Spring Security gateway, you will need to install the special servlet filter class `FilterToBeanProxy` in `web.xml`, as shown in Listing 6-1.

Listing 6-1. `web.xml` *Fragment*

```
<filter>
        <filter-name>springSecurityFilterGateway</filter-name>
        <filter-class>org.springframework.security.util.FilterToBeanProxy
        </filter-class>
        <init-param>
            <param-name>targetClass</param-name>
            <param-value>org.springframework.security.util.FilterChainProxy
            </param-value>
        </init-param>
</filter>
```

```
<filter-mapping>
        <filter-name>springSecurityFilterGateway</filter-name>
        <url-pattern>/*</url-pattern>
</filter-mapping>
```

Note that the filter in Listing 6-1 uses the initialization parameter `targetClass`. The servlet filter delegates the actual processing to this `FilterChainProxy`. On initialization, the Spring Security filter gateway looks for a bean of type `FilterChainProxy` in the Spring web application context. It then delegates all the handling to this filter chain proxy. You can configure multiple filter chain proxies. In that case, the one found first will be used. If no filter chain proxy object is found, an exception will be raised. It is possible to set the `targetBean` initialization parameter instead of `targetClass`. This will allow the gateway filter to look for a bean with the given name in the application context. But this can lead to a bug that's hard to detect. If you rename this bean in the Spring configuration, you will have to do the same in `web.xml` as well. The filter mapping configuration in Listing 6-1 forces all web requests to be passed through this filter.

For Spring Security to work, the Spring application context must be loaded. Since the goal all along has been to separate security concerns from presentation concerns, `ContextLoaderListener` will load the application context for Spring Security. This will load the parent Spring web application context. The dispatcher servlet described in Chapter 2 will load its own application context with the presentation tier beans. This application context is a child of the context loaded by the servlet context listener, as shown in Listing 6-2. The parent web application context will be loaded from the classpath resource `applicationContext-security.xml`. Note that the Spring web application context is bound to the servlet context, so there is no performance concern here because you're not reloading the context for each request.

Listing 6-2. `web.xml`

```
<?xml version="1.0" encoding="UTF-8"?>
<web-app version="2.4" xmlns=http://java.sun.com/xml/ns/j2ee
 xmlns:xsi=http://www.w3.org/2001/XMLSchema-instance
 xsi:schemaLocation="http://java.sun.com/xml/ns/j2ee
 http://java.sun.com/xml/ns/j2ee/web-app_2_4.xsd">

    <context-param>
        <param-name>contextConfigLocation</param-name>
        <param-value>
            classpath:/WEB-INF/applicationContext-security.xml
```

```
        </param-value>
    </context-param>



    <filter>
        <filter-name>springSecurityFilterChain</filter-name>
        <filter-class>org.springframework.security.util.FilterToBeanProxy
        </filter-class>
        <init-param>
            <param-name>targetClass</param-name>
            <param-value>org.springframework.security.util.FilterChainProxy
            </param-value>
        </init-param>
    </filter>

    <filter-mapping>
        <filter-name>springSecurityFilterChain</filter-name>
        <url-pattern>/*</url-pattern>
    </filter-mapping>

    <listener>
        <listener-class>org.springframework.web.context.ContextLoaderListener
        </listener-class>
    </listener>



    <servlet>
        <servlet-name>insurance</servlet-name>
        <servlet-class>
            org.springframework.web.servlet.DispatcherServlet
        </servlet-class>
        <load-on-startup>1</load-on-startup>
    </servlet>


    <servlet-mapping>
        <servlet-name>insurance</servlet-name>
        <url-pattern>*.do</url-pattern>
    </servlet-mapping>
```

```
<jsp-config>
    <taglib>
        <taglib-uri>/spring</taglib-uri>
        <taglib-location>
            /WEB-INF/tld/spring-form.tld
        </taglib-location>
    </taglib>
</jsp-config>
</web-app>
```

Now that I have shown how to set up the security gateway of the web application and registered it with the web server, it's time to focus on the Spring side of things. On the Spring side, the FilterChainProxy receives a request for security processing from the gateway filter. The FilterChainProxy can then pass this request through a series of filters configured in the Spring application context. Listing 6-3 shows this FilterChainProxy configuration. ContextLoaderListener uses this configuration file to start the root Spring application context.

Listing 6-3. applicationContext-security.xml

```
<?xml version="1.0" encoding="UTF-8"?>
<!DOCTYPE beans PUBLIC "-//SPRING//DTD BEAN//EN"
"http://www.springframework.org/dtd/spring-beans.dtd">

<beans>

<bean name="filterChainProxy"
        class="org.springframework.security.util.FilterChainProxy">
  <property name="filterInvocationDefinitionSource">
    <value>
      CONVERT_URL_TO_LOWERCASE_BEFORE_COMPARISON
      PATTERN_TYPE_APACHE_ANT
      /**=httpSessionContextIntegrationFilter,authenticationProcessingFilter,➥
anonymousProcessingFilter,exceptionTranslationFilter,➥
filterInvocationInterceptor
    </value>
  </property>
</bean>
</beans>
```

The `filterInvocationDefinitionSource` is the key property for the `FilterChainProxy`. It defines a ruleset for invoking the filters. As shown in Listing 6-3, it will convert an incoming request URL to lowercase before any comparison. It will use Apache Ant–based pattern matching to map an incoming request to the Spring Security filters. In this example, all the incoming requests will pass through five filters. (I will get into the core of Spring Security in a while and explain the functions of each of these filters.) There are several other concrete filter implementations provided by Spring. You can refer to the Spring Security documentation at `http://static.springframework.org/spring-security/site/index.html` for more details about them. For our purposes in this section, these five will be sufficient.

The `httpSessionContextIntegrationFilter` filter will be the first filter to be executed when the request reaches `FilterChainProxy`. The ordering is important because one filter may depend on the value set by the preceding or succeeding ones. In other words, setting the filters in a different order may lead to unpredictable results. Figure 6-3 shows the filter chaining.

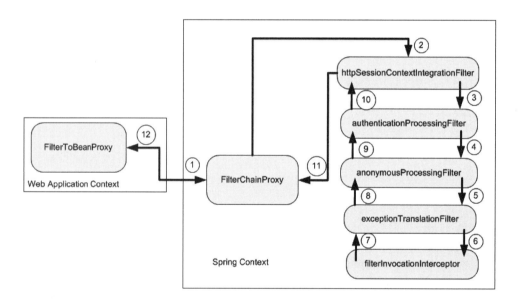

Figure 6-3. *Filter chaining in Spring Security*

Session Context Integration Filter (SCIF)

This is the first of the five filters in the chain that is executed in Spring Security. SCIF checks whether an `HttpSession` has been started, and it contains a security context object. If the `SecurityContext` object is not found, it creates a new instance of this object. SCIF puts the security context object in a temporary placeholder called a *security context holder* for the other filters in the chain to access and update important information such as user identity and roles. It then invokes the next filter in the chain. Once the control returns, SCIF puts the security context back on to the HTTP session and clears the temporary placeholder. Listing 6-4 shows the SCIF configuration.

Listing 6-4. applicationContext-security.xml

```
<?xml version="1.0" encoding="UTF-8"?>
<!DOCTYPE beans PUBLIC "-//SPRING//DTD BEAN//EN"
"http://www.springframework.org/dtd/spring-beans.dtd">

<beans>

<!—Other beans -->

<bean id="httpSessionContextIntegrationFilter"

class="org.springframework.security.context.HttpSessionContextIntegrationFilter"/>

</beans>
```

Authentication Processing Filter (APF)

The primary responsibility of APF is to authenticate a user's identity. Several such filters are available with Spring, as shown in the class diagram in Figure 6-4.

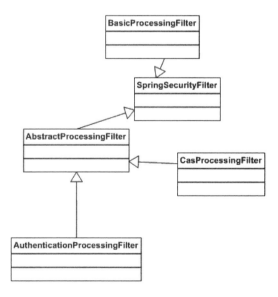

Figure 6-4. *Class diagram: authentication processing filter*

Spring Security offers a variety of authentication-processing choices. The BasicProcessingFilter supports HTTP basic authentication with the user information stored in the request header. CasProcessingFilter is used for identity verification with JA-SIG's Central Authentication Service (CAS) SSO solution. You can read more about CAS at http://www.ja-sig.org/products/cas/. There are other options such as the DigestProcessingFilter for HTTP digest authentication, whereas X509ProcessingFilter processes authentication with X.509 certificates.

In this book, I will concentrate on the simpler HTTP form-based authentication supported by AuthenticationProcessingFilter. This will help you grasp the key concepts easily and apply them to different situations. With Spring Security, this would primarily involve configuration. The sole responsibility of this filter is to invoke the underlying authentication provider. It inherits from the AbstractProcessingFilter, which implements the core workflow associated with authentication. The SpringSecurityFilter implements the javax.servlet.Filter interface. It implements the doFilter method defined by this interface and delegates the actual processing to an abstract method doFilterHttp, which should be implemented by all subclasses.

Before proceeding, I will introduce the sign-on page, as shown in Listing 6-5.

Listing 6-5. /WEB-INF/jsp/login.jsp

```
<%@ taglib prefix="form" uri="http://www.springframework.org/tags/form" %>
<html>

<head>
<title>Login</title>
</head>
<body>
<form action="j_spring_security_check" method="POST">
    <form:errors path="*" cssClass="errorBox" />
  <table>
    <tr>
      <td>User:</td>
        <td><input type='text' name='j_username' />
        </td>
    </tr>
    <tr>
      <td>Password:</td>
      <td><input type='password' name='j_password' /></td>
    </tr>
```

```
    <tr><td colspan='2'><input name="submit" type="submit" /></td></tr>
    <tr><td colspan='2'><input name="reset" type="reset" /></td></tr>
  </table>
</form>
</body>
</html>
```

This login form is specific to the application, and hence I will configure this to work with the front controller servlet, as shown in Listing 6-6.

Listing 6-6. `insurance-servlet.xml`

```xml
<?xml version="1.0" encoding="UTF-8"?>

<beans xmlns="http://www.springframework.org/schema/beans"
      xmlns:xsi="http://www.w3.org/2001/XMLSchema-instance"
      xsi:schemaLocation="http://www.springframework.org/schema/beans
      http://www.springframework.org/schema/beans/spring-beans-2.5.xsd">

    <bean id="viewResolver"
        class="org.springframework.web.servlet.view.InternalResourceViewResolver">
      <property name="viewClass"
                value="org.springframework.web.servlet.view.JstlView" />
      <property name="prefix" value="/WEB-INF/jsp/" />
      <property name="suffix" value=".jsp" />
    </bean>

    <bean name="/login.do"
        class="org.springframework.web.servlet.mvc.UrlFilenameViewController">

    </bean>
    <!--  other beans to be shown later    -->

</beans>
```

As shown in Listing 6-5, this is a simple login form. If you fill in the two text fields and submit this form, it will result in the following URL: `http://localhost/eInsureWeb/ j_spring_security_check?j_username=value1&j_password=value2`.

This request will be intercepted by the Spring Security filter and delegated to the Spring-managed filter chain. Once SCIF is done with the preprocessing of the request, it's APF turn to act on it. The APF is configured in the root application context, as shown in Listing 6-7.

Listing 6-7. `applicationContext-security.xml`

```xml
<?xml version="1.0" encoding="UTF-8"?>
<!DOCTYPE beans PUBLIC "-//SPRING//DTD BEAN//EN"
"http://www.springframework.org/dtd/spring-beans.dtd">

<beans>

<!—Other beans -->

<bean id="authenticationProcessingFilter" class="org.springframework.security.ui.➥
webapp.AuthenticationProcessingFilter">
  <property name="authenticationManager" ref="authenticationManager"/>
  <property name="authenticationFailureUrl" value="/login.do?errorId=1"/>
  <property name="defaultTargetUrl" value="/secure/app/createPolicy.do"/>
  <property name="filterProcessesUrl" value="/j_spring_security_check"/>

 </bean>

</beans>
```

The first decision that APF needs to make is whether the incoming request needs authentication. For this it depends on the property `filterProcessesUrl`. APF will extract the URI using the `HttpServletRequest.getRequestURI` method. In this case, the method returns `/eInsureWeb/j_spring_security_check`. This returned value is then compared to the context root and `filterProcessUrl` combination to determine whether this URL has to be processed for authentication. You may want to customize the names of the two text fields in Listing 6-5. I have used the default values. To use custom values, you will need to configure the properties `passwordParameter` and `usernameParameter` of the authentication processing filter.

Now, in the scenario under consideration, the APF determines that the incoming request does need authentication. So, it will attempt to carry out the actual authentication. For this it will use the `authenticationManager` property. The authentication managers are pluggable helpers that carry out the actual authentication; they implement the `AuthenticationManager` interface. This interface defines a single method named `authenticate`. This method accepts an `Authentication` object containing the user's principal and credential. On successful authentication, this method returns the `Authentication` object with the user's role list. This will be required later during authorization.

The authenticated user is redirected to the URL specified by the property `defaultTargetUrl`. In this case, the user is directed to the web page for underwriting a new policy. If the authentication fails, an `AuthenticationException` will be raised. In this case, the user is redirected to the URL set in the property `authenticationFailureUrl`. In this example, the user is redirected to the login page. The `errorId` specified in the `authenticationFailureUrl` flags the `login.jsp` file in Listing 6-5 to display the error messages because of an authentication failure.

Spring Security provides one custom authentication manager implementation in the form of the `ProviderManager` class. This in turn delegates to authentication providers. Authentication providers are adapters for the underlying authentication technology. With this strategy, it is possible to authenticate with any identity management system. The `ProviderManager` class can be configured to work with multiple authentication providers. It will iterate through the list of authentication providers until the user is authenticated by one of them or the provider collection is exhausted. Listing 6-8 shows the provider manager configuration.

Listing 6-8. `applicationContext-security.xml`

```xml
<?xml version="1.0" encoding="UTF-8"?>
<!DOCTYPE beans PUBLIC "-//SPRING//DTD BEAN//EN"
"http://www.springframework.org/dtd/spring-beans.dtd">

<beans>

<!–Other beans -->
<bean id="authenticationManager"
        class="org.springframework.security.providers.ProviderManager">
  <property name="providers">
    <list>
      <ref local="daoAuthenticationProvider"/>
    </list>
  </property>
</bean>

</beans>
```

Note that in Listing 6-8, the provider manager works with a single authentication provider. Spring provides several out-of-the-box providers, as shown in Figure 6-5.

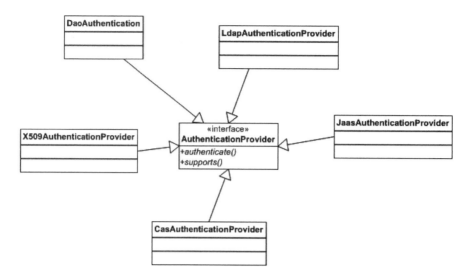

Figure 6-5. *Class diagram: authentication provider*

The providers implement the AuthenticationProvider interface. It defines two methods. The authenticate method is used to trigger the actual authentication process. The authentication manager invokes this method and passes a reference to the Authentication object. The supports method checks whether the authentication provider can work with the given Authentication object. As shown in Figure 6-5, Spring provides several concrete implementations catering to most security requirements. Listing 6-9 shows the authentication provider for the current example.

Listing 6-9. applicationContext-security.xml

```
<?xml version="1.0" encoding="UTF-8"?>
<!DOCTYPE beans PUBLIC "-//SPRING//DTD BEAN//EN"
"http://www.springframework.org/dtd/spring-beans.dtd">

<beans>

<!-Other beans -->
<bean id="authenticationManager"
        class="org.springframework.security.providers.ProviderManager">
  <property name="providers">
    <list>
      <ref local="daoAuthenticationProvider"/>
      </list>
```

```
  </property>
</bean>

<bean name="daoAuthenticationProvider"
class="org.springframework.security.providers.dao.DaoAuthenticationProvider">
      <property name="userDetailsService" ref="userDetailsService"/>

</bean>
</beans>
```

In this case I am going to use a data access object–based authentication provider: `DaoAuthenticationProvider`. This provider assumes that the user's identity is stored in a relational database. To retrieve this information, it employs a data access object. The DAO is configured using the `userDetailsService` property.

The principal and credential combination fetched from the database is matched with the one passed by the provider manager in the `Authentication` object. If there's a successful match, an `Authentication` object with the user role list will be passed to the provider manager. A failure results in an `AuthenticationException` being raised, indicating a failed identity validation.

The DAOs used by the `DaoAuthenticationProvider` should implement the `UserDetailsService` interface. This again is a single method interface and defines the method `loadUserByUsername`. Spring Security provides two ready-made implementations of this interface, as shown in Figure 6-6.

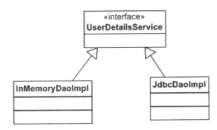

Figure 6-6. *Class diagram: user details service*

`InMemoryDaoImpl` is suitable for quick prototyping and testing. For real-world use, you need to use `JdbcDaoImpl` or provide a custom implementation. The `UserDetailsService` also needs to be wired up in the Spring application context, as shown in Listing 6-10.

Listing 6-10. applicationContext-security.xml

```xml
<?xml version="1.0" encoding="UTF-8"?>
<!DOCTYPE beans PUBLIC "-//SPRING//DTD BEAN//EN"
"http://www.springframework.org/dtd/spring-beans.dtd">

<beans>

<!--Other beans -->
<bean id="authenticationManager"
        class="org.springframework.security.providers.ProviderManager">
  <property name="providers">
    <list>
      <ref local="daoAuthenticationProvider"/>
      </list>
  </property>
</bean>

<bean name="daoAuthenticationProvider" class="org.springframework.➥
security.providers.dao.DaoAuthenticationProvider">
        <property name="userDetailsService" ref="authenticationDao "/>

</bean>

<bean name="authenticationDao"
class="org.springframework.security.userdetails.jdbc.JdbcDaoImpl">
<property name="dataSource" ref="dataSource"/>
</bean>

<bean id="datasource" class="org.springframework.jndi.JndiObjectFactoryBean">
        <property name="jndiName" value="einsureDatasource" />
        <property name="jndiEnvironment">
            <props>
                <prop key="java.naming.factory.initial">
                    org.jnp.interfaces.NamingContextFactory
                </prop>

                <prop key="java.naming.provider.url">
                    jnp://localhost:1099
                </prop>
                <prop key="java.naming.factory.url.pkgs">
```

```
                org.jboss.naming.client
            </prop>
        </props>
    </property>
</bean>


</beans>
```

As shown in Listing 6-10, the `JdbcDaoImpl` requires a `DataSource` reference to execute its query. The `JdbcDaoImpl` assumes you have set up two tables in the database as shown in Figure 6-7.

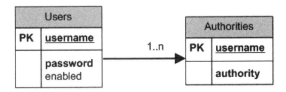

Figure 6-7. *Spring Security: database tables*

To retrieve data from these tables, the `JdbcDaoImpl` uses the default SQL statements shown in Listing 6-11.

Listing 6-11. `applicationContext-security.xml`

```
<?xml version="1.0" encoding="UTF-8"?>
<!DOCTYPE beans PUBLIC "-//SPRING//DTD BEAN//EN"
"http://www.springframework.org/dtd/spring-beans.dtd">

<beans>

<!—Other beans -->

<bean name="daoAuthenticationProvider" class="org.springframework.➥
security.providers.dao.DaoAuthenticationProvider">
        <property name="userDetailsService" ref="authenticationDao "/>

</bean>
```

```xml
<bean id="authenticationDao"
class="org.springframework.security.userdetails.jdbc.JdbcDaoImpl">
<property name="dataSource" ref="dataSource"/>

<property name="userByUserNameQuery" >
<value>
SELECT username, password, enabled
FROM users
WHERE username=?
</value>

</property>

<property name="authoritiesByUserNameQuery" >
<value>
SELECT username, authority
FROM authorities
WHERE username=?
</value>

</property>


</bean>
</beans>
```

If your tables and column names were different, it is possible to supply your custom queries by overriding the userByUserNameQuery and authoritiesByUserNameQuery properties. You need to use proper aliases for the columns that have different names than the default tables because Spring retrieves data from the resultset using default column names. eInsure used the e-mail address instead of the username and role in the place of authority. Listing 6-12 shows the configuration of the custom queries with aliases.

Listing 6-12. applicationContext-security.xml

```xml
<?xml version="1.0" encoding="UTF-8"?>
<!DOCTYPE beans PUBLIC "-//SPRING//DTD BEAN//EN"
  "http://www.springframework.org/dtd/spring-beans.dtd">

<beans>
```

```xml
<!--Other beans -->

<bean name="daoAuthenticationProvider" class="org.springframework.➥
security.providers.dao.DaoAuthenticationProvider">
        <property name="userDetailsService" ref="authenticationDao "/>

</bean>

<bean id="authenticationDao"
class="org.springframework.security.userdetails.jdbc.JdbcDaoImpl">
<property name="dataSource" ref="dataSource"/>

<property name="userByUserNameQuery" >
<value>
SELECT email as username, password, enabled
FROM t_users
WHERE email=?
</value>

</property>

<property name="authoritiesByUserNameQuery" >
<value>
SELECT email as username, role as authority
FROM t_user_role
WHERE email=?
</value>

</property>

</bean>
</beans>
```

Thus, with Spring Security, a few lines of configuration are enough to set up your authentication component. Once the user is successfully authenticated, the request is forwarded to the URL specified by the `defaultTargetURL`, which in this case is `/secure/app/createPolicy.do`.

Anonymous Processing Filter (ANPF)

This is the third filter in the chain. Its sole purpose is to set an anonymous `Authentication` object in the security context. This will allow you to browse certain URLs that are not secure and can be viewed without verifying user's identity with the application. ANPF can be configured as shown in Listing 6-13.

Listing 6-13. `applicationContext-security.xml`

```xml
<?xml version="1.0" encoding="UTF-8"?>
<!DOCTYPE beans PUBLIC "-//SPRING//DTD BEAN//EN"
"http://www.springframework.org/dtd/spring-beans.dtd">

<beans>

<!--Other beans -->

<bean id="anonymousProcessingFilter" class="org.springframework➥
.security.providers.anonymous.AnonymousProcessingFilter">
        <property name="key" value="changeThis"/>
        <property name="userAttribute" value="anonymousUser,ROLE_ANONYMOUS"/>
    </bean>

</beans>
```

Exception Translation Filter (ETF)

ETF handles any exception raised during authentication or authorization. It is configured in the application context as shown in Listing 6-14.

Listing 6-14. `applicationContext-security.xml`

```xml
<?xml version="1.0" encoding="UTF-8"?>
<!DOCTYPE beans PUBLIC "-//SPRING//DTD BEAN//EN"
"http://www.springframework.org/dtd/spring-beans.dtd">

<beans>

<!--Other beans -->

<bean id="exceptionTranslationFilter"
class="org.springframework.security.ui.ExceptionTranslationFilter">
        <property name="authenticationEntryPoint" ref="authenticationEntryPoint" />
        <property name="accessDeniedHandler"  ref="accessDeniedHandler" />
```

```
        </bean>

<bean name ="authenticationEntryPoint" class="org.springframework.➥
security.ui.webapp.AuthenticationProcessingFilterEntryPoint">
                <property name="loginFormUrl" value="/login.do"/>
                <property name="forceHttps" value="false"/>
</bean>
<bean name="accessDeniedHandler" class="org.springframework➥
.security.ui.AccessDeniedHandlerImpl">
                <property name="errorPage" value="/denied.do"/>
 </bean>

</beans>
```

The task of this filter is simple. In the case of an authentication exception, ETF uses the `authenticationEntryPoint` property to redirect the user to the login page. If there is an authorization failure, the user is redirected to the access-denied page.

Filter Security Interceptor (FSI)

This is another pivotal filter in Spring Security along with the authentication processing filter. The primary responsibility of the FSI is to assist in authorization. If an unauthenticated user tries to access a secured resource, FSI should prevent the user and force him to either an access-denied page or a login page. Even an authenticated user may have access to only a subset of the resources. The FSI ensures that a valid user accesses only the resources available to his role. It also allows users to access certain pages anonymously. The sign-on page, for example, should be available to all the users. The FSI is configured in the Spring application context, as in Listing 6-15.

Listing 6-15. `applicationContext-security.xml`

```
<?xml version="1.0" encoding="UTF-8"?>
<!DOCTYPE beans PUBLIC "-//SPRING//DTD BEAN//EN"
"http://www.springframework.org/dtd/spring-beans.dtd">

<beans>

<!—Other beans -->
   <bean id="filterInvocationInterceptor"
       class="org.springframework.➥
       security.intercept.web.FilterSecurityInterceptor">
       <property name="authenticationManager" ref="authenticationManager"/>
       <property name="accessDecisionManager" name="accessDecisionManager" />
```

```
        <property name="objectDefinitionSource">
            <value>
                CONVERT_URL_TO_LOWERCASE_BEFORE_COMPARISON
                PATTERN_TYPE_APACHE_ANT
                /secure/admin/**=ROLE_ADMIN
                /secure/**=IS_AUTHENTICATED_REMEMBERED
                /**=IS_AUTHENTICATED_ANONYMOUSLY
            </value>
        </property>
    </bean>

</beans>
```

The first property that I will focus on with the FSI is `objectDefinitionSource`. In Spring Security, secured resources are called *object definitions*. The name is generic because Spring Security can be applied to method invocation and object creation in addition to web applications. The `objectDefinitionSource` is composed of directives and URL pattern to role mapping. The directives are same as the ones used for the filter chain proxy in Listing 6-3.

A user with `ROLE_ADMIN` has access to all URLs starting with `/secure/admin`. Only authenticated users are allowed entry into all URLs starting with `/secure`. All other URLs can be accessed anonymously or if the user is already authenticated. Note that the URL mappings will be processed in the same order as they are defined. Also, you are free to define any role that you want for your application.

The property `authenticationManager` uses the same Spring bean that I used with the APF. It can be used to reauthenticate a request. This can hurt application performance, so you need to set it carefully, and you can control this by setting the `alwaysReauthenticate` property of the FSI to `false`. The property `accessDecisionManager` works like authentication managers and is responsible for making the actual authorization decision. The access decision manager is wired up as shown in Listing 6-16.

Listing 6-16. `applicationContext-security.xml`

```
<?xml version="1.0" encoding="UTF-8"?>
<!DOCTYPE beans PUBLIC "-//SPRING//DTD BEAN//EN"
"http://www.springframework.org/dtd/spring-beans.dtd">

<beans>

<!—Other beans -->
```

```
<bean name="accessDecisionManager"
        class="org.springframework.security.vote.AffirmativeBased">
         <property name="decisionVoters">
            <list>
                 <bean class="org.springframework.security.vote.RoleVoter"/>
                 <bean class="org.springframework.security.vote.AuthenticatedVoter"/>
            </list>
         </property>
    </bean>

</beans>
```

The access decision managers implement the `AccessDecisionManager` interface. In this case, I am using the `AffirmativeBased` access decision manager. This access decision manager is controlled by a list of voters. It is similar to voting in an election. These voters decide whether a user can actually access a particular protected resource. The access decision manager will poll each voter for a vote. The possible values are `ACCESS_DENIED`, `ACCESS_GRANTED`, and `ACCESS_ABSTAIN` (when the voter is unsure). Once the voting is done, the `AffirmativeBased` access decision manager executes a simple algorithm to arrive at the result. If any of the voters vote with `ACCESS_GRANTED`, the user is granted access.

The access decision manager supplies each voter with the `Authentication` object and the `objectDefinitionSource` to make their decisions. The `RoleVoter` scans through the list of URL pattern to role mappings. For the matched URL, it will check the roles. It will vote if it finds a role starting with the prefix `ROLE`. You can alter this value by setting the `rolePrefix` property. If it finds a matching role, it votes `ACCESS_GRANTED`; otherwise, it votes `ACCESS_DENIED`. The `AuthenticatedVoter` will vote if it finds a predefined role in any of the matched URL to role mapping. One such predefined value is `IS_AUTHENTICATED_ANONYMOUSLY`. It will probe the `Authentication` object to determine whether the user has been authenticated anonymously. A positive finding will result in `ACCESS_GRANTED` being voted.

Consequences

Benefits

- Spring Security can be enabled and altered by mere configuration.

- Only users with valid identities are allowed access to the system.

- Spring Security does not intrude into the application code. In fact, it can be applied without the application code having any knowledge about it.

- Authenticated users can access only a subset of the application resources based on their roles.

Concerns

- You need to know about a lot of classes, interfaces, and above all configuration items. This adds to the development and maintenance overhead.

Audit Interceptor

Problem

The auditing of business tier method invocation is a common requirement in most enterprise applications. This involves tracing the input arguments as well as the return values. The audit trail information can be later utilized for analysis in the case of any security lapses. Because this data may be needed for future reference, it is stored in a permanent store such as a filesystem or database. The audit trailing feature is applied at the business tier because it is the gateway to the business logic and can be accessed by a variety of clients.

Since eInsure handled sensitive financial data, it too implemented an audit trail feature. This was used in the SLSBs. The audit trail API saved the method arguments and returned results in the database. This was also inflexible and mixed the business logic with the security concerns. This coupling led to frequent code changes as eInsure tried to fit in a customer-specific audit trail requirement. The SLSB in the eInsure application internally invoked multiple other session bean methods, each of which also used the audit trail API. Since the audit data was saved in the database, it increased the transactional overhead and degraded response time.

The eInsure audit trail API was hardly configurable. As a result, it was difficult to switch on/off the audit trailing as and when required. It also did not allow the flexibility to filter what was being logged. For example, in certain cases you may not be interested to log only the values being passed to a method as arguments and not the value returned by the method. Also, you may not want to log all the values in the returned object. The eInsure audit trail also required that the incoming and outgoing objects must implement the `toString` method. Though this is a good practice, it often clutters code with long lines of calls to `StringBuffer.append` or those using `String` concatenation.

Forces

- Apply the audit trailing transparently on the business service.

- The audit trailing must be configurable.

- Allow an audit trace of requests, responses, and exceptions raised from a service.

Solution

Implement a centralized *audit interceptor* that can be declaratively used to apply the auditing of the business service invocations.

Strategies with the Spring Framework

You can easily develop an audit interceptor with Spring AOP support. With AOP, you can build the audit trail component as an independent reusable component and then apply it transparently with configuration. Since the audit interceptor needs to support the pre- and postprocessing of methods along with the exceptions, the first step to building the interceptor is to develop an *advice*. An advice denotes a reusable piece of code that can be applied transparently to the actual application code. Since the SLSBs are container-managed components, I will apply the interceptor on the application service POJOs. Listing 6-17 shows the audit interceptor advice.

Listing 6-17. `AuditAdviseInterceptor.java`

```java
public class AuditAdviseInterceptor implements MethodInterceptor {

    private AuditRules rules;
    private boolean auditOn = true;
    private AuditLog auditLog;

    public Object invoke(MethodInvocation invocation) throws Throwable {
        Object returnVal = null;
        String eventCode = "";
        Object arguments[] = null;

        try {
            returnVal = invocation.proceed();
        } catch (Exception exp) {
```

```
            //handle exception
            throw e;
        } finally {
            //post process
            if (this.auditOn) {
                eventCode = getEventCode();
                arguments = invocation.getArguments();
                AuditRule rule = rules.getRule(eventCode);
                if(rule!=null && rule.isApplyRule()){
                    String thisMethod = invocation.getMethod().getName();
                    if(thisMethod.equals(rule.getRuleDefinition())){
                        AuditEvent ae = new AuditEvent(eventCode,arguments,
                results,exp);

                        auditLog.log(ae);
                    }
                }
            }
        }
        return returnVal;
    }

    private String getEventCode() {
        String eventCode = "";
        StackTraceElement[] stack = Thread.currentThread().getStackTrace();

        eventCode = stack[7].getMethodName();
        return eventCode;
    }

    public AuditRules getRules() {
        return rules;
    }

    public void setRules(AuditRules rules) {
        this.rules = rules;
    }

    public boolean isAuditOn() {
        return auditOn;
    }
```

```
    public void setAuditOn(boolean auditOn) {
        this.auditOn = auditOn;
    }
}
```

A lot is going on in this class. This class implements the Spring AOP class
MethodInterceptor to provide around advice. The key here is the invoke method. This
method is called before and after the invocation of the target business method that you
want to audit. The audit trail operation happens in the finally block. The property
auditOn can be used to globally stop the audit trail.

If the audit trail flag is set to true, then an event code is determined by the invoke
method. Here, for simplicity, I have assumed that coarse-grained session facade method
name as the event code. This event code should be unique and used to look up an audit
rule from the audit rule list. If an audit rule is found for this event code and this rule is
not disabled, then the rule definition is consulted to see whether it is applicable to the
current application service method. Finally, the data in the audit event is traced by an
audit logger. Listing 6-18 shows how this class is wired in the Spring configuration.

Listing 6-18. audit-config.xml

```
<?xml version="1.0" encoding="UTF-8"?>
<beans xmlns="http://www.springframework.org/schema/beans"
       xmlns:xsi="http://www.w3.org/2001/XMLSchema-instance"
       xsi:schemaLocation="http://www.springframework.org/schema/beans
http://www.springframework.org/schema/beans/spring-beans-2.5.xsd">

    <!--advice -->
    <bean name="auditAdvice"
          class="com.apress.einsure.security.audit.AuditAdviseInterceptor">

<property name="rules" >
            <bean class="com.apress.einsure.security.audit.AuditRules" >
                <property name="ruleMap" >
                    <map>
                        <entry>
                            <key><value>underwriteNewPolicy</value></key>
                            <bean
class="com.apress.einsure.security.audit.AuditRule" >
                                <property name="ruleDefinition" value="com.apress➥
.einsure.business.impl.UnderwritingApplicationService.underwriteNewPolicy" />
                                <property name="applyRule" value="true"></property>
```

```
                              </bean>
                          </entry>
                      </map>
                  </property>
              </bean>
          </property>
      </bean>

      <!--other beans -->

  </beans>
```

The `rules` property is used to externalize the rules that are applicable for a particular audit event. The `AuditRules` class acts as a container for the audit rules, as shown in Listing 6-19.

Listing 6-19. `AuditRules.java`

```java
public class AuditRules{
    public Map ruleMap;
    public AuditRule getRule(String key){
        return (AuditRule)ruleMap.get(key);
    }

    public Map getRuleMap() {
        return ruleMap;
    }

    public void setRuleMap(Map ruleMap) {
        this.ruleMap = ruleMap;
    }
}
```

Each rule is an instance of the class `AuditRule`. In the current example, I'm using a very simple rule. I just check whether the current method being intercepted is in the rule definition. There is also a fine-grained control to turn off this rule. You can do this by setting the `applyRule` property. Listing 6-20 shows the `AuditRule` class.

Listing 6-20. `AuditRule.java`

```java
public class AuditRule {
    private String ruleDefinition;
    private boolean applyRule = true;
    public boolean isApplyRule() {
        return applyRule;
    }

    public void setApplyRule(boolean applyRule) {
        this.applyRule = applyRule;
    }

    public String getRuleDefinition() {
        return ruleDefinition;
    }

    public void setRuleDefinition(String ruleDefinition) {
        this.ruleDefinition = ruleDefinition;
    }

}
```

The `AuditEvent` class is a simple bean that stores the data that has to be logged as part of audit trail. It is shown in Listing 6-21. The `ToStringBuilder` class is part of the Jakarta Commons-lang project and can be used to simplify the `toString` method.

Listing 6-21. `AuditEvent.java`

```java
public class AuditEvent {
    private String eventCode;
    private String fullMethodName;
    private Object arguments[];
    private Object result;
    public String toString(){
        return ToStringBuilder.reflectionToString(this);
    }
}
```

Now that you have collected the audit data, it has to be logged. You can adopt various strategies to store this data. It can be stored in a database, filesystem, Microsoft Windows Event Log, or Unix syslog. Hence, this component needs to be pluggable. I will follow the simple principle of program to interface for this purpose. The AuditLog interface just defines the single method log, which accepts an AuditEvent object. You can implement this interface to provide a custom implementation. I have used an Apache Commons Logger–based implementation to log the messages to the console, as shown in Listing 6-22.

Listing 6-22. CommonsLoggingAuditLogImplt.java

```java
public class CommonsLoggingAuditLogImpl implements AuditLog{
    private final Log _LOG = LogFactory.getLog(getClass());
    public void log(AuditEvent event) {
        _LOG.info(event);
    }
}
```

An instance of this logger is injected into the audit advices, as shown in Listing 6-23.

Listing 6-23. audit-config.xml

```xml
<?xml version="1.0" encoding="UTF-8"?>
<beans xmlns="http://www.springframework.org/schema/beans"
       xmlns:xsi="http://www.w3.org/2001/XMLSchema-instance"
       xsi:schemaLocation="http://www.springframework.org/schema/beans
http://www.springframework.org/schema/beans/spring-beans-2.5.xsd">

    <!--advice -->
    <bean name="auditAdvice"
          class="com.apress.einsure.security.audit.AuditAdviseInterceptor">

    <property name="auditLog" ref="auditLogger" />

            <!- - other properties    -->

    </bean>

    <bean name="auditLogger" class="com.apress.einsure.security.audit.AuditRule"  />

    <!--other beans -->

</beans>
```

To apply this audit advice, you need a *pointcut*. In AOP, a pointcut determines where to apply this advice. You can combine an advice and pointcut into an advisor. Listing 6-24 shows the advisor for this example.

Listing 6-24. `audit-config.xml`

```xml
<?xml version="1.0" encoding="UTF-8"?>
<beans xmlns="http://www.springframework.org/schema/beans"
       xmlns:xsi="http://www.w3.org/2001/XMLSchema-instance"
       xsi:schemaLocation="http://www.springframework.org/schema/beans
http://www.springframework.org/schema/beans/spring-beans-2.5.xsd">

    <!--advisor -->
        <bean id="auditAdvisor"
           class="org.springframework.aop.aspectj.AspectJExpressionPointcutAdvisor">
          <property name="advice" ref="auditAdvice" />
          <property name="expression" value="execution(* *.underwrite*(..))" />
    </bean>

    <!–other beans -->

</beans>
```

As shown in Listing 6-24, the audit advice is applicable to any method starting with the word `underwrite`. Finally, you need to create proxies for the beans matching the expression property of the advisor. Listing 6-25 shows the automatic proxy creator bean.

Listing 6-25. `audit-config.xml`

```xml
<?xml version="1.0" encoding="UTF-8"?>
<beans xmlns="http://www.springframework.org/schema/beans"
       xmlns:xsi="http://www.w3.org/2001/XMLSchema-instance"
       xsi:schemaLocation="http://www.springframework.org/schema/beans
http://www.springframework.org/schema/beans/spring-beans-2.5.xsd">

    <!--advisor -->
        <bean id="auditAdvisor"
           class="org.springframework.aop.aspectj.AspectJExpressionPointcutAdvisor">
          <property name="advice" ref="auditAdvice" />
          <property name="expression" value="execution(* *.underwrite*(..))" />
    </bean>
```

```
    <bean class="org.springframework.aop.framework.autoproxy➥
    .DefaultAdvisorAutoProxyCreator" />
  <!—other beans -->

</beans>
```

Note that this bean does not require a name or ID attribute because it will be used by the Spring AOP module internally. It will check beans for method names matching the advisor and will create appropriate proxies to intercept calls to the method.

Consequences

Benefits

- With Spring AOP support, the audit trail can be applied declaratively on the POJO application service components.

- It has support for a variety of options for logging the audit trail.

- The Spring AOP–based audit trail has no impact on the application code.

Concerns

- Upfront knowledge of AOP is required, which is considered difficult for junior developers.

- Spring AOP makes extensive use of proxies and bytecode generation. This adds to performance overhead.

Domain Service Owner Transaction

Problem

Transaction management is a critical concern for any enterprise application. It is essential to maintain the consistency of enterprise data. Transaction management is a complex system concern because it involves interacting with a variety of enterprise information systems. In Java EE servers, the applications can leverage the EJB container's robust support for distributed transaction. All the different types of EJBs—session, entity, and message-driven beans—can subscribe to transactions declaratively. This often puts the application designers in a dilemma when they get down to devising strategies for transaction management. Consider the cases when your session bean accesses a number of entity beans or when a message-driven bean invokes remote methods on a session bean. Even with declarative Java EE transaction support, it becomes difficult to make crucial decisions such as where to start a transaction, how to propagate a transaction, and where to end it.

Sometimes Java EE applications are required to support non-web-based clients such as Java Swing–based desktop software. These clients more often than not resort to client-managed transactions. This is done programmatically with JTA. This, however, dilutes the core goal of the Swing clients to act only as the view tier. This also results in multiple fine-grained calls to the business logic on the server, which leads to a surge in network traffic. This also greatly reduces the benefits of server-based distributed computing. Developing, testing, and maintaining applications with client tier programmatic transaction are complicated tasks.

In Chapter 4, I mentioned a client of eInsure who wanted us to deploy the entire application on Apache Tomcat, which is a web server and servlet container. Tomcat does not have an EJB container. So, the EJBs did not work in Tomcat, and there was no transaction management support. An immediate option was to use JDBC-based transaction support. But this would be cumbersome and would require a lot of code to be written as well as refactored. Another solution was to use open source transaction monitors such as ObjectWeb JOTM or Atomikos Essentials. But using them would pose the same problems as with client-managed transactions.

Forces

- Avoid client-managed transactions wherever possible.

- Support declarative transaction management to be applied transparently.

- Declarative transaction management should work outside the EJB container as well.

Solution

Deploy a *domain service owner transaction* to declaratively apply transactions both in and out of the EJB container.

Strategies with the Spring Framework

In a Java EE application, an SLSB implements the domain service for a remote client. The SLSB is the most useful EJB component and can be used extensively for remoting and transaction support. However, as shown in Chapter 4, writing and maintaining an EJB is cumbersome because it involves a lot of classes and metadata. Also, they have little importance if your application needs to run out of an EJB container or in a web container. Moreover, a session facade intercepts only a remote business logic request, so in a strict sense the application service actually implements the domain service.

With the Spring Framework, it is possible to provide declarative transaction support even to POJO application service components. This makes an application highly portable. You can now deploy this application in a web container with just a few configuration changes. This application, with the POJO domain service, can also continue to run in the EJB container and subscribe to container-managed transactions. Thus, with the Spring Framework, you do not need an EJB to support transactions.

The Spring Framework neither implements any transaction monitor nor tries to directly manage transactions. Instead, it delegates to the underlying transaction implementation through an abstraction called a *platform transaction manager*. There are transaction manager implementations for most of the widely used platforms—JDBC, object-relational mapping such as Hibernate and TopLink, JTA, JCA, and all major application servers. In the next few sections, I will review some frequently used transaction managers.

Plain JDBC Transactions

The DataSourceTransactionManager handles all the transactional requirements if straight JDBC or Spring DAO is being used in the application. It can be configured in the Spring application context as shown in Listing 6-26.

Listing 6-26. transaction-config.xml

```
<beans>
<bean id="datasourceTransactionManager" class="org.springframework.➥
jdbc.datasource.DataSourceTransactionManager">
<property name="dataSource" ref="dataSource"/>
</bean>
<beans>
```

The DataSourceTransactionManager works with a javax.sql.DataSource object. It ensures that the same Connection object is retrieved from the DataSource and used in a transaction. If the transaction is successful, the commit method is invoked on the Connection object. If the transaction is a failure, the rollback method will be used. In short, this transaction manager delegates the actual transaction processing to the database.

Hibernate Transactions

HibernateTransactionManager can be used to manage transactions if your application uses Hibernate ORM to manage application persistence. This transaction manager works with the Hibernate SessionFactory object. It delegates the transaction handling to the org.hibernate.Transaction object retrieved from the Hibernate Session object. The commit and rollback methods will be called on this Transaction object depending on successful and failed transactions, respectively. The HibernateTransactionManager is wired in the Spring configuration, as shown in Listing 6-27.

Listing 6-27. `transaction-config.xml`

```
<beans>
<bean id="hibernateTransactionManager" class="org.springframework.➥
orm.hibernate.HibernateTransactionManager
">
<property name="sessionFactory
" ref="hibernateSessionFactory
"/>
</bean>
<beans>
```

JPA Transactions

The Java Persistence API is the new persistence standard in EJB 3, replacing the widely disliked entity beans. Spring also supports JPA transactions through the JpaTransactionManager. This is configured in the Spring application context, as in Listing 6-28.

Listing 6-28. `transaction-config.xml`

```
<beans>
<bean id="jpaTransactionManager"
class="org.springframework.orm.jpa.JpaTransactionManager">
<property name="entityManagerFactory"
ref="entityManagerFactory" />
</bean>
</beans>
```

Note that this transaction manager needs an entity manager factory, that is, an implementation of the `javax.persistence.EntityManagerFactory`. This factory provides the `EntityManager`. The `JpaTransactionManager` uses this `EntityManager` to coordinate transactions.

JTA Transactions

The transaction managers described earlier are not very suitable for distributed XA transactions. XA describes a protocol to coordinate transactions involving multiple transaction and resource managers. BEA WebLogic Server and JBoss Application Server (AS) are examples of transaction managers. They manage transactions involving multiple resource managers such as databases, messaging providers such as IBM MQ Series, mainframes, and so on.

In such scenarios you will need to use the `JTATransactionManager`. It generally delegates the transaction handling responsibility to the underlying JTA implementation provided by BEA WebLogic Server, JBoss AS, ObjectWeb JOTM, or Atomikos. Listing 6-29 shows the configuration of `JTATransactionManager`.

Listing 6-29. `transaction-config.xml`

```
<beans>
<bean id="transactionManager" class="org.springframework.➡
transaction.jta.JtaTransactionManager">
<property name="transactionManagerName"
value="java:/TransactionManager" />
</bean>
</beans>
```

`JtaTransactionManager` works with the `javax.transaction.UserTransaction` and `javax.transaction.TransactionManager` objects, delegating responsibility for transaction management to those objects. A successful transaction will be committed with a call to the `UserTransaction.commit` method. Likewise, if the transaction fails, the `UserTransaction.rollback` method will be called.

Application Server Transaction

`JTATransactionManager` can work with application server transaction support. However, application servers differ significantly with regard to their transaction management implementation. They also provide varying degrees of transaction optimizations. To leverage them, Spring comes with a few application-server specific transaction managers: `WeblogicJtaTransactionManager` (BEA WebLogic), `WebsphereUowTransactionManager` (IBM WebSphere), and `OC4JtaTransactionManager` (Oracle Application Server).

Declarative Transaction

Declarative transaction management support is immensely useful for applications because it has the least impact on source code. It is nonintrusive and allows transaction to be applied to a component transparently. The Spring Framework supports declarative transaction management through its AOP module. In the next few sections, I will show how Spring declarative transactions can be applied to the application service classes discussed in Chapter 4.

The first step to using Spring declarative transaction is to create an advice. In the case of transaction management, the transaction manager applies an advice, as shown in Listing 6-30.

Listing 6-30. `transaction-config.xml`

```xml
<?xml version="1.0" encoding="UTF-8"?>
<beans xmlns="http://www.springframework.org/schema/beans"
    xmlns:xsi="http://www.w3.org/2001/XMLSchema-instance"
    xmlns:aop="http://www.springframework.org/schema/aop"
    xmlns:tx="http://www.springframework.org/schema/tx"
    xsi:schemaLocation="
    http://www.springframework.org/schema/beans
http://www.springframework.org/schema/beans/spring-beans-2.5.xsd
    http://www.springframework.org/schema/tx
http://www.springframework.org/schema/tx/spring-tx-2.5.xsd
    http://www.springframework.org/schema/aop
http://www.springframework.org/schema/aop/spring-aop-2.5.xsd">

  <!-- this is the service object on which the transaction has to be applied -->
  <bean name="uwrAppService"
```

```
                class="com.apress.einsure.business.impl.➥
            UnderwritingApplicationServiceImpl">
    </bean>

    <!-- the transactional advice decides what needs to be done -->
    <tx:advice id="txAdvice" transaction-manager="txManager">
            <!- - More - - >
    </tx>



    <!--  DataSource -->
    <bean id="dataSource" class="org.apache.commons.➥
        dbcp.BasicDataSource" destroy-method="close">
    <property name="driverClassName" value="oracle.jdbc.driver.OracleDriver"/>
    <property name="url" value="jdbc:oracle:thin:@eInsureDev:1525:eInsure"/>
    <property name="username" value="scott"/>
    <property name="password" value="tiger"/>
    </bean>

    <!--  Platform Transaction Manager, in this straight jdbd -->
    <bean id="txManager" class="org.springframework.jdbc.➥
        datasource.DataSourceTransactionManager">
    <property name="dataSource" ref="dataSource"/>
    </bean>

    <!-- other beans -->

</beans>
```

Note that I have introduced the namespace and schema for simplifying AOP and transaction configuration. In the previous example, I have assumed the application uses straight JDBC for persistence and hence configured the DataSourceTransactionManager. This will be used to apply transactional advice on the POJO application service. If you want to use another platform transaction manager, it's just a matter of configuration.

As you saw earlier with AOP, an advice needs to be combined with a pointcut to form an advisor, as shown in Listing 6-31.

Listing 6-31. `transaction-config.xml`

```xml
<?xml version="1.0" encoding="UTF-8"?>
<beans xmlns="http://www.springframework.org/schema/beans"
     xmlns:xsi="http://www.w3.org/2001/XMLSchema-instance"
     xmlns:aop="http://www.springframework.org/schema/aop"
     xmlns:tx="http://www.springframework.org/schema/tx"
     xsi:schemaLocation="
     http://www.springframework.org/schema/beans
http://www.springframework.org/schema/beans/spring-beans-2.5.xsd
     http://www.springframework.org/schema/tx
http://www.springframework.org/schema/tx/spring-tx-2.5.xsd
     http://www.springframework.org/schema/aop
 http://www.springframework.org/schema/aop/spring-aop-2.5.xsd">

  <!-- this is the service object on which the transaction has to be applied -->
   <bean name="uwrAppService"
            class="com.apress.einsure.business.➥
        impl.UnderwritingApplicationServiceImpl">
    </bean>

  <!-- the transactional advice decides what needs to be done -->
  <tx:advice id="txAdvice" transaction-manager="txManager">

     <!- - More - ->
  </tx>
  <!--  DataSource -->
  <bean id="dataSource" class="org.apache.commons.dbcp.BasicDataSource"
        destroy-method="close">
  <property name="driverClassName" value="oracle.jdbc.driver.OracleDriver"/>
  <property name="url" value="jdbc:oracle:thin:@eInsureDev:1525:eInsure"/>
  <property name="username" value="scott"/>
  <property name="password" value="tiger"/>
  </bean>

  <!--  Platform Transaction Manager, in this case straight jdbc -->
  <bean id="txManager"
        class="org.springframework.jdbc.➥
               datasource.DataSourceTransactionManager">
  <property name="dataSource" ref="dataSource"/>
  </bean>
```

```
<aop:config>
  <aop:pointcut id="uwrServiceMethods" expression="execution➥
(* com.apress.einsure.business.*.Underwriting*.*(..))"/>
  <aop:advisor advice-ref="txAdvice" pointcut-ref="uwrServiceMethods"/>
</aop:config>

<!-- other beans -->
```

```
</beans>
```

Finally, I will set up the transaction attributes applicable to the methods of the application service, as shown in Listing 6-32.

Listing 6-32. transaction-config.xml

```
<?xml version="1.0" encoding="UTF-8"?>
<beans xmlns="http://www.springframework.org/schema/beans"
    xmlns:xsi="http://www.w3.org/2001/XMLSchema-instance"
    xmlns:aop="http://www.springframework.org/schema/aop"
    xmlns:tx="http://www.springframework.org/schema/tx"
    xsi:schemaLocation="
 http://www.springframework.org/schema/beans
http://www.springframework.org/schema/beans/spring-beans-2.5.xsd
http://www.springframework.org/schema/tx
http://www.springframework.org/schema/tx/spring-tx-2.5.xsd
http://www.springframework.org/schema/aop
http://www.springframework.org/schema/aop/spring-aop-2.5.xsd">

  <!-- this is the service object on which the transaction has to be applied -->
  <bean name="uwrAppService"
          class="com.apress.einsure.business.impl.➥
      UnderwritingApplicationServiceImpl">
  </bean>

  <!-- the transactional advice decides what needs to be done -->
  <tx:advice id="txAdvice" transaction-manager="txManager">

  <tx:attributes>
      <!-- all methods starting with 'list' fetch data from db, hence read-only -->
      <tx:method name="list*" read-only="true"/>
```

```
    <!-- other methods use the default transaction propagation attribute REQUIRES
-->
    <tx:method name="underwrite*"/>

    <tx:method name="update*" propagation="REQUIRES_NEW"/>

    </tx:attributes>

  </tx:advice>

  <!-- DataSource -->

  <!-- Platform Transaction Manager, in this straight jdbd -->
  <bean id="txManager" class="org.springframework.jdbc➥
      .datasource.DataSourceTransactionManager">
  <property name="dataSource" ref="dataSource"/>
  </bean>

  <aop:config>
    <aop:pointcut id="uwrServiceMethods" expression="execution(*➥
com.apress.einsure.business.*.Underwriting*.*(..))"/>
    <aop:advisor advice-ref="txAdvice" pointcut-ref="uwrServiceMethods"/>
  </aop:config>


  <!-- other beans -->

</beans>
```

The transaction attributes have been set with the AOP advice. All methods starting with `list` are read-only and do not participate in transactions. Methods starting with `underwrite` are associated with a default transactional propagation attribute of `REQUIRED`. This is similar to the EJB transaction setting. An invocation of the `underwriteNewpolicy` method on `UnderwritingApplicationService` will result in this method, either starting a new transaction or joining an existing transaction. Similarly, any update method will run in a new transaction scope.

Unlike in EJBs, the Spring Framework supports a declarative rollback configuration as well. In general, if a `Runtime` exception (or its subclass) is thrown from the POJO application service method, Spring will mark that transaction for rollback. It is possible to specify the exceptions that will result in rollback. You can also configure the exceptions that will not cause a rollback, as shown in Listing 6-33.

Listing 6-33. `transaction-config.xml`

```xml
<?xml version="1.0" encoding="UTF-8"?>
<beans xmlns="http://www.springframework.org/schema/beans"
    xmlns:xsi="http://www.w3.org/2001/XMLSchema-instance"
    xmlns:aop="http://www.springframework.org/schema/aop"
    xmlns:tx="http://www.springframework.org/schema/tx"
    xsi:schemaLocation="
    http://www.springframework.org/schema/beans
http://www.springframework.org/schema/beans/spring-beans-2.5.xsd
ttp://www.springframework.org/schema/tx
http://www.springframework.org/schema/tx/spring-tx-2.5.xsd
http://www.springframework.org/schema/aop
http://www.springframework.org/schema/aop/spring-aop-2.5.xsd">

  <!-- this is the service object on which the transaction has to be applied -->
   <bean name="uwrAppService"
           class="com.apress.einsure.business.impl.➥
       UnderwritingApplicationServiceImpl">
    </bean>

  <!-- the transactional advice decides what needs to be done -->
  <tx:advice id="txAdvice" transaction-manager="txManager">

   <tx:attributes>
       <!-- all methods starting with 'list' fetch data from db, hence read-only -->
       <tx:method name="list*" read-only="true"/>

       <!-- other methods use the default transaction propagation
         attribute REQUIRES -->
     <tx:method name="underwrite*" rollback-for="ProductRuleViolationException"/>

     <tx:method name="update*" propagation="REQUIRES_NEW" ➥
      no-rollback-for="TruncatedFirstNameException"/>

   </tx:attributes>

  </tx:advice>

  <!-- other beans -->

</beans>
```

Consequences

Benefits

- Declarative transaction support has no impact on existing source code.

- With the Spring declarative transaction and different transaction manager support, the same application can be switched from the application server to the web server with few configuration changes.

- Spring transactions have configurable rollback support.

- Stand-alone applications are no longer required to use programmatic transactions. These applications can now leverage Spring declarative transaction support outside the container as well.

Concerns

- Transaction and AOP concepts are difficult to grasp for less experienced developers. So, a significant learning curve is involved in using Spring or even EJB declarative transactions.

Summary

In this chapter, I discussed some critical Java EE application aspects that are generally ignored or are mostly afterthoughts. Security design is of utmost importance for any enterprise application, and much has been written on this subject. This is especially important for Java EE applications because they service a variety of clients. The Authentication and Authorization Enforcer pattern can be used to prevent any malicious access to system resources. With out-of-the-box support from Spring Security, you can set up a security layer with mere configuration.

An audit trail is another widely used but often ignored concern in Java EE applications. With Spring AOP-based interceptor support, it is possible to deploy a robust, nonintrusive, and declarative audit trail system. Although EJB containers provide comprehensive transaction support, it comes with a price. Your codebase will not run outside the EJB container, thus severely limiting portability. With Spring AOP-based declarative transaction support, the domain service objects run almost seamlessly in EJB containers, web containers, and stand-alone components.

Finally, with the crosscutting patterns, I will end the journey of exploring Java EE patterns with the Spring Framework. In the next chapter, I will apply the concepts explored so far to build the architecture and design of an order management system. So, read on because I will introduce some interesting design and architecture artifacts in the process.

CHAPTER 7

■■■

Case Study: Building an Order Management System

I explored the architecture and design of Java EE applications in the earlier chapters. I also explained the Java EE design patterns with regard to the Spring Framework. Now it's time to put all the concepts you've learned so far together to build a basic application. In this chapter, I will apply the Spring Java EE patterns in the context of an order management system (OMS). This is a simplified version of an OMS that I once built for a telecom company that was used by their customers to register for value-added services such as ringtones, video broadcasting, voicemail, and so on. Using this OMS, users can sign in and then look up and order services. They can also search, cancel, and suspend their orders. The primary focus will be on building a lightweight architecture and design. I will also demonstrate the steps to develop, test, and deploy this application.

For this example OMS, I will borrow heavily from extreme programming (XP) principles. When applied properly, XP offers immense flexibility for project teams compared to other methodologies that stress planning and invest significant effort on up-front architecture and design. An application framework such as Spring, backed by IDE support, is best suited for agile software development. If you are new to XP, then you can visit `http://www.extremeprogramming.org` for a quick tour of the features and workflow. In the rest of this chapter, I will go through a customized XP iteration to develop the foundation of the order management system. As you read on, you will see that in some parts of this chapter I will leave some solution or development tasks as an exercise for you. I've done this to get you to think about what you have learned in the previous chapters. It also makes reading this chapter more interesting and interactive. If you want to validate your solutions and development tasks, then visit `http://www.opengarage.org`, where I have posted the entire solution and code for this chapter.

Requirements

To start any software development project, you need some documented business requirements. XP employs *user stories* for documenting requirements. Each user story describes how the system is going to solve a business problem. Each is a very short description of the requirement and is often accompanied by acceptance test cases. Thus, there is a clear traceability from the requirements to the tests. A user story is written on a *story card*.

   With agile processes, it is not necessary that you have all the requirements in place before starting a project. To start the first iteration, you need just a few requirements. The user stories coming after the start of the first iteration are added to the requirements backlog. A few of them will be picked from the backlog based on their priority for implementation in a future iteration until the backlog has been cleared. For the OMS in this chapter, I have picked up three requirements with the highest priority for the first iteration. The priority is set by the customer, and it is used to determine whether a requirement will be taken up from the backlog for implementation in the next iteration. The user stories for these requirements are described in the next sections.

Story Card: Sign In Users

The system allows only registered users to sign in with a username and password. In the case of a sign-in failure, the user will be notified with a generic error message and prompted to sign in again. On successful sign-in, the user is taken to the home page with a link to save the order.

   Acceptance test set: AT-01

   Priority: 1

Story Card: Look Up Services

The system should provide a facility to look up services available to order for authenticated users only. This opens in a new pop-up window. When the user selects a service, this pop-up closes, supplying the appropriate values to the parent page.

   Acceptance test set: AT-02

   Priority: 1

Story Card: Save Order

The system allows authenticated users to save an order with a unique order identifier. This identifier can be used later to search an order. The users need to use a lookup function to select the order items. In the first release, the system will allow only one item per order.

Acceptance test set: AT-03

Priority: 1

Iteration Planning

Once the requirements are identified, it's time for *iteration planning*. Iteration planning generally produces a plan for the programming and unit testing tasks to be carried out for the current iteration. You should also add architecture, design, coding standards compliance, and refactoring to the iteration plan. Each iteration lasts 14 to 21 working days on average. In the first couple of iterations, more time is spent on architecture and design evolutions. You should not spend more than two to three iterations baselining your architecture and design, after which the programming tasks should take precedence.

You can use advanced software such as Microsoft Project for your project management and planning needs. However, keeping with the XP philosophy of simplicity and flexibility, you can use spreadsheet software such as Microsoft Excel or OpenOffice Calc for quick planning and tracking. Figure 7-1 shows the plan and tracker for the first iteration of the example OMS created using Microsoft Excel.

St#	Task	Estimated Hour	Hours Used	Remaining	Actual Hours Used	Start Date	End Date	Actual End Date	Variance	Status	Remarks	Resource
1	Architecture	24	1	23	1	14-Jul-08	16-Jul-08		-0.95833	IN PROGRESS		DHRUBO
2	Design	32	0	32	0	17-Jul-08	22-Jul-08		-1	TO START		DHRUBO
3	Dev + Unit Test - Login	32	0	32	0	23-Jul-08	28-Jul-08		-1	TO START		DHRUBO
4	Dev + Unit Test - Lookup Services	24	0	24	0	29-Jul-08	31-Jul-08		-1	TO START		SUDIP
5	Dev + Unit Test - Save Order	24	0	24	0	29-Jul-08	31-Jul-08		-1	TO START		PROSENJIT
6	Integration and Release	16	0	16	0	1-Aug-08	4-Aug-08		-1	TO START		DHRUBO

Figure 7-1. *Plan and tracker for iteration 1*

As shown in Figure 7-1, each row in the tracker represents a task that needs to be carried out in the iteration. As part of the planning and tracking, you have the generic attributes such as estimated hours, actual hours, start date, end date, and so on. You can also see the resource or person who has been entrusted with a particular task. One important attribute worth noting in this planner is *variance*. Variance helps keep track of the "health" of the iteration. A positive variance generally indicates that a task has taken longer than initially estimated. You can also maintain an overall project summary tracker, as shown in Figure 7-2. This gives a quick snapshot of the overall progress of a project.

Order Management Tracker Summary						
Iteration	Total Planned Hours	Hours Consumed	Hours Remaining	Actual Hours Consumed	Variance	Health
1	152	1	151	1	-0.99342	

Figure 7-2. *Overall project summary tracker*

Architecture

Traditional projects tend to build a complete application architecture in a planned way. However, experience has shown that this big-bang approach often results in failures. Application architecture depends on a variety of factors including the functional and nonfunctional requirements. It is not always possible to think and incorporate all the issues that affect architecture in advance. As the customers business requirements change and the team gets deep into the development phase, the cracks in the architecture are revealed.

XP, on the contrary, believes in evolutionary architecture. Architecture-related tasks consume a significant portion of the time in the first few iterations. The project starts with a base architecture that evolves through the iterations. Figure 7-3 shows the architecture for the example OMS.

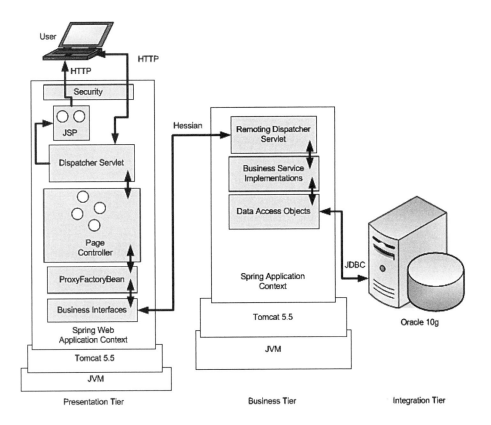

Figure 7-3. *Architecture of the example OMS*

As shown in Figure 7-3, the OMS is divided into three distinct tiers. Each tier is divided into layers with distinct roles.

Presentation Tier

The presentation tier is primarily responsible for processing the incoming request and preparing the HTML-based view to be rendered on the browser. It is also responsible for invoking the business logic. The data returned by the business tier is then used to produce the response for the client.

Security

This component is responsible for allowing secured access to the presentation tier resources.

JSP

Java Server Pages (JSP) provides the view components of the OMS application.

Dispatcher Servlet

The dispatcher servlet intercepts all the incoming requests that cross the security layer. It invokes the appropriate page controller for each user action. It is also responsible for picking up the appropriate view component and merging it with the model to prepare the final response.

Page Controller

A page controller is invoked by the dispatcher servlet for each action triggered by the user. The page controller in turn interacts with the business tier components. It takes the model returned by the business tier and a logical reference to the next view and passes them to the dispatcher servlet.

Proxy Factory Bean and Business Interfaces

The proxy factory bean and the business interfaces are used to generate proxy objects to access the business tier components. The proxy objects hide the networking details for accessing remote business objects. The business interfaces are used by page controllers to invoke methods on the business object proxy. The business interfaces play a role similar to EJB home interfaces.

Business Tier

The business tier is responsible for executing the business rules. Distributing the business logic components is one important decision that can be made up front. This will help you choose the appropriate remoting technology. For the example OMS, the customer wants to expose the business logic only to external retail outlets over some form of HTTP remoting. Also, the team is not conversant with EJB. Hence, I have decided to use the fast, lightweight Hessian remoting, which is based on HTTP. It can be used to export

POJOs as remote business services. Later, if required, these POJO business components can also be exposed as web services.

The business services also need security services if they are exposed to external clients such as the Java Swing-based desktop application used by the retail outlets. This consideration can be factored into the architecture later, when the customer makes the final decision on this. Since the remoting is being done over HTTP using servlets, the same security component used in the presentation tier can be reused in the business tier.

Remote Dispatcher Servlet

This dispatcher servlet intercepts all the remote business logic invocations over the Hessian protocol. It dispatches the actual invocation on POJO business components.

Business Service Implementations

This layer implements the business interfaces and provides the actual implementation of the business logic. The business service or the application service layer for the OMS application will be developed as POJOs.

Data Access Objects

Data access objects (DAOs) encapsulate the interaction with the integration tier. In this case, the DAOs connect and manipulate data stored in the Oracle RDBMS. For this they use the JDBC API.

Integration Tier

The integration tier is hosted on an Oracle 10*g* database. The DAOs are responsible for interfacing with this tier. They pass SQL commands to retrieve and manipulate the data stored in the RDBMS. Note that OMS will not use any stored procedure because the application does not require any bulk or long-running database operation.

A careful observation of Figure 7-3 will reveal a few missing pieces in the architecture. For example, you may have noticed that I did not include any description about transaction or logging. Since this is only the first iteration of the project, I was still deliberating about these two system aspects. In the case of transactions, the customer was keen to embed the ObjectWeb JOTM transaction manager. However, I was confident that the Spring Framework's data source transaction manager implementation would be sufficient in this case. Hence, I decided to implement the second option as part of the development task. This would enable me to highlight its benefits such as robustness and ease of use to convince the end client. The selected approach can be applied in a subsequent iteration to refactor the evolutionary architecture. Note that in this book I will discuss only the first iteration. Interested readers can take this up as an exercise for architecture refactoring. You can also visit `http://www.opengarage.org` to see the outcome of this exercise.

Design

In the first pass of architecture, I managed to divide the application into tiers. Each tier was decomposed into smaller layers with distinct functions. Now I will get down to the design of the OMS application. It is important to educate the project development team on the design of the application. This helps speed up development because it is now based on best practices and established guidelines and patterns. Hence, before getting into the actual design aspects, I will touch upon a very convenient yet powerful way to publish design instructions.

I generally produce an HTML-based design directive as an agile design artifact. Figure 7-4 shows a design directive composed in Javadoc style.

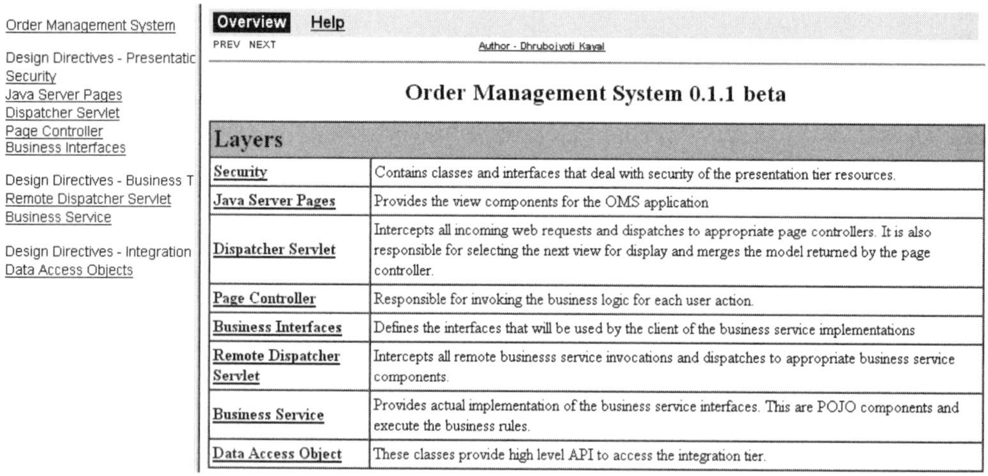

Figure 7-4. *Design directive order management system*

The design directive is composed just like a Javadoc. Each element in the Javadoc describes a design concern. Since design aims to provide a high-level solution to the problem at hand, each design concern is documented using the pattern template discussed in Chapter 2. In the next few sections, I will cover some of these design concerns and address them using the Spring Java EE patterns discussed earlier in this book.

Security

Problem

The OMS application requires that only authenticated users can search for services and place orders. Anonymous users should be prevented from pasting a URL in the browser's address bar and accessing a page in the application.

Forces

- Only valid users are allowed entry into the application.

- All different entry points into an application should be guarded by authentication.

- All authenticated users should have the appropriate roles/authority to access secure system resources.

Solution

All these forces probably are familiar to you. You guessed right—you will need to implement the Authentication and Authorization Enforcer design pattern to solve this problem. I will not delve much into the details of this solution because the entire problem can be addressed by this pattern described in Chapter 6.

Java Server Pages

Problem

The OMS application needs to display dynamic data to the end users. It also needs to show controls such as text fields and buttons for the users to interact with the application. The dynamic data and controls must be presented in a particular layout. It should be easy to rearrange the position of the data and controls in the layout with configuration. The layout should be flexible enough to add or remove new content.

Forces

- Users need to view dynamic data and different HTML controls in their browsers.

- There needs to be flexible layout support.

Solution

The dynamic data can be displayed using the View Helper design pattern. In the case of the order management application, I will use JSTL tags to retrieve and display dynamic data. To render the different controls, you can use the Spring form tags. You can read more about the Spring form tags at `http://static.springframework.org/spring/docs/2.5.x/reference/view.html#view-jsp-formtaglib`.

   You can apply the Composite View pattern to include the JSP-based view in a flexible layout. The layout in the example OMS will be built using Apache Tiles 2. The Spring documentation provides comprehensive details about the integration with the Tiles layout framework; you can access it at `http://static.springframework.org/spring/docs/2.5.x/reference/view.html#view-tiles`. If you are interested to know more about layouts and the Tiles framework in general, read all about it at `http://tiles.apache.org/`.

Page Controller

Problem

The event generated by each user action needs to be handled outside the front controller. This will enable the front controller to concentrate on the core task of acting as the single point of entry into the application and hence conform to SRP. Once the request is received, the front controller delegates the actual request processing to some other components. These components should also be responsible for retrieving a model by invoking the business logic component.

Forces

- Remove the code that invokes business logic in response to user action to reusable components.

- Identify the reusable components based on the request URL.

- Deploy one reusable component per user action.

Solution

Obviously, you will use the Page Controller pattern discussed in Chapter 3 to solve this design issue. The OMS application will extensively use page controller implementations that extend the `SimpleFormController`. However, the home page controller that will be used for redirection on successful authentication will use a `UrlFilenameViewController`. This is because this page controller does not define a complete workflow and is used only to render a simple home page now. Figure 7-5 shows the page controller class diagram.

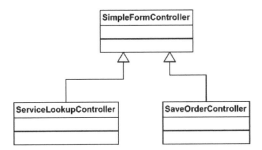

Figure 7-5. *OMS class diagram for page controllers in iteration 1*

The `ServiceLookupController` produces a list of matching services as per the search inputs supplied by the user. Similarly, the `SaveOrderController` saves the order information by invoking the business tier components.

By now you must have observed the similarity between the design directives and the patterns presented earlier in this book. I have not shown the consequences for using the different solutions. This is deliberate. I am sure you can make out the consequences from the Spring Java EE patterns that were applied for a particular design issue. A consequences section with a benefit and concern analysis is a must when you deliver a design directive to a development team or customer. Also, I prefer to add a UML package diagram (besides class and sequence diagrams) in my design directives, because it helps reveal the coupling in the application.

By now you should have a clear idea about the OMS application design. Table 7-1 points you to the appropriate Spring Java EE design patterns for the rest of the design issues. You can try to elaborate on these design directives as well as add the "Consequences" section to the previous examples.

Table 7-1. *Design Directive Pointers*

Design Issue	Spring Java EE Pattern
Dispatcher servlet	Front Controller
Business interfaces	Business Interface
Remote dispatcher servlet	Web Service Broker
Business service	Application Service
Data access object	Data Access Object

Development

Once the design is in place, the next step is to start the development. Before you get started, though, it's imperative that you set up the team development environment. For the example OMS, I decided to use Blazon ezJEE 1.0.0, which is based on the Eclipse Ganymede release. It is a comprehensive agile Java EE development environment and comes bundled with all the essential plug-ins, including support for the Spring Framework. If you are familiar with the Eclipse IDE, then getting started with Blazon ezJEE will be a breeze. You can get Blazon ezJEE by following the download link at `http://www.opengarage.org`.

Once you are done with the download, go through the quick-start guide to get started with this IDE. I will use Apache Maven (included in Blazon ezJEE) to build and deploy the web application artifacts. Maven is a useful tool for agile project development. It makes it easy to develop, build, and deploy projects in a very flexible and modular way. It promotes test-driven development by directly including unit test runs in the build process. It can also be used with Continuum (`http://continuum.apache.org/`) to support continuous integration. In the next few sections, I will explain how you can use Blazon ezJEE to set up the different projects required for the OMS application in the workspace.

Setting Up the Workspace

When you launch Blazon ezJEE for the first time, it will prompt you to select a workspace. Simply, a *workspace* is a folder in which you will keep your other Eclipse project directories. Because I am developing this OMS on the Windows platform, I will supply the fully qualified folder name as `c:\omsworkspace`, as shown in Figure 7-6.

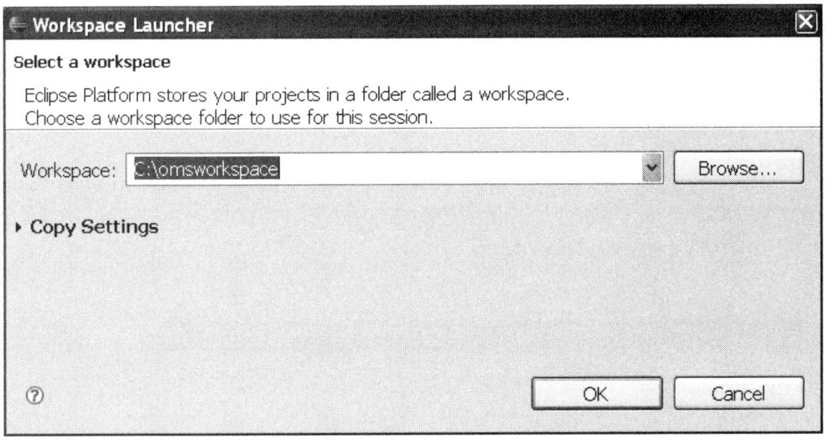

Figure 7-6. *Workspace selection*

So, now ezJEE is ready with a clean workspace to create projects for the OMS application. Because I will use Apache Maven 2 to build this project, you will need to turn off the automatic build option to follow along by selecting the Project menu and deselecting Build Automatically, as shown in Figure 7-7. If you are new to Maven, then visit `http://maven.apache.org/` to learn more about Maven concepts. Maven is one of the best build tools available, especially for large projects with lots of modules that need incremental and versioned releases.

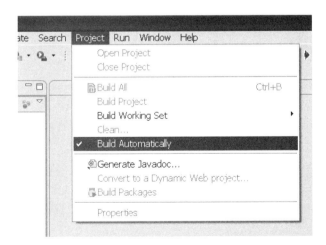

Figure 7-7. *Turning off the automatic build*

Setting Up the Projects

The first project that I will show how to set up is the simplest one. This project contains the JavaBeans that will be used to transfer data across layers and then across tiers. Here are the step-by-step instructions for creating this project:

1. Create a new project by selecting File ➤ New ➤ Project in ezJEE. This displays the New Project Wizard, as shown in Figure 7-8.

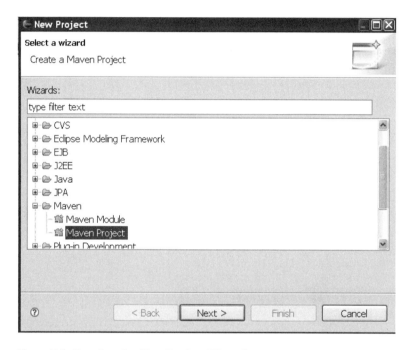

Figure 7-8. *Starting the New Project Wizard*

2. In the New Project Wizard, select Maven Project, and click Next to move to the Select Project Name and Location screen. On this screen, do not make any changes. Just click Next to move to the Select An Archetype screen, as shown in Figure 7-9.

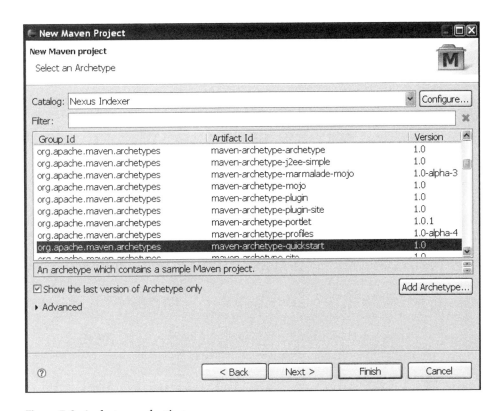

Figure 7-9. *Archetype selection*

3. Select `maven-archetype-quickstart`, and click Next. This will take you to the screen where you can specify the archetype parameters, as shown in Figure 7-10.

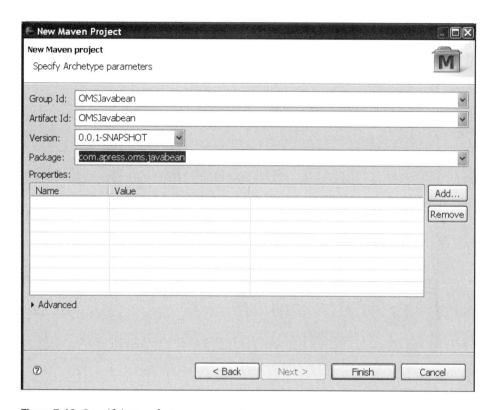

Figure 7-10. *Specifying archetype parameters*

4. Enter the values shown in Figure 7-10, and click Finish.

With these four steps you have created a Maven-based Java project in Blazon ezJEE. You will need to repeat these four steps to set up a few other Maven 2 projects, as listed in Table 7-2.

Table 7-2. *Maven 2 Java Project Setup*

Project Name	Description	Package Name
OMSJavabean	Contains the JavaBean classes used as data container	`com.apress.oms.javabean`
OMSBusinessAPI	Contains the business service interfaces	`com.apress.oms.business.api`

Project Name	Description	Package Name
OMSBusinessImpl	Contains the actual business logic implementations	`com.apress.oms.business.impl`
OMSPersistence	Contains the data access objects	`com.apress.oms.persistence`
OMSBusinessRemote	Contains the components required to export the business services as remote objects	`com.apress.oms.remoting`
OMSWeb	Contains the presentation	`com.apress.oms.web.controller`

The last two projects in Table 7-2 should be created as Maven 2 web projects. The steps to create these projects are the same except the archetype selection. To set up web projects with Maven, you will need to select `maven-archetype-webapp` on the Select an Archetype screen.

Adding Dependencies

So far, all the Maven projects have been set up independently. But in order for these projects to compile and produce the final build, you will need to add dependencies amongst projects as well other frameworks. Table 7-3 lists the dependencies.

Table 7-3. *Maven 2 Project Dependencies*

Project	Dependency
OMSJavabean	None
OMSBusinessAPI	OMSJavabean
OMSBusinessImpl	OMSBusinessAPI, OMSJavabean
OMSBusinessRemote	OMSBusinessAPI, OMSBusinessImpl, OMSJavabean, Spring Framework
OMSPersistence	OMSJavabean, Spring Framework
OMSWeb	OMSJavabean, OMSBusinessAPI, Spring Framework (2.5.4), JSTL 1.1.2

I will show you the steps that need to be followed to add Maven project dependencies in Blazon ezJEE for the OMSWeb project. You can follow the same steps to add dependencies for other projects. To add dependencies, you must first build all the projects in your workspace using Maven. You can do this by selecting the individual `pom.xml` file and running the Maven install goal, as shown in Figure 7-11.

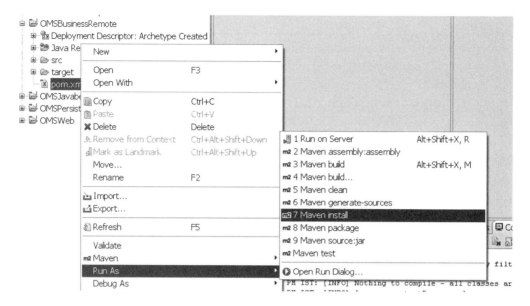

Figure 7-11. *Running the Maven 2 install goal*

Now to add dependencies, select pom.xml in the project OMSWeb, and click Add Dependency, as shown in Figure 7-12.

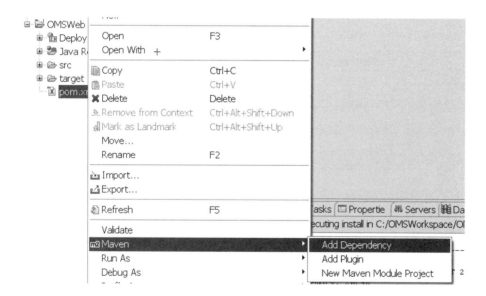

Figure 7-12. *Adding Maven 2 dependency*

This displays the Add Dependency dialog box. In the query input box search for Spring, select the appropriate version of the product, and click OK, as shown in Figure 7-13. This will now add the Spring project dependency to the OMSWeb project. The version of the dependent project that you select may be critical. This is because the dependent project—Spring in this case—can in turn have dependencies on other projects.

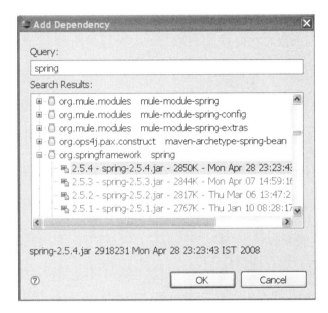

Figure 7-13. *Searching and adding Maven 2 projects as dependency*

Following the same steps, you can add dependencies for other projects as listed in Table 7-3. You are now ready to start coding and unit testing for the OMS application.

Constructing the Project

As shown in the Resource column of the tracker in Figure 7-1, I will now start with the login service and setup of the security layer. The security layer is added primarily by the configuration to the OMSWeb project to provide secured access to system resources to authenticated users. All the development tasks that follow from now on are in the OMSWeb project unless mentioned otherwise.

The first step to setting up the OMSWeb project is to add Maven dependencies with other projects. You can do this by following the steps outlined earlier. Listing 7-1 shows the pom.xml file that results from adding the dependent projects of OMSWeb.

Listing 7-1. pom.xml

```xml
<?xml version="1.0" encoding="UTF-8"?>
<project xsi:schemaLocation="http://maven.apache.org/POM/4.0.0
http://maven.apache.org/maven-v4_0_0.xsd"
xmlns:xsi="http://www.w3.org/2001/XMLSchema-instance">
    <modelVersion>4.0.0</modelVersion>
    <groupId>OMSWeb</groupId>
    <artifactId>OMSWeb</artifactId>
    <packaging>war</packaging>
    <version>0.0.1-SNAPSHOT</version>
    <name>OMSWeb Maven Webapp</name>
    <url>http://maven.apache.org</url>
    <dependencies>
        <dependency>
            <groupId>junit</groupId>
            <artifactId>junit</artifactId>
            <version>3.8.1</version>
            <scope>test</scope>
        </dependency>
        <dependency>
            <groupId>org.springframework</groupId>
            <artifactId>spring</artifactId>
            <version>2.5.4</version>
        </dependency>
        <dependency>
            <groupId>org.springframework.security</groupId>
            <artifactId>spring-security-core</artifactId>
            <version>2.0.3</version>
        </dependency>
        <dependency>
            <groupId>org.springframework</groupId>
            <artifactId>spring-webmvc</artifactId>
            <version>2.5.4</version>
        </dependency>
    <dependency>
    <groupId>OMSBusinessAPI</groupId>
    <artifactId>OMSBusinessAPI</artifactId>
    <version>0.0.1-SNAPSHOT</version>
</dependency>
```

```
  <dependency>
    <groupId>OMSJavabean</groupId>
    <artifactId>OMSJavabean</artifactId>
    <version>0.0.1-SNAPSHOT</version>
  </dependency>
<dependency>
      <groupId>jstl</groupId>
      <artifactId>jstl</artifactId>
      <version>1.1.2</version>
  </dependency>
 </dependencies>
   <build>
       <finalName>OMSWeb</finalName>
   </build>
</project>
```

As shown in the pom.xml file in Listing 7-1, running the Maven install goal will produce a web application archive (WAR) file. I will now show how to modify web.xml to
register the Spring dispatcher or front controller servlet. As mentioned in Chapter 3, this
servlet will load the Spring configuration from an XML configuration file starting with
the name of the servlet in web.xml. The Spring application context loaded by this servlet
will be a child of the parent application context loaded by the Spring context listener.
The parent application context is loaded from the classpath resource
applicationContext-security.xml. Listing 7-2 shows web.xml.

Listing 7-2. web.xml

```
<?xml version="1.0" encoding="UTF-8"?>
<web-app version="2.4" xmlns="http://java.sun.com/xml/ns/j2ee"
xmlns:xsi="http://www.w3.org/2001/XMLSchema-instance"
xsi:schemaLocation="http://java.sun.com/xml/ns/j2ee
http://java.sun.com/xml/ns/j2ee/web-app_2_4.xsd">

    <context-param>
        <param-name>contextConfigLocation</param-name>
        <param-value>
            /WEB-INF/applicationContext-security.xml
        </param-value>
    </context-param>
```

```xml
<filter>
    <filter-name>springSecurityFilterChain</filter-name>
    <filter-class>org.springframework.security.util.FilterToBeanProxy
    </filter-class>
    <init-param>
        <param-name>targetClass</param-name>
        <param-value>org.springframework.security.util.FilterChainProxy
        </param-value>
    </init-param>
</filter>

<filter-mapping>
    <filter-name>springSecurityFilterChain</filter-name>
    <url-pattern>/*</url-pattern>
</filter-mapping>


<listener>
    <listener-class>org.springframework.web.context.ContextLoaderListener
    </listener-class>
</listener>


<servlet>
    <servlet-name>oms</servlet-name>
    <servlet-class>
        org.springframework.web.servlet.DispatcherServlet
    </servlet-class>
    <load-on-startup>1</load-on-startup>
</servlet>


<servlet-mapping>
    <servlet-name>oms</servlet-name>
    <url-pattern>*.do</url-pattern>
</servlet-mapping>


<jsp-config>
    <taglib>
        <taglib-uri>/spring</taglib-uri>
```

```
            <taglib-location>
                /WEB-INF/tld/spring-form.tld
            </taglib-location>
        </taglib>
    </jsp-config>

</web-app>
```

As shown in Listing 7-2, I have installed the Spring Security filter. This filter interacts with its security counterpart in the Spring application context. Listing 7-3 shows the Spring Security application context configuration.

Listing 7-3. /WEB-INF/applicationContext-security.xml

```
<?xml version="1.0" encoding="UTF-8"?>
<!DOCTYPE beans PUBLIC "-//SPRING//DTD BEAN//EN"
"http://www.springframework.org/dtd/spring-beans.dtd">

<beans>


    <bean id="filterChainProxy"
class="org.springframework.security.util.FilterChainProxy">
        <property name="filterInvocationDefinitionSource">
            <value>
                CONVERT_URL_TO_LOWERCASE_BEFORE_COMPARISON
                PATTERN_TYPE_APACHE_ANT
                /**=httpSessionContextIntegrationFilter,authenticationProcessing➥
Filter,anonymousProcessingFilter,exceptionTranslationFilter, ➥
filterInvocationInterceptor➥
            </value>
        </property>
    </bean>

    <bean id="httpSessionContextIntegrationFilter"
        class="org.springframework.security.context➥
.HttpSessionContextIntegrationFilter"/>


    <bean id="authenticationProcessingFilter" class="org.springframework.➥
security.ui.webapp.AuthenticationProcessingFilter">
```

```xml
            <property name="authenticationManager" ref="authenticationManager"/>
            <property name="authenticationFailureUrl" value="/login.do?errorId=1"/>
            <property name="defaultTargetUrl" value="/secure/home.do"/>
            <property name="filterProcessesUrl" value="/j_spring_security_check"/>

    </bean>


    <bean id="anonymousProcessingFilter" class="org.springframework.security.➥
providers.anonymous.AnonymousProcessingFilter">
        <property name="key" value="changeThis"/>
        <property name="userAttribute" value="anonymousUser,ROLE_ANONYMOUS"/>
    </bean>

    <bean id="exceptionTranslationFilter" class="org.springframework.security.➥
ui.ExceptionTranslationFilter">
        <property name="authenticationEntryPoint">
            <bean class="org.springframework.security.ui.webapp.➥
AuthenticationProcessingFilterEntryPoint">
                <property name="loginFormUrl" value="/login.do"/>
                <property name="forceHttps" value="false"/>
            </bean>
        </property>
        <property name="accessDeniedHandler">
            <bean class="org.springframework.security.ui.AccessDeniedHandlerImpl">
                <property name="errorPage" value="/denied.jsp"/>
            </bean>
        </property>
    </bean>

    <bean id="filterInvocationInterceptor" class="org.springframework.security.➥
intercept.web.FilterSecurityInterceptor">
        <property name="authenticationManager" ref="authenticationManager"/>
        <property name="accessDecisionManager" ref="accessDecisionManager" />

        <property name="objectDefinitionSource">
            <value>
                CONVERT_URL_TO_LOWERCASE_BEFORE_COMPARISON
                PATTERN_TYPE_APACHE_ANT
                /secure/admin/**=ROLE_ADMIN
                /secure/**=IS_AUTHENTICATED_REMEMBERED
```

```xml
                    /**=IS_AUTHENTICATED_ANONYMOUSLY
            </value>
        </property>
    </bean>

    <bean name="accessDecisionManager"
class="org.springframework.security.vote.AffirmativeBased">
        <property name="allowIfAllAbstainDecisions" value="false"/>
        <property name="decisionVoters">
            <list>
                <bean class="org.springframework.security.vote.RoleVoter"/>
                <bean class="org.springframework.security.vote.AuthenticatedVoter"/>
            </list>
        </property>
    </bean>


    <bean id="authenticationManager"
class="org.springframework.security.providers.ProviderManager">
        <property name="providers">
            <list>
                <ref local="daoAuthenticationProvider"/>
            </list>
        </property>
    </bean>

    <bean id="daoAuthenticationProvider" class="org.springframework.security➥
.providers.dao.DaoAuthenticationProvider">
        <property name="userDetailsService" ref="userDetailsService"/>
    </bean>

    <bean id="userDetailsService" class="org.springframework.➥
security.userdetails.memory.InMemoryDaoImpl">
        <property name="userProperties">
            <bean class="org.springframework.beans.factory.config➥
.PropertiesFactoryBean">
                <property name="location" value="/WEB-INF/users.properties"/>
            </bean>
        </property>
    </bean>

</beans>
```

As shown in Listing 7-3, I have used an in-memory DAO for now. This is because the customer was unsure of the security provider. When the first iteration started, they were still deciding between an OpenID provider and an LDAP server. However, this did not affect the progress of the project. You can easily set up an in-memory DAO security provider for testing purposes. Spring Security provides support to easily switch to either an OpenID or an LDAP authentication provider. Note that in order to use the in-memory DAO, you need to create the user.properties file in the WEB-INF folder. Listing 7-4 shows a sample user.properties file. This file also stores the role or authorities of the user as a comma-separated list.

Listing 7-4. /WEB-INF/users.properties

```
dhrubo=kayal,ROLE_USER
harry=potter,ROLE_ADMIN
peter=parker,ROLE_USER
```

You are familiar with most of the configuration shown in Listing 7-3 from Chapter 6. The application-specific beans are configured in the dispatcher servlet application context. This application context is loaded from the configuration file, as shown in Listing 7-5.

Listing 7-5. /WEB-INF/oms-servlet.xml

```xml
<?xml version="1.0" encoding="UTF-8"?>
<beans xmlns="http://www.springframework.org/schema/beans"
       xmlns:xsi="http://www.w3.org/2001/XMLSchema-instance"
        xsi:schemaLocation="http://www.springframework.org/schema/beans
       http://www.springframework.org/schema/beans/spring-beans-2.5.xsd
       "
       >

    <bean id="viewResolver"
         class="org.springframework.web.servlet.view.InternalResourceViewResolver">
        <property name="viewClass"
                value="org.springframework.web.servlet.view.JstlView" />
        <property name="prefix" value="/WEB-INF/jsp/" />
        <property name="suffix" value=".jsp" />
    </bean>

    <bean name="/login.do"
        class="org.springframework.web.servlet.mvc.UrlFilenameViewController">
```

```
    </bean>

    <bean name="/secure/home.do"
          class="org.springframework.web.servlet.mvc.UrlFilenameViewController">

    </bean>

</beans>
```

As shown in Listing 7-5, `UrlFileNameViewController` is used to display both the login page and the home page. You may later want to use a different controller implementation for the home or login page depending on requirement changes. The home page, for instance, may require displaying the list of all the pending orders when the user signs on. The home page shown in Listing 7-6 displays a simple form to place an order. It also contains a link to launch a pop-up window to search and select a service. Note that `home.jsp` has been placed in the secure folder.

Listing 7-6. `/WEB-INF/jsp/secure/home.jsp`

```
<%@ taglib prefix="form" uri="http://www.springframework.org/tags/form" %>
<html>

<head>
<title>Place an Order</title>
</head>
<body>
<form action="saveOrder.do" method="POST">
    <form:errors path="*"  />
  <table>
    <tr>
      <td>Item Id:</td>
      <td><input type='text' name='itemId' readonly="readonly"/></td>
      <td><input value="Find Item" name="FindItem"
type="button" onClick="openItemSearchWindow()"/></td>
    </tr>
    <tr>
      <td>Item Name</td>
      <td><input type='text' name='ItemName' /></td>
    </tr>
    <tr>
      <td>Item Description</td>
```

```
            <td><input type='text' name='ItemDesc' /></td>
        </tr>

        <tr><td colspan='2'><input value="Save" name="Save"
type="submit" /></td></tr>

    </table>
</form>
</body>
</html>
```

Since Spring Security is installed, any unauthorized or unauthenticated access will redirect the user to the login page. Listing 7-7 shows the login page.

Listing 7-7. /WEB-INF/jsp/login.jsp

```
<%@ taglib prefix="form" uri="http://www.springframework.org/tags/form" %>
<html>

<head>
<title>Login</title>
</head>
<body>
<form action="j_spring_security_check" method="POST">
    <form:errors path="*" cssClass="errorBox" />
  <table>
    <tr>
      <td>User:</td>
        <td><input type='text' name='j_username' />
        </td>
    </tr>
    <tr>
      <td>Password:</td>
      <td><input type='password' name='j_password' /></td>
    </tr>

    <tr><td colspan='2'><input value="Sign In" type="submit" /></td></tr>

  </table>
</form>
</body>
</html>
```

This page just sets up form-based user authentication. Note that this code also uses the Spring form tags as view helpers to display error messages resulting from login failures.

Now that some code is in place, you need to build and test this application on the Tomcat 5.5 web server. To build the OMSWeb application, you need to select the project and run the Maven install goal as shown earlier in this chapter. The install goal will also run any JUnit tests that you may have written. By default, Maven uses JUnit for unit tests. You can also use any other testing framework, such as TestNG, as well. On a successful build, the install goal generates a WAR file. In the next section, I will present a step-by-step guide to install this WAR file on Tomcat 5.5. To follow the next section, you will need to download, install, and start the Tomcat web server. You can get detailed instructions for this at `http://tomcat.apache.org/`.

Deploying the Project

Maven 2 provides a plug-in to deploy the generated WAR file in the Tomcat 5.5 server. You need to install this plug-in before you can actually use it. The steps to adding this plug-in are the same as setting up the dependencies. To add the Maven 2 Tomcat plug-in, right-click the OMSWeb project to launch the context menu. In the context menu, select Maven ➤ Add Plugin. This is shown in Figure 7-14.

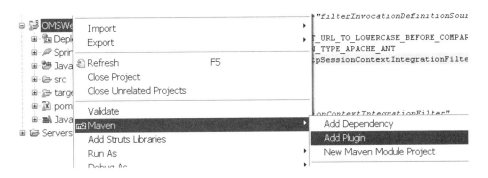

Figure 7-14. *Adding the Maven 2 plug-in*

On the Add Plugin screen that appears, type **tomcat** in the Query box. Select the Tomcat Maven plug-in as shown in Figure 7-15, and click OK. This automatically downloads the relevant JAR files required by this plug-in.

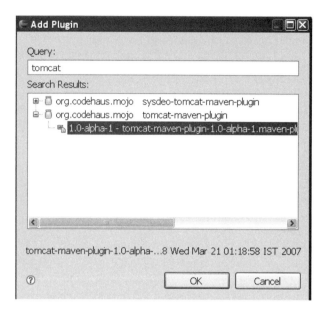

Figure 7-15. *Searching and adding the Maven 2 plug-in*

The Maven 2 Tomcat plug-in assumes a default Tomcat Manager URL (http://localhost:8080/manager) to connect and deploy the WAR file. For authentication, it assumes that the manager's username is admin with no password. So, in order to get this working, you may need to alter the tomcat-users.xml file to change the password of the admin user. The Maven goals for this plug-in are not available explicitly. So, you need to create a new run configuration as shown in Figure 7-16 to execute the Tomcat Maven plug-in goals.

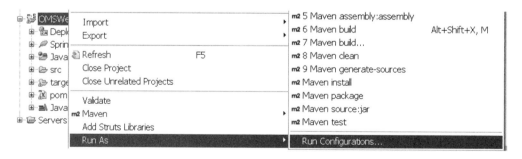

Figure 7-16. *Creating run configurations*

This opens the screen to create a new configuration, as shown in Figure 7-17. On this screen, double-click Maven Build to create a new Maven configuration. Fill in the values as shown in Figure 7-17, except Goals.

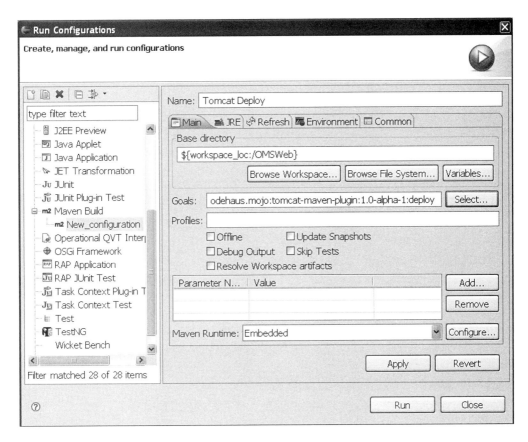

Figure 7-17. *New run configuration for Maven build*

For the goals, click Select, and in the goal search window that appears, query for **tomcat,** as shown in Figure 7-18. You will need to select the deploy task and click OK. This populates the text box in Figure 7-17 with the appropriate values for the Tomcat deploy goal.

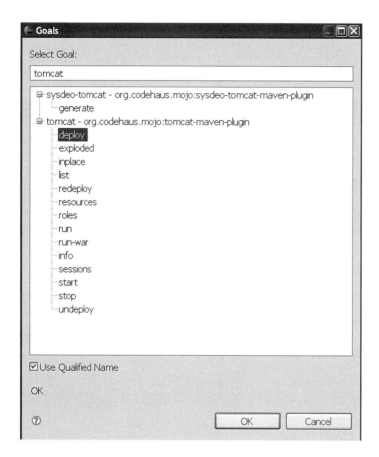

Figure 7-18. *Searching and selecting a goal*

Once the goal is selected, click Apply to save this configuration (for future use) and then click Run to execute this goal and install the OMSWeb.war file on the Tomcat server.

Setting up and using the Maven plug-in for Tomcat is a complex task. Moreover, you may have reservations about using an alpha version of the plug-in. Also, you may not like the idea of changing the Tomcat manager user password and setting it to be blank. This plug-in has been around for some time now and has worked despite its alpha status. It is especially useful if you do not use continuous integration and in staging environments where you do not have access to Eclipse and need to execute all Maven goals from the command line.

Simplified Deployment

There is a simpler way to deploy the OMSWeb project. I assume that you have already executed the Maven install goal to create the WAR file and have downloaded and installed Tomcat 5.5. Since I am on Windows, I have installed Tomcat at `c:\tomcat5.5`. Note that you should not download and use the Tomcat Windows Service installer; instead, choose the simple zipped distribution.

As a first step to this new deployment strategy, you will need to set up the target runtime (or the server on which the web application will run) for the OMSWeb project. For this, right-click the OMSWeb project to launch the context menu, and select Properties, as shown in Figure 7-19.

Figure 7-19. *Selecting OMSWeb project properties*

On the project properties screen for OMSWeb, select Targeted Runtimes. In the Targeted Runtimes view, click New, as shown in Figure 7-20.

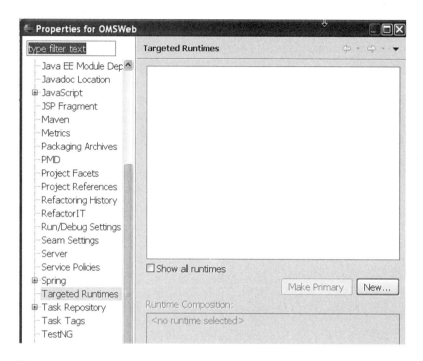

Figure 7-20. *New target runtime*

On the New Server Runtime Environment screen, select Apache Tomcat 5.5, and check the Create a New Local Server option, as shown in Figure 7-21. Then click Next to move to the next screen to select the Tomcat installation directory.

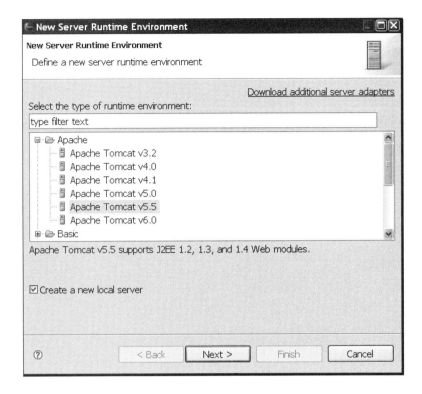

Figure 7-21. *New server runtime: Apache Tomcat 5.5*

On the Tomcat installation directory selection screen, you need to browse to and select the Tomcat installation home directory. Alternatively, you can also choose to download and install Tomcat from this screen. Since I have already installed Tomcat 5.5, I will choose `c:\tomcat5.5`, as shown in Figure 7-22. Click Finish to complete the installation of Tomcat 5.5 and the local server.

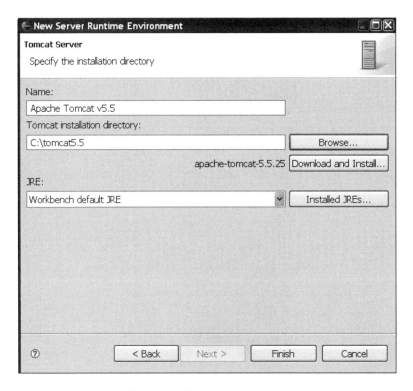

Figure 7-22. *Tomcat directory selection*

Once complete, you are back again on the project properties screen. The newly created Tomcat runtime is now shown in this screen. You will need to select this new runtime and click OK, as shown in Figure 7-23.

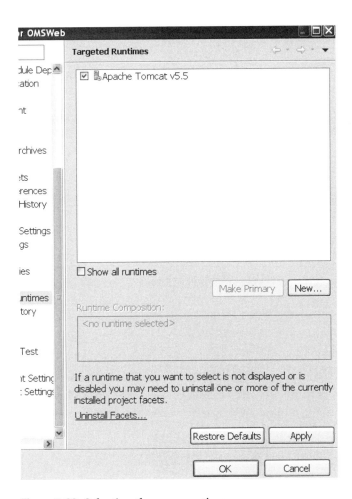

Figure 7-23. *Selecting the new runtime*

You're not done yet. You need to create a new server from the local server configuration created just now. You can do this in the server control panel. For this you need to select Window ➤ Show View ➤ Servers in Blazon ezJEE IDE, as shown in Figure 7-24.

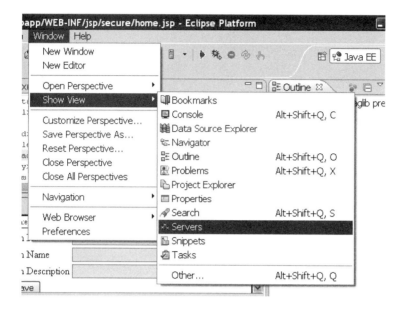

Figure 7-24. *Enabling a Servers view*

Once the Servers view is enabled, it opens a blank server control panel. The server control panel has buttons to start, stop, and restart a server. On the server control panel, right-click to launch the context menu, and select New ➤ Server, as shown in Figure 7-25.

Figure 7-25. *Server control panel: new server setup*

In the New Server dialog box that appears, select Apache Tomcat 5.5, and click Finish, as shown in Figure 7-26.

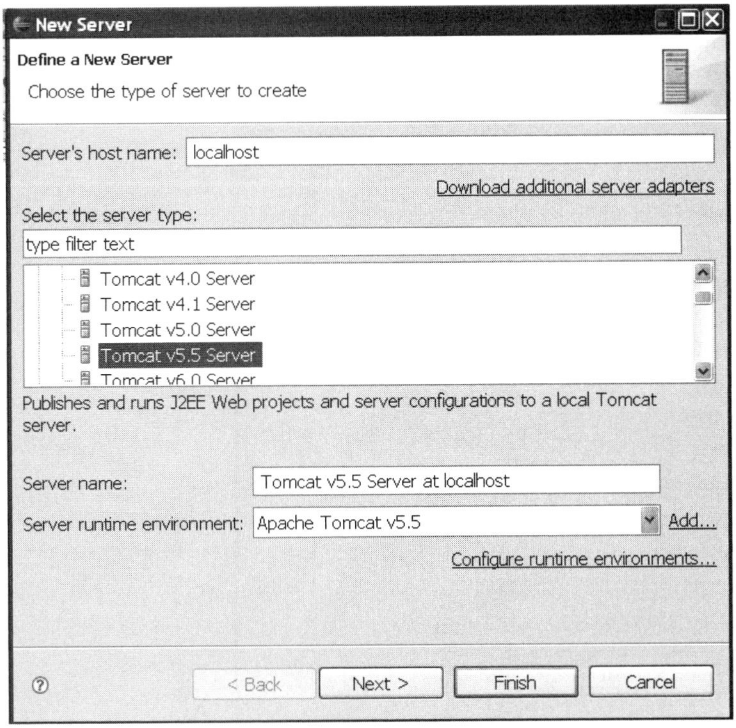

Figure 7-26. *Tomcat server setup*

The Tomcat server now appears in a stopped state in the server control panel. Right-click it to add the OMSWeb project by selecting the Add and Remove Projects option, as shown in Figure 7-27.

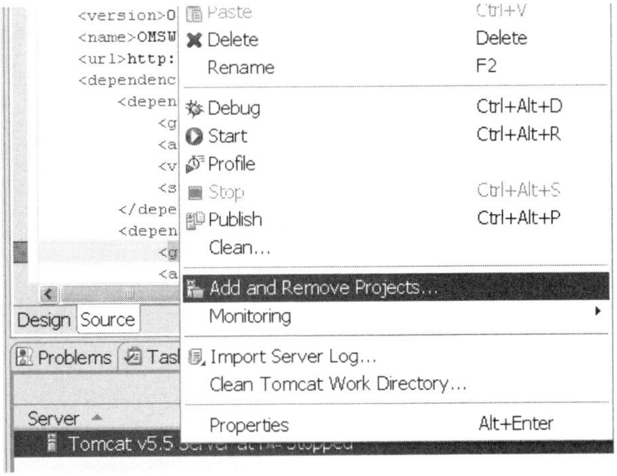

Figure 7-27. *Adding and removing web projects on the Tomcat server*

In the Add and Remove Projects dialog box, select the OMSWeb project, and click Finish, as shown in Figure 7-28.

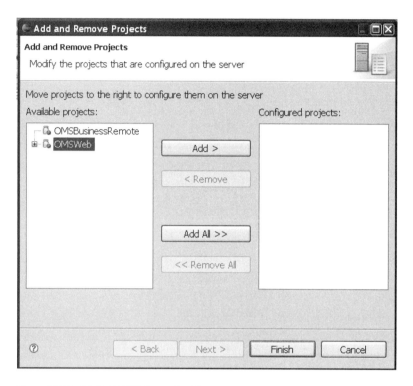

Figure 7-28. *Add OMSWeb on the Tomcat server*

Now you can start the Tomcat server from the Blazon ezJEE server control panel. This will also deploy the OMSWeb project on the server. You can now browse to `http://localhost:8080/OMSWeb/login.do` to view the login screen, as shown in Figure 7-29.

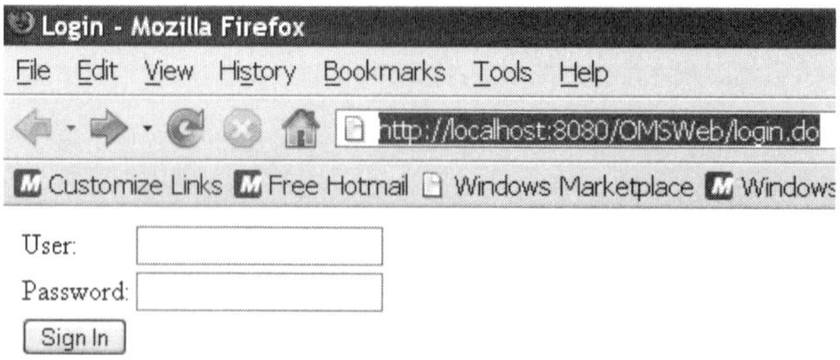

Figure 7-29. *Login screen*

You can now test the login screen by supplying the values for the user and password setup in the `users.properties` file in Listing 7-4. On successful authentication, the user is redirected to the home page, as shown in Figure 7-30.

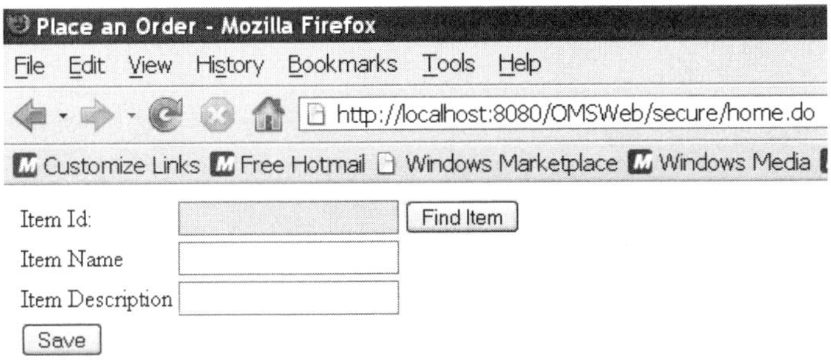

Figure 7-30. *Placing an order*

I will leave the rest of the tasks in the tracker for you to complete. Any agile Java EE project must set up a source control, continuous integration server, as well as a few source code analysis and refactoring tools. You can try these different options in Blazon ezJEE to take this project forward. I will take this project forward on my web site at `http://www.opengarage.org`.

Summary

In this chapter, I showed how to build the basic structure for an order management system in an interactive way. Although I provided most of the foundation, I left enough for you to try to experience the application design and development with the Spring Framework and Java EE patterns. I also introduced you to user stories for agile requirements gathering. Then I discussed the strategies that should be adopted by describing the architecture and design for projects in a flexible way. Finally, I presented a quick tour to get started on the development using Blazon ezJEE, which is an Eclipse Ganymede-based agile development environment.

As they say, all good things must come to an end. With this chapter, we've finished our journey of Java EE design patterns with the Spring Framework. I will keep updating and adding to this catalog, and you can find useful supplementary information related to Java EE Spring patterns on my web site at `http://www.opengarage.org`.

Index

- (minus sign) in class diagrams, 15
* (asterisk) as wildcard, 58
? (question mark) for positional bind
    variables, 187
+ (plus sign) in class diagrams, 15

A

AbstractCachingViewResolver class, 60
AbstractCommandController class, 74–78
AbstractController class, 71–74
AbstractEnterpriseBean class, 158, 200
AbstractHandlerMapping, 54
AbstractMessageDrivenBean class, 200
AbstractProcessingFilter, 234
AbstractStatelessSessionBean, 158
AbstractTemplateViewResolver class,
    60–61
AbstractWizardFormController class, 89
access decision manager (Spring
    Security), 228
accessDecisionManager property,
    246–247
Acegi Security, 223–224
action/command handling (application
    controller), 52–56
action handlers
  page controllers and, 51
  sequence, 54
  using (application controller), 56–58
advices, audit interceptor, 249
AffirmativeBased access decision
    manager, 247
afterCompletion callback method, 104
aggregation relationship (UML), 17
Alur, Deepak, 1, 223
ANPF (Anonymous Processing Filter),
    243–244

AOP module (Spring), 34, 37
Apache Axis web services framework, 210
Apache Maven, 280–285
Apache Struts framework, 23
Apache Tiles framework, 122, 278
Apache Tomcat, 257
APF (Authentication Processing Filter),
    233–243
application contexts (Spring), 33
Application Controller pattern
  action/command handling, 52–56
  action handlers, using, 56–58
  for action-view management, 50–52
  background, 50–51
  benefits and concerns, 68
  strategies with Spring framework, 52
  view handlers, 59–62, 62–68
application server transactions, 261
application servers, 138
application service implementation class,
    164
Application Service pattern
  benefits and concerns, 167
  to concentrate business logic in POJO
    classes, 162–163
  strategies with Spring framework,
    164–167
applicationContext-security.xml, 229
applicationScope object, 128
architecture
  container, 6–8
  layered, 10
  OMS application, 272–275
architecture, Java EE
  n-tier, 4–5
  overview, 5–6
  single-tier, 2

three-tier, 4

two-tier, 3

aspect-oriented programming (AOP), 33

association relationship (UML), 16

asynchronous report processing, 204

asynchronous service requests, 199–200

audit interceptors

   to apply auditing of business service invocations, 248–249

   benefits and concerns, 256

   strategies with Spring framework, 249–256

AuditEvent class, 253

AuditLog interface, 254

AuditRules class, 252–253

authentication

   Authentication Processing Filter (APF), 233–243

   authenticationEntryPoint property, 245

   authenticationManager property, 246

   AuthenticationProvider interface, 238

   defined, 224

   manager (Spring Security), 228, 236–237

Authentication and Authorization Enforcer pattern

   high-level components of, 226

   OMS application and, 277

   Spring Security framework components, 228

   strategies with Spring framework, 226

   to verify user identity, 224–226

authorization, defined, 225

automatic proxy creator bean, 255–256

■B

BasicProcessingFilter, 234

BEA WebLogic Server, 260

beans

   bean factory (Spring), 29–32

   BeanFactoryLocator implementation, 160

   beanNameHandlerMapping, 106

BeanNameUrlHandlerMapping, 54, 56–57, 127

BeanNameUrlHandlerMapping class, 48

BeanNameViewResolver class, 60

   defined, 29

   entity, 135

   factory bean, defined, 140

   form, 74–76

Beck, Kent, 41

bind variables, 187–188

Blazon ezJEE 1.0.0 development environment, 280

Burlap protocol, remoting with, 217–220

BurlapServiceExporter, 219

business

   interfaces, 274

   layers, 2

   logic, 195

   service layer (OMS application), 275

Business Delegate pattern

   as adapter to invoke business objects, 151

   benefits and concerns, 154–155

   business delegate object, 131

   strategies with Spring framework, 151–154

Business Interface pattern

   benefits and concerns, 176

   to consolidate business methods, 168–169

   strategies with Spring framework, 169–175

business tier design patterns

   Application Service pattern. *See* Application Service pattern

   Business Delegate pattern. *See* Business Delegate pattern

   Business Interface pattern. *See* Business Interface pattern

   business tier method invocation, auditing, 248

business tier (Spring application), 37–38
OMS application, 274–275
overview, 135
Service Locator pattern. *See* Service
    Locator pattern
Session Facade pattern. *See* Session
    Facade pattern

■ **C**

cache, service locator, 161
callbacks, Spring DAO, 188–194
CasProcessingFilter, 234
catalog, Java EE design pattern, 12–14
Central Authentication Service (CAS) SSO
    solution, 234
Chedgey, Chris, 22
class diagrams, UML, 15–17
Clickstream (Open Symphony), 102
command classes, 74
compile-time checks, 169–171
components, code, 22
Composite GOF design pattern, 118–119
composite view
    Apache Tiles framework, 122
    benefits and concerns, 123
    to group and deploy subview
        components, 117–118
    OMS application, 278
    SiteMesh web page layout, 119
    strategies with Spring framework,
        118–122
composition relationship (UML), 17
ConnectionFactory object, 204
constructor injection, 32
container architecture, 6–8
Context Object pattern
    benefits and concerns, 98
    to encapsulate and share form data,
        90–91
    strategies with Spring framework, 91–98
ContextJndiBeanFactoryLocator class, 160
ContextLoaderListener, 229, 231
Continuum, 280

controller component (MVC), 8
Controller interface (Spring framework),
    71–72
controller layers, 8
Core J2EE Design Pattern (Prentice Hall), 1,
    11–12, 223
Core module (Spring)
    application contexts, 33
    bean factory, 29–32
    DI (Dependency Injection), 26–29
    IOC (Inversion of Control), 25–26
Core Security Patterns (Prentice Hall),
    223–224
createBinder method, 96–97
crosscutting design patterns
    audit interceptors. *See* audit
        interceptors
    Authentication and Authorization
        Enforcer pattern. *See*
        Authentication and Authorization
        Enforcer pattern
    defined, 14
    domain service owner transactions. *See*
        domain service owner transactions
    overview, 223–224
Crupi, John, 223
custom queries with aliases (security), 242

■ **D**

DAO, Spring, 38, 34
DaoAuthenticationProvider, 239
data access layers, 2
Data Access Object (DAO) pattern
    benefits and concerns, 194
    bind variables, 187–188
    to encapsulate data access logic,
        180–183
    OMS application, 275
    Spring DAO callbacks, 188–194
    strategies with Spring framework,
        183–186
data transfer objects (DTOs), 180
DataSourceTransactionManager, 258

declarative container-managed
    transaction (CMT) support, 156
declarative transactions, 261–265
declarative validators (Spring MVC), 85
declareParameter method, 197
DefaultMessageListenerContainer, 208
dependencies, adding (OMS application),
    285–287
Dependency Injection (DI). *See* DI
    (Dependency Injection), Spring
deployment, OMS application, 297–309
design patterns
    business tier. *See* business tier design
        patterns
    crosscutting. *See* crosscutting design
        patterns
    design pattern directive, Spring Java EE,
        38–39
    *Elements of Reusable Object-Oriented
        Software* (Addison Wesley), 11
    Java EE, 11–14
    presentation tier. *See* presentation tier
        design patterns
Destination object, 204
DI (Dependency Injection), Spring, 26–29
diagrams, UML, 14–18
DigestProcessingFilter, 234
direct instantiation, 26
Dispatcher View pattern
    benefits and concerns, 130
    to process static/semistatic views,
        123–124
    strategies with Spring framework,
        124–128
DispatcherServlet, 46–49, 274
display, form, 78–80
Displaytag tag library, 116
distributed computing, 2–10
distributed objects, design of, 11
documented business requirements (OMS
    application), 270–271
doDispatch method, 55

doFilter method, 103, 234
domain service owner transactions
    application server transactions, 261
    benefits and concerns, 267
    declarative transactions, 261–265
    to declaratively apply transactions,
        256–257
    Hibernate transactions, 259
    JDBC transactions, 258–259
    JPA transactions, 259–260
    JTA transactions, 260–261
    strategies with Spring framework, 258
doSubmitAction method, 82

■ **E**

Eclipse IDE, 280
EJB (Enterprise Java Beans)
    deploying business components with,
        11
    EJB 2.0, 157
    EJB 3 lookup, 144
    EJB containers, 7
    ejb-jar.xml deployment descriptor,
        159–160
    EJBObject/EJBLocalObject interfaces,
        168
    local EJB 2.x lookup, 143–144
    remote EJB 2.x lookup, 140–142
    session beans, 136
endpoints, SOAP-based, 210
entity beans, 135
EntityManager, 260
ETF (Exception Translation Filter),
    244–245
evolutionary architecture, 272
Exception Translation Filter (ETF),
    244–245
*Expert One-on-One J2EE Design and
    Development* (Wrox), 21
Expert Spring MVC and Web Flow (Apress),
    79
extreme programming (XP), 269

F

factory bean, defined, 140
factory helper, 27–28
filters
    filter chaining in Spring Security, 232
    Filter Security Interceptor (FSI),
        245–247
    FilterChainProxy bean, 229, 231
    filterInvocationDefinitionSource
        property, 232
    filterProcessesUrl property, 236
    FilterToBeanProxy servlet filter class,
        228
    servlet, 99–103
    Spring Security, 291
forms
    beans, 74–76
    display, 78–80
    submission, 81–83
    tags, Spring, 278
    validation, 85–89
Foundations of AOP for J2EE Development
    (Apress), 34, 224
Fowler, Martin, 41
Front Controller pattern
    benefits and concerns, 49
    front controller servlet, 42–46
    strategies with Spring framework, 46–49
FSI (Filter Security Interceptor), 245–247

G

Gamma, Eric, 11
Gang of Four (GOF). *See* GOF (Gang of
    Four)
Gateway Servlet pattern, 46
generalization relationship (UML), 16
GET requests, 72
getEJBHome method, 138
getHandler method, 55
getHibernateTemplate method, 194
getObject method, 140
getParameter method, 74

GOF (Gang of Four)

    command pattern, 46
    Decorator design pattern, 119
    patterns, 11
    Strategy GOF design pattern, 118–119
    Template Method design pattern, 204

H

HandlerAdapter interface, 54
handleRequest method, 48–49
HandlerExecutionChain, 54
HandlerInterceptor interface, 103–106
HandlerInterceptorAdapter class, 104
HandlerMapping interface, 48, 54
Headway Software, 22
Helm, Richard, 11
Hessian remoting protocol, 217, 274–275
Hibernate
    and container support, 23
    HibernateDaoSupport base class,
        193–194
    HibernateTransactionManager, 259
    SessionFactory, 192
    transactions, 259
home interface (session beans), 157
HTTP (HyperText Transfer Protocol)
    exposing services over, 217
    HttpServletRequest, 71
    HttpServletRequest object, 74
    HttpServletRequest.getRequestURI
        method, 236
    httpSessionContextIntegrationFilter
        filter, 232

I

if-else blocks, 68–69
injection
    constructor, 32
    setter, 28, 30–31
InMemoryDaoImpl, 239
instantiation, direct, 26

integration tier design patterns
 OMS application, 275–276
 overview, 179
 Spring application, 38
Intercepting Filter pattern
 to apply reusable processing, 98–99
 benefits and concerns, 106
 servlet filters, 99–102
 Spring interceptors, 103–106
 strategies with Spring framework,
  99–106
interceptors, Spring, 103–106
InternalResourceView class, 49
InternalResourceViewResolver, 60–61,
  67–68
invoke method, 251
IOC (Inversion of Control), Spring, 25–26
iteration planning (OMS application),
  271–272

■J

Jakarta Commons-lang project, 253
JasperReportsViewResolver, 60–61
Java
 Authorization and Authentication
  Service (JAAS) API, 223–224
 Blueprints (Sun), 11, 223
 JavaBean view helper, 108–110
 Javadoc, 276
 javax.servlet.Filter interface, 234
 object (POJO) programming, 14
 Persistence API. *See* JPA (Java
  Persistence API)
 Server Faces (JSF), 37
 Server Pages (JSP). *See* JSP (Java Server
  Pages)
 Transaction API (JTA). *See* JTA (Java
  Transaction API)
 Transaction Design Strategies
  (Lulu.com), 224
 Virtual Machine (JVM), 7

Java EE
 APIs, 8
 application server, 7
 design pattern directive (Spring), 38–39
 Java EE 2 platform, 6
 Java EE 5, 6
Java EE application architecture
 container architecture, 6–8
 distributed computing, 2–10
 layered architecture, 10
 MVC (Model-View-Controller), 8–9
 overview, 1, 5–6
 with UML, 14–18
Java EE application design
 design pattern catalog, 12–14
 overview, 11
 simplifying with patterns, 11–12
 with UML, 14–18
JAX-RPC
 JaxRpcPortProxyFactoryBean, 216
 web services with, 210–216
JBoss
 Application Server (AS), 260
 server, 142
 -specific deployment descriptor, 161,
  203
JDBC (Java DataBase Connectivity)
 API, 34, 38, 181–182, 275
 JDBC/DAO module (Spring), 34
 JdbcDaoImpl, 239, 241
 JdbcDaoSupport class, 184
 JdbcTemplate class, 184–185
 transactions, 258–259
JEE module (Spring), 35
jee tag (Spring 2.x), 148–149
JMS (Java Messaging Service)
 JmsTemplate class, 204, 206
 objects, lookup of, 145–150
JNDI (Java Naming and Directory
  Interface)
 directory service, 136
 JndiAccessor class, 140

JndiObjectFactoryBean service locator class, 140–144, 146, 149
object lookup, 136–139
registry service, 28
Johnson, Ralph, 11
Johnson, Rod, 21
JPA (Java Persistence API)
JpaTransactionManager, 259
transactions, 259–260
JSP (Java Server Pages)
as controllers, 45
JSTL Expression Language (EL), 111–112
OMS application, 277–278
Standard Tag Library (JSTL), 64, 84, 111–113
view components in OMS application, 273–274
JTA (Java Transaction API)
JTATransactionManager, 260–261
transactions, 260–261

L

Lai, Ray, 223–224
Lampson, Butler W., 151–152
layers
defined, 2
layered application, building with Spring, 35–38
layered architecture, 10
layout element (views), 117
layout frameworks, 119–122
lifelines, object, 18
local EJB 2.x lookup, 143–144
LocalSessionFactoryBean, 193
LocalStatelessSessionProxyFactoryBean, 174
log method, 254
Logger, Apache Commons, 254
login form, 235, 295–297
lookup
EJB 3, 144
of JMS objects, 145–150
local EJB 2.x, 143–144
remote EJB 2.x, 140–142
services (OMS application), 270

M

Magic Servlet antipattern, 44
Malks, Dan, 223
Map objects, 188, 190, 197
Maven, Apache, 280, 297–300
message-driven beans (MDBs), 135–136, 200–201
message-driven POJOs (MDPs), 207–208
message listener container, 207–208
MessageCodesResolver implementation, 88
MessageCreator interface, 182
MessageDrivenContext object, 200
MessageListenerAdapter, 207
MethodInterceptor Spring AOP class, 251
MethodNameResolver class, 89
model component (MVC), 8
ModelAndView object, 71
MultiActionController class, 89
MVC (Model-View-Controller)
basics, 8–9
Java EE architecture with, 9
web MVC module (Spring), 35

N

n-tier architecture, 4–5
Nagappan, Ramesh, 223–224
NamedParameterJdbcDaoSupport class, 188
network computing, 2

O

objects
lifeline of, 18
object definitions, 246
Object Management Group (OMG), 14
objectDefinitionSource property (FSI), 246
in sequence diagrams, 18

OC4JtaTransactionManager (Oracle
    Application Server), 261
OMS (order management system). *See*
    order management system (OMS)
    application
Oracle Database, 183
order management system (OMS)
    application
    application architecture, 272–275
    business tier, 274–275
    dependencies, adding, 285–287
    design of, 276
    development overview, 280
    documented business requirements,
        270–271
    integration tier, 275–276
    iteration planning, 271–272
    JSP, 277–278
    look up services, 270
    order saving, 270
    Page Controller pattern, 278–279
    presentation tier, 273–274
    project construction, 287–297
    project deployment, 297–309
    project setup, 282–285
    security, 277
    story cards, 270–271
    user sign in, 270
    workspace setup, 280–281
order saving (OMS application), 270
Ordered interface, 54, 68
org.springframework.beans.factory.
    BeanFactory interface, 29
org.springframework.web.servlet.mvc.
    Controller interface, 48–49
ORM (Object-Relational Mapping)
    module (Spring), 35

■P

Page Controller pattern
    AbstractCommandController class,
        74–78
    AbstractController class, 71–74
AbstractWizardFormController class, 89
    benefits and concerns, 89
    to consolidate user action processing,
        68–69
    implementation class, 70–71
    MultiActionController class, 89
    OMS application, 278–279
    SimpleFormController class, 78–89
    strategies with Spring framework, 70
page controllers
    defined, 36–37
    OMS application, 274
    in presentation tier, 151
patterns, Java EE design, 11–14. *See also*
        Java EE, design pattern directive
        (Spring)
Pawlak, Renaud, 224
persistence logic, 195
platform transaction manager, 258
pointcuts (AOP), 255
POJO (Plain Old Java Object)
    business components, 138, 150
    business objects, 37
    components, 164, 167
    message-driven (MDPs), 207–208
postHandle method, 104
preHandle method, 104
PreparedStatementSetter callback
        interface, 189
presentation layers, 2
presentation tier design patterns
    Application Controller pattern. *See*
        Application Controller pattern
    composite view. *See* composite view
    Context Object pattern. *See* Context
        Object pattern
    Dispatcher View pattern. *See* Dispatcher
        View pattern
    eInsure application background, 41–42
    Front Controller pattern. *See* Front
        Controller pattern
    Intercepting Filter pattern. *See*
        Intercepting Filter pattern

OMS application, 273–274

Page Controller pattern. *See* Page
   Controller pattern

Service to Worker. *See* Service to Worker
   pattern

Spring application, 36–37

View Helper pattern. *See* View Helper
   pattern

Procedure Access Object pattern

   benefits and concerns, 199

   to invoke stored procedures, 195

   strategies with Spring framework,
      196–197

program to interface (P2I), 27, 184

programmatic transaction management,
   224

programmatic validators (Spring MVC), 85

property placeholder support (Spring),
   142

ProviderManager class, 237

proxy creator bean, automatic, 255–256

proxy factory beans, 150, 219, 274

proxy service locators, 174–175

pull dependency injection, 28, 30

push dependency injection, 28, 30

R

RdbmsOperation, 196

Reenskaug, Trygve, 8

*Refactoring: Improving the Design of
   Existing Code* (Addison-Wesley), 41

registry service, JNDI, 28

remoting

   with Burlap protocol, 217–220

   remote dispatcher servlet (OMS
      application), 275

   remote EJB 2.x lookup, 140–142

   remote interface (session beans), 157

reports

   generation of, 199–200

   ReportingMDB, 204

   scheduled, 199

   synchronous, 200

ResourceBundleViewResolver, 60–65

Retaillé, Jean-Philippe, 224

return values of sequence diagram
   messages, 18

reusability, 44, 50, 68, 89, 98, 106, 123

Richards, Mark, 224

rolePrefix property, 247

RowMapper interface, 190

Runtime exceptions, 152, 265

S

SaveOrderController, 279

scheduled reports, 199

SCIF (Session Context Integration Filter),
   232–233

security. *See also* Spring Security
   framework

   context holders, 232–233

   design patterns, 14

   filter, Spring, 291

   interceptor (Spring Security), 228

   OMS application, 277

   Spring. *See* Spring Security framework

Seinturieris, Lionel, 224

sequence diagrams, UML, 18

servers

   Java EE application, 7

   Tomcat web server, 297–309

Service Activator pattern

   benefits and concerns, 208–209

   message-driven POJOs (MDPs),
      207–208

   to receive/carry out asynchronous
      service requests, 199–200

   strategies with Spring framework,
      200–207

Service Locator pattern

   benefits and concerns, 150–151

   EJB 3 lookup, 144

   to encapsulate JNDI object lookup,
      136–139

   local EJB 2.x lookup, 143–144

   lookup of JMS objects, 145–150

remote EJB 2.x lookup, 140–142
strategies with Spring framework,
139–140
service requests, asynchronous, 199–200
Service to Worker pattern
benefits and concerns, 132
to coordinate request processing
workflow, 130–131
strategies with Spring framework, 131
ServiceLookupController, 279
servlets
Apache Axis servlet, 211–214
controllers, 9
dispatcher, 274
filters, 99–103, 228
front controller, 42–46
remote dispatcher (OMS application),
275
ServletEndpointSupport base class, 210
session beans
building, 157
subscribing to container services, 159
Session Context Integration Filter (SCIF),
232–233
Session Facade pattern
benefits and concerns, 162
to encapsulate business logic remotely,
155–156
strategies with Spring framework,
156–161
SessionContext object, 158
SessionFactory, Hibernate, 192
SessionFactory object, Hibernate, 259
setBeanFactoryLocator method, 160
setSessionContext method, 160
setter injection, 28, 30–31
Simple Object Access Protocol (SOAP), 210
SimpleControllerHandlerAdapter class, 54
SimpleFormController class, 78–89, 279
SimpleRemoteStatelessSessionProxy
FactoryBean class, 172, 174
SimpleUrlHandlerMapping, 54, 58, 127

simplified deployment (OMS application),
301–309
single responsibility principle (SRP), 45
single-tier architecture, 2
SiteMesh web page layout (Open
Symphony), 119
Spring Framework
action management component, 56
AOP documentation, 224
AOP module, 34
application controller strategies with,
52
application service strategies with,
164–167
audit interceptors strategies with,
249–256
Authentication and Authorization
Enforcer pattern strategies with,
226
building layered application with, 35–38
business delegate strategies with,
151–154
business interface strategies with,
169–175
composite view strategies with, 118–122
contact object strategies with, 91–98
Core module. See Core module (Spring)
DAO callbacks, 188–194
data access object (DAO) strategies
with, 183–186
dispatcher view strategies with, 124–128
domain service owner transactions
strategies with, 258
form tags, 278
front controller strategies with, 46–49
importance of, 22–24
intercepting filter strategies with,
99–106
interceptors, 103–106
Java EE design pattern directive, 38–39
JDBC/DAO module, 34
JEE module, 35
module overview, 24

ORM module, 35, 192

overview, 21

page controller strategies with, 70

patterns catalog, Java EE, 12

procedure access object strategies with, 196–197

service activator strategies with, 200–207

Service Locator pattern strategies with, 139–140

service to worker strategies with, 131

session facade strategies with, 156–161

Spring 2.x, 148

tags, 113–115

view helper strategies with, 108–116

web MVC module, 35

web service broker strategies with, 210–220

Spring Security framework

ANPF (Anonymous Processing Filter), 243–244

APF (Authentication Processing Filter), 233–243

authentication and authorization with, 228–232

benefits and concerns, 247–248

components, 228

ETF (Exception Translation Filter), 244–245

filter chaining in, 232

FSI (Filter Security Interceptor), 245–247

high-level components of, 228

SCIF (Session Context Integration Filter), 232–233

Security filter, 234, 291

SqlCall class, 196

SQLException, 185

SRP (single responsibility principle), 45

stateless session beans (SLSBs), 135, 150, 155, 157

Steel, Christopher, 223–224

stereotypes (UML), 14

stored procedures

PAO to invoke, 195

StoredProcedure abstract class, 196

support classes, 196

story cards (OMS application), 270–271

Strategy GOF design pattern, 118–119

Structure101 software, 22

Struts framework, 37, 52

submission, form, 81–83

synchronous reports, 200

■T

tags

JSP Standard Tag Library (JSTL), 64, 111–113

library view helper, 111

Spring, 113–115

third-party libraries, 116

test-driven development (TDD), 28

ThemeChangeInterceptor, 104

thick clients, 3

third-party tag libraries, 116

three-tier architecture, 4

ThrowawayController, 71

ThrowawayController interface, 91–97

tiers, defined, 2

Tiles framework, 278

Tomcat web server, 297–309

toString method, 248

ToStringBuilder class, 253

transaction management. *See* domain service owner transactions

transactional design patterns, 14

two-tier architecture, 3

■U

UML (Unified Modeling Language)

Java architecture and design with, 14–18

package diagram, 279

UML Distilled Third Edition (Addison Wesley), 14

UrlBasedViewResolver, 60–61

UrlFilenameViewController class, 74, 125, 279, 295
users
    generated reports by, 199
    identity, verifying, 224–226, 233
    sign in (OMS application), 270
    userDetailsService property, 239
    user.properties file, 294
    UserRoleAuthorizationInterceptor, 104

■**V**

validation
    form, 85–89
    ValidationUtils class, 85–86
    Validator interface, 85–86
    validators, programmatic/declarative (Spring MVC), 85
variance attribute, 272
view component (MVC), 8, 117
view handlers
    application controller and, 59–62, 62–68
    page controllers and, 51
View Helper pattern
    to adapt model data with view components, 107
    benefits and concerns, 116
    JavaBean view helper, 108–110
    JSP Standard Tag Library (JSTL), 111–113
    OMS application, 278
    Spring tags, using, 113–115
    strategies with Spring framework, 108–116
    tag library view helper, 111
    third-party tag libraries, 116
View/ViewResolver interfaces, 59
Vlissides, John, 11

■**W**

web application context, 33
web containers, 7
WEB-INF/applicationContext.xml, 213–214
web MVC module (Spring), 35
Web Service Broker pattern
    benefits and concerns, 221
    to expose business services to external clients, 209–210
    remoting with Burlap protocol, 217–220
    strategies with Spring framework, 210–220
    web services with JAX-RPC, 210–216
web services
    with JAX-RPC, 210–216
    Web Service Description Language (WSDL), 210
web sites, for downloading
    Blazon ezJEE 1.0.0, 280
    Clickstream (Open Symphony), 102
    Continuum, 280
    Displaytag tag library, 116
    Headway Software, 22
    SiteMesh web page layout, 119
    Tomcat web server, 297
    UML 2.0, 14
web sites, for further information
    Apache Maven, 281
    Central Authentication Service (CAS) SSO solution, 234
    Hibernate, 192
    Magic Servlet antipattern, 44
    OMS application solution and code, 269
    property placeholder support (Spring), 142
    single responsibility principle (SRP), 45

Spring 2.5 documentation, 33
Spring AOP documentation, 34, 224
Spring documentation, 278
Spring form tags, 278
Spring Security documentation, 232
Tiles framework, 278
XP, 269
WebContentGenerator superclass, 72
WeblogicJtaTransactionManager (BEA
    WebLogic), 261
WebsphereUowTransactionManager (IBM
    WebSphere), 261
web.xml, modifying, 289–291
workspace setup (OMS application),
    280–281

X

X509ProcessingFilter, 234
XML (Extensible Markup Language)
    deployment descriptors, 157
    messages, 210
    XmlBeanFactory class, 29
    XmlViewResolver, 60–61, 65–66
XP (extreme programming), 269, 272

Z

zero-argument constructor, 30

You Need the Companion eBook

Your purchase of this book entitles you to buy the companion PDF-version eBook for only $10. Take the weightless companion with you anywhere.

We believe this Apress title will prove so indispensable that you'll want to carry it with you everywhere, which is why we are offering the companion eBook (in PDF format) for $10 to customers who purchase this book now. Convenient and fully searchable, the PDF version of any content-rich, page-heavy Apress book makes a valuable addition to your programming library. You can easily find and copy code—or perform examples by quickly toggling between instructions and the application. Even simultaneously tackling a donut, diet soda, and complex code becomes simplified with hands-free eBooks!

Once you purchase your book, getting the $10 companion eBook is simple:

❶ Visit **www.apress.com/promo/tendollars/**.

❷ Complete a basic registration form to receive a randomly generated question about this title.

❸ Answer the question correctly in 60 seconds, and you will receive a promotional code to redeem for the $10.00 eBook.

Apress®
THE EXPERT'S VOICE™

2855 TELEGRAPH AVENUE | SUITE 600 | BERKELEY, CA 94705

Offer valid through 02/09.